LOS ANGELES PRINTS

LOS ANGELES PRINTS

1883–1980

Ebria Feinblatt and Bruce Davis

Los Angeles County Museum of Art

PART I: September 4–November 30, 1980
PART II: June 25–September 20, 1981

Library of Congress
Cataloging in Publication Data

Feinblatt, Ebria.
Los Angeles Prints, 1883–1980.

Bibliography: p.
CONTENTS: September 4–November 30, 1980.—June 25–September 20, 1981.
1. Prints, American—California—Los Angeles—Exhibitions. 2. Prints—19th century—California—Los Angeles—Exhibitions. 3. Prints—20th century—California—Los Angeles—Exhibitions. I. Davis, Bruce, 1951– joint author. II. Los Angeles Co., Calif. Museum of Art, Los Angeles. III. Title.

NE538.L67F44 769.9794'94'074019494 80-19539
ISBN 0-87587-097-X

Published by the Los Angeles County Museum of Art
5905 Wilshire Boulevard
Los Angeles, California 90036

CONTENTS

LENDERS

Stephen Anaya

Edward Biberman

Dorothy and Michael Blankfort

Mildred Bryant Brooks

Cirrus Editions Ltd.

Douglas S. Cramer

Richard Diebenkorn

Lorser Feitelson Revocable Trust

The Fine Arts Museums of San Francisco, Achenbach Foundation for Graphic Arts, California State Library Long Loan

Gemini G.E.L.

Gene Gill

Green Altar Corporation

Grunwald Center for the Graphic Arts, University of California, Los Angeles

Janus Gallery

Lynton R. Kistler

Margo Leavin

Margo Leavin Gallery and Brooke Alexander, Inc.

Helen Lundeberg

Mekler Gallery

Joseph and Nancy Moure

The Oakland Museum

Dr. and Mrs. Pratapaditya Pal

Carl Parsons

Mr. and Mrs. Monroe E. Price

Betye Saar

San Diego Museum of Art

Abe Tankenson in memory of Mary Donovan Tankenson

Takako and Irwin Weinberg

Anonymous lenders

LOS ANGELES PRINTS: 1883–1980

PREFACE On the occasion of the bicentennial of the founding of the city of Los Angeles, the Los Angeles County Museum of Art has undertaken a limited survey of prints produced by artists of the greater Los Angeles area over the last century.[1] In the past thirty years or more, Los Angeles has assumed a position as a prime center of American art, no less of graphic art. While the present study—only an introductory outline of a still unexplored subject—for logistical reasons cannot include photography, it will attempt a brief sketch of prints by Southern California artists as seen in the context of an ever changing and developing cultural environment. Due to the limitations of space, however, the exhibition merely offers an overview of these printmakers; regrettably many more artists have been omitted. The majority of the works included are from the Museum's own collection.

As this exhibition was being organized, many earlier, "forgotten" printmakers of Los Angeles came to light. Their works encapsulate the flavor of a period that was quite self-contained, almost insulated in its own environment. It recalls the "innocent" cultural youth of the city and contrasts with its productive maturity. It also admittedly affords an excursion into the charm of nostaglia, as some of the prints have been revived here to document our historical past. This opens to view a partial picture of the outlook and creations that for some time were expressive of the area's cultural objectives. Several earlier Los Angeles printmakers undoubtedly merit further study, which would show their works in greater range and place them in sharper perspective. Others made prints as only an occasional activity. Unfortunately, it has not been possible to recover rare early graphic works by artists such as Knud Merrild and Man Ray.

The exhibition is shown in two parts. The first, covering the years between 1883 and 1959, has been my responsibility; the second, 1960–1980, that of Bruce Davis, assistant curator of prints and drawings. Given the difficulty of finding material from the early years of the twentieth century, the exhibition must be incomplete. Yet it is possibly sufficient in scope to reveal the contrast, not to say chasm, between prints before and after World War II. The works themselves are eloquent proof of the profound upheaval that took place in the goals and philosophy of printmakers working in the greater Los Angeles area over a period of almost a century. The prints produced since 1960 reflect the marked changes that occurred in Southern California as the area evolved as an art center. Indeed, Los Angeles has been at the forefront of the increased interest by contemporary artists in printmaking, primarily due to the leadership and innovations provided by the great trio of workshops: Tamarind, Gemini, and Cirrus.

Although in the catalog the prints are discussed according to medium, they are illustrated and exhibited for the greater part chronologically, the several techniques having been intermingled to afford a sequential idea of their changes and development over a considerable span of time.

As for the question of local residency, the organizers of the exhibition decided that, given the frequent changes that have occurred, continuous or at least fairly prolonged residence and work in Southern California would be the criteria for identification of Los Angeles printmakers. Many prints, particularly in the contemporary section, however, were not necessarily executed in Los Angeles. With the worldwide interest in printmaking, as well as increased ease of travel, some artists, such as Sam Francis, might travel as far as Switzerland to produce their graphic art.

ACKNOWLEDGMENTS The concept and plan for this exhibition arose in the course of discussions by the Museum's professional staff on programs for the celebration of the bicentennial of the founding of Los Angeles. For their support of the proposal of the present exhibition, the curators of the department wish to thank Dr. Pratapaditya Pal, former acting director, and the Museum's Board of Trustees.

Before leaving the Museum last year, Joseph E. Young, former assistant curator of prints and drawings, had begun to work on the exhibition. Young was uniquely equipped to treat the history of prints executed by Los Angeles artists, for this was an integral part of his specialized interest in American and contemporary art. We would like to acknowledge the contribution he made to the plan of the exhibition and catalog. For a brief period, the department was fortunate in the assistance of Judy Larson, to whom we express our gratitude. Bruce Davis, present assistant curator of prints and drawings, has assumed various burdens of the exhibition in addition to curating its second part.

Other curators, colleagues, and friends who have taken time from busy schedules to assist us most generously include Clinton Adams; Edward Biberman; E. Maurice Bloch and Lucinda Gedeon; Mildred Bryant Brooks; Helen Lundeberg Feitelson; Janet Flint; Ruth Hatfield; Therese Heyman; Robert Flynn Johnson; Lynton R. Kistler; Joseph Landacre; Kirk Martin; Adam Mekler; Lisa Mosher; Nancy Moure; Martin E. Petersen; Aimée Brown Price; Ward Ritchie; Elizabeth Roth; Walter G. Silva; Esther Sparks; and Jake Zeitlin. Finally we must acknowledge the cooperation and assistance of many Museum staff members, without whom this catalog and exhibition would not be possible: Victoria Blyth and the conservation department; John Gebhard and the photography department; Jeanne D'Andrea and Jeffrey Mueller and the publications and graphic design department; Research Librarian Eleanor Hartman and her staff; Registrar Patricia Nauert and her staff; and Head of Operations James Peoples and his staff.

EBRIA FEINBLATT

1. A well-documented study of the development of art and related cultural activity in Southern California has not yet seen the light. (This gap may now be filled by Nancy Moure's *Painting and Sculpture in Los Angeles, 1900–1945*, in publication.) Previously pointed out in a University of California, Los Angeles, doctoral dissertation (1964) by Winifred H. Higgins, *Art Collecting in the Los Angeles Area, 1910–1960*, microfilmed in 1974; more recently Fidel Danieli in "Nine Senior Southern California Painters," *Journal of the Los Angeles Institute of Contemporary Art*, 1974, noted that "There does not exist even the barest accurate published outlines on the subject of Los Angeles art, its historical development." In consequence of such lacunae, efforts to proceed with a subject along these lines must of necessity be fragmentary rather than total.

INTRODUCTION Joseph E. Young, who pioneered in reconstructing the history of early printmaking in Southern California, discerned two tendencies in that art toward the close of the nineteenth century. One was "an inclination toward romantic realism . . . and [the other] the opposing impressionist faction."[2] Most printmakers of the 1920s and 1930s inclined toward romantic realism. Some also revealed the influences of Japanese prints, Art Deco, and the modern Mexican school.

In the thirteenth Print Makers Society International Exhibition, held in 1932 at the Los Angeles County Museum in Exposition Park, the top prizes went to two artists of the English school, Malcolm Osborne and Stanley Anderson. Such master technicians of the clear, definite line and of structure were admired by the conservative jury. In reviewing the show, the society's secretary and organizer, Howell Brown, noted that it included only one lithograph, a Matisse, from France, while among the etchings he listed works by Picasso and Matisse together with those by Beaufrère, Brouet, Lévy, Moreau, and Guillaume; he lamented the absence of inspiration and development in the French school.[3] Criticized for the small representation of "modernist" prints in the show, Brown asked why his society should "displace good conservative work to make place for something we do not like?" He concluded by asserting that he could not see "why the so-called moderns pride themselves on doing 'something different.' They are just as much conventional in their way as any others and it has become as easy to recognize a [Peggy] Bacon, Bruton, Fay, Handforth, Pinto or Lozowick as it is an Osborne, Anderson, Roth, Sturges or Benson. The only difference is that the latter are more carefully composed and drawn and are submitted in clean mats while the more radical a print the dirtier the mat."[4]

This astonishingly naive conservatism and complacency characterized certain dominant elements of the art world in Los Angeles in the 1920s and 1930s. The unresponsiveness of the Print Makers Society to new directions in creative printmaking ultimately led to its loss of standing in the community. But despite the restraints of the society, the work of the city's modern artists continued to reflect their diversity and independence.

It is difficult to define or to speak of a native or indigenous tradition of printmaking in Los Angeles and its environs. From the earliest period of the twentieth century, the majority of American etchers from the Midwest and the Eastern seaboard studied in Paris, and most of them concentrated on producing the "picturesque," that is, Old World views, villages, cities, landscapes, monuments. An occasional exception was the Swedish-born B. Olsson-Nordfelt who, in addition to the traditional European themes, found stimulation for his etchings in the industrialization of Chicago and in the individual character of San Francisco. But the major influences upon early twentieth-century American etchers were the modern nineteenth-century masters: Whistler, Meryon, and Haden. Other admired etchers included Frank Short and D. Y. Cameron.

Serious printmaking in Southern California grew out of the presence at the Panama-Pacific International Exposition of 1915 of two American artist-etchers, Ernest Haskell (1876–1925) and Cadwallader Washburn (1866–1965). "Prior to 1915," wrote Arthur Millier, the earliest chronicler of Los Angeles printmakers, "the West Coast could boast little of its prints. . . . A copper-plate firm was persuaded to import etchings supplies. Erwin H. Furman[5] took over the Print Rooms from Hill Tolerton in Pasadena and installed a press for the use of etchers. Soon a number were at work and the California Society of Etchers was founded in 1913."[6] In 1913, Hill Tolerton was furnishing biographical sketches of the American etchers illustrated in the catalog published by Albert Roullier Art Galleries in Chicago.

"From Monterey [where he had settled]," wrote Millier, "Haskell set a standard, etching and engraving his magnificent series of Monterey cypress, redwood trees, and those glowing plates of hills studded with live oaks. With his admiration for Dürer, Rembrandt, and Legros, no feat of craftsmanship was too laborious for him."[7]

Lithography, which was to become one of the most dominant and important print techniques in the first heyday of Los Angeles printmaking, took hold fairly late in the city. Lithographic landscape views were made for surveying purposes in the late nineteenth century, but photography led as the medium most involved in recording the westward expansion. Adam Clark Vroman, a book dealer in Pasadena, began to make photographs in 1892. He was active in the same period as was another photographer, Charles Fletcher Lummis, who worked to improve the conditions of the California Indians. In 1914, eleven Los Angeles photographers formed an organization which came to be known as the Camera Pictorialists of Los Angeles. Among its founding members were Edward Weston, Louis Fleckenstein, and Margrethe Mather. International exhibitions of the Camera Pictorialists were held at the Los Angeles County Museum from the 1920s until the late 1940s.

During this period, the California Art Club, a conservative organization dominated by the landscape painter William Wendt and his wife, Julia, a sculptor, was the only group in Los Angeles that represented artists. Unalterably opposed to "modernism," and secure in its annual members' exhibitions at the Los Angeles County Museum, the Club ran into difficulties with the appearance of an extremely modern and vocal artist on the scene, the celebrated co-founder of Synchromism, Stanton Macdonald-Wright. In 1920, the Los Angeles County Museum had held its first exhibition of avant-garde art organized by the Virginia-born Macdonald-Wright. From the gallery of Alfred Stieglitz and others in New York, it offered works by John Marin, Arthur Dove, Alfred Maurer, Georgia O'Keeffe, Henry McFee, Edwin Dickinson, Charles Demuth, Charles Sheeler, Abraham Walkowitz, Morgan Russell, and other leading Ameri-

---

2. J. E. Young, "Contemporary Southern California Printmaking," *Print Review*, vol. 2, 1973, p. 49.

3. H. Brown, "The Thirteenth International Print Makers' Exhibition," *Prints*, vol. 2, 1931–32, pp. 22–24.

4. Ibid.

5. Furman was an agent of Lieutenant General Munthe, founder of the Peking police department and collector of Chinese art. See Higgins, *Art Collecting*, p. 94.

6. A. Millier, "Far-Western Print Makers," *Prints*, vol. 1, no. 2, 1931, p. 11.

7. Ibid.

can artists. Stanton Macdonald-Wright recalled many years later that the show "was the cause of near riots." At the same time, the exhibition eventually brought significant changes, stimulating awareness of new trends in modern art and opening the way for their teaching and practice in Los Angeles and vicinity. Six years later, the indomitable founder of the Blue Four, Galka Scheyer, arranged an exhibition of their works at the Los Angeles County Museum. The art of Paul Klee, Lyonel Feininger, Vasilii Kandinsky, and Alexei Jawlensky "hit Los Angeles like a bombshell."[8]

In 1922–23, the Los Angeles Group of Independent Artists printed a manifesto that pointed up the conditions in which certain artists found themselves. Addressed to "all workers in the graphic arts who rebel against the rule of thumb in art," it protested the actions of conservative juries in preventing the exhibition of artists who supported Cubism, Dynamism, and Expressionism as against academism and what the Group called "dead form." Among the well-known members of the committee was Boris Deutsch, newly arrived from Europe. The Group's first exhibition was held in the Taos building, at First and Broadway in downtown Los Angeles, and included works by members such as Stanton Macdonald-Wright, Nick Brigante, and Peter Krasnow as well as works lent by William Zorach, Morgan Russell, Rex Slinkard, and Thomas Hart Benton, among others.

About 1923–24, some of the modern artists in Los Angeles—Peter Krasnow, Stanton Macdonald-Wright, Edward Vysekal, and others—decided to form a modern art society. Most of the group clustered around Macdonald-Wright, who had a studio in the North Broadway area and held classes. But a factor that mitigated against creating a cohesive center of art was the notorious size of the Los Angeles territory, which led to a division into several cultural centers. The Harvard-educated photographer, champion of Indian rights, and Southern California cultural leader Charles Fletcher Lummis was responsible for the first artist colony in the greater Los Angeles area. It revolved around his residence in Highland Park, adjoining the wealthy community of "old money and first families," Pasadena. Among contributors to his magazine, *Land of Sunshine,* were the educator David Starr Jordon; the poets Edwin Markham and Ina Coolbrith; and the writer Mary Austin.

Pasadena was also the site of a club called the Print Makers of Los Angeles, organized by the painter-etcher Benjamin Chambers Brown, together with his brother, Howell, in 1914. In 1921, the club changed its name to the Print Makers Society of California and began holding international exhibitions. Edward Hopper was one of the winners in the Fourth International show for his etching *East Side Interior* (1923).

Despite Pasadena's predominance as a cultural site, with its celebrated orange groves and wealthy resort visitors, it was in Los Angeles proper that art schools and commercial art galleries took root. In 1905, the *Los Angeles Times* art critic, Anthony Anderson, and the artist Hanson Puthoff organized the Art Students' League of Los Angeles, which continued to exist even after the founding of the Otis Art Institute in 1919. Otis was the first among the influential art training schools in the city. The residence of the owner and publisher of the *Los Angeles Times,* General Harrison Gray Otis, it was given by him to the County of Los Angeles to advance art in the area and was originally a part of the Los Angeles County Museum.

Specializing in fine and industrial arts, Otis did not incorporate a class in etching into the curriculum until 1943–44. The class instructor was the *Los Angeles Times* art critic, Arthur Millier. In 1948, the University of Southern California led the way for planographic printing with the appointment of Jules Heller as instructor in lithography. In 1952, the well-known artist, muralist, and designer Millard Sheets—for many years director of the Fine Arts Exhibition of the Los Angeles County Fair—became director at Otis, with Jarvis Barlow as assistant. Soon afterward, Ernest Freed, a former student of Mauricio Lasansky at the celebrated intaglio center at the University of Iowa, became head of the Graphic Arts Department at Otis. The University of California, Los Angeles, followed suit, appointing another Lasansky pupil, John Paul Jones, as the head of its Graphic Arts Department. These departments signaled a new stimulus for printmaking activities in the Los Angeles area.

Originally intending to teach a design class at Otis, the indefatigable Nelbert (Nellie) Chouinard arrived in Los Angeles in 1920 from New York where she had graduated from the Pratt Institute. The following year she opened the art institute that bore her name. Aware that art students in Los Angeles did not know what was going on in the East, Chouinard hired internationally known artists such as Morgan Russell, Hans Hofmann, Alexandr Archipenko, Lorser Feitelson, and Jean Charlot as instructors. In a politically conservative period, she courageously brought in David Siqueiros to teach the art of fresco. Such infusions contributed to the widening of art horizons in the area.

A student at Chouinard, Herbert Jepson, a Chicagoan, became an influential instructor at the institute in 1931. Like Otis, Chouinard was geared to practical, commercial goals. Eventually dissatisfied with these directions, Jepson broke away in 1945 and started his own school which lasted for eight years. Jepson's school became the focal point for the more intellectually oriented, internationally cultured artists. Among the instructors on its staff were Rico Lebrun, Howard Warshaw, and William Brice, artists who can be considered among the most influential of their period in Los Angeles.

Another school of importance in Los Angeles for many years was the more commercially oriented Art Center School. Among its well-known instructors have been the pioneer abstractionist, both post-surrealist and "hard-edge," Lorser Feitelson and the muralist and painter of social concerns Edward Biberman. While Feitelson concentrated on the practice of classical

8. Higgins, *Art Collecting,* p. 190.

draftsmanship, he also appreciated and collected Old Master prints and drawings.

This brief survey of the original art schools in Los Angeles reveals that instruction in printmaking appeared fairly late in their curricula. Drawing, fashion, and commercial design were taught here earlier. Indeed, printmaking has rarely functioned as a consistent means of livelihood for any local artist, with the possible exception of the pioneering California lithographer Sam Francis.

A prime factor in the alteration, or development, of the art scene in Los Angeles through the later 1930s was the introduction of the Federal Art Project in 1935. This WPA project encouraged artists to produce prints for which they were remunerated. Under this program, six thousand lithographs and twelve hundred woodcuts were made in Southern California.

Another positive contribution to the development of art in the Los Angeles area was the opening of a number of vital commercial art galleries. The two best known of the earlier period were the Dalzell Hatfield Gallery, originally located a block from Chouinard, and the Earl Stendahl Gallery, then located in the Ambassador Hotel. Millard Sheets, a key figure in Los Angeles art, relates that at Hatfield's he saw his first Van Gogh and Matisse and that the experience was "pretty shocking to a kid growing up in the 'California eucalyptus school.' "[9] In addition to modern art, Earl Stendahl introduced pre-Columbian art, a genre then completely unknown to Los Angeles residents. During the Depression, a group of artists rented the art gallery in the Biltmore Hotel. Eventually they were bought out by Alexander Cowie, an Easterner, who ran the gallery for about a quarter of a century, featuring artists of the Los Angeles area.

While these galleries concentrated on painting and sculpture, the pioneer Los Angeles book dealer Jake Zeitlin introduced local and international prints to the area.[10] As early as the late 1920s, Zeitlin's shop was exhibiting Paul Landacre, and in the 1930s he was the first to show the work of Henrietta Shore as well as other Los Angeles lithographers. For more than a half century Zeitlin's bookshop has been a center for the exhibition, appreciation, and collection of Southern California graphic art.

Although several of the early Los Angeles printmakers worked in motion picture studios, and while many renowned art collections were beginning to be formed in the motion picture colony, one of the direct contributions to the art life of Los Angeles was made by the popular actor, art collector, and patron Vincent Price, who in the early 1940s co-directed the Little Gallery in Beverly Hills and was one of the founders of the Modern Institute of Art there in 1947. Price, together with the art dealer Frank Perls, was responsible for encouraging the careers of Howard Warshaw and William Brice, among others.

About the time of the founding of the Modern Institute of Art, Associated American Artists of New York opened a lavish branch in Beverly Hills for the exhibition and sale of contemporary American printmakers. Like the Modern Institute, it lasted no more than a few years. National exposure for Los Angeles printmakers was provided by the 1942 Whitney Museum exhibition *Between Two Wars, 1914–1941,* which showed 261 American prints. Of these, twenty-one were by Californians, about half from the Los Angeles area.

The post-World War II period saw significant changes in the art life of Los Angeles. This was caused in part by the growing circle of European artists, musicians, and writers who injected cosmopolitan values into the largely self-contained community. Yet as late as 1947, the Los Angeles County Museum's Eighth Annual Exhibition of Paintings and Sculpture by Artists of Los Angeles and Vicinity was the occasion of protests and picketing by a number of rejected artists who denounced the show as "radical, degenerate, subversive and un-American." The California Art Club and other groups, however, favoring what they termed "traditional American art," gradually lost ground under the steady advance and victories of contemporary art. By the early 1950s, abstract art had won its battle, and most of the significant artists of Los Angeles had sloughed off traditional forms and values. Even for those who continued with the figurative and "representational" there was a massive reinterpretation that lent new vigor and meaning to the delineation of the human form and the human condition.

ETCHING With rare exceptions until the mid-1850s, printmaking in the United States was stylistically under the influence first of England, then of Italy and Germany. Only occasionally did American etchers of this period attempt originality of expression, since at this time their medium was generally employed as a preliminary stage for line engraving on steel plates. Original etching really did not begin to be practiced in the United States until well after the middle of the nineteenth century, spurred on by the increasing influence of French art with its emphasis upon individualism and by Seymour Haden's lectures on etching delivered in New York, Philadelphia, and other Eastern cities from 1882 to 1884.

Although the first intimations of graphic work in the Los Angeles area were in photography, the earliest significant etcher in Southern California was the little-studied artist Henry Chapman Ford. In 1883, in Santa Barbara, Ford produced a highly ambitious, pioneering effort in the form of twenty-four etchings depicting the *Franciscan Missions of California.* Published in New York by the Studio Press in an edition of fifty on Japan paper, Ford's etchings were based on oil sketches he made of remaining portions of the buildings, combined with his study of photographs, drawings, and published descriptions. Advanced in terms of their originality, the prints were also remarkable in slightly antedating the appearance of Helen Hunt Jackson's legendary novel *Ramona,* which created a mythic mission lore throughout the Southland, not to say, the country. Yet it is interesting that Frank Weitenkampf, in his still standard book

9. *Los Angeles Art Community: Group Portrait/Millard Sheets,* Oral History Program, University of California, Los Angeles, 1977, vol. 1, p. 166.

10. A print gallery had been initiated at the original Dawson's Book Shop in 1912.

11. B. E. Jacques, "A glance backwards," *The Print Collectors' Chronicle,* vol. 1, no. 3, 1939, p. 12.

12. The Achenbach Foundation in San Francisco has an impression of the print that differs in intensity of color from the Los Angeles example. It also bears another title, *The Red Boat—Oakland Mole.* The variation of color in these two impressions of the same subject indicates that Brown was experimenting with his unusual technique.

American Graphic Art of 1912, did not refer to Ford's prints. His omission points up the fact that few people in the late nineteenth century thought of the Far West in terms of graphic art. The centers for etching in those years were New York, Boston, and Philadelphia where clubs and societies for the propagation of the medium were formed. In 1939 it was noted that among the American etchings in the Chicago Columbian Exposition of 1893, "There was no representation from the West whence much of the finest and most virile work now comes."[11]

Ford's *Mission* etchings were highly sophisticated technically for the period and place in which they were created. Multiple bitings of the plates, selective use of drypoint, and retroussage were employed to produce romantic images of atmospheric landscapes. The etchings document a series of historic buildings that contributed to making the state famous and stand as perhaps the most significant "remembrance" of the era of Spanish California.

After Ford, little is heard of etching in Southern California in the early years of the twentieth century. An Arkansas-born painter who studied at the Académie Julien in Paris, Benjamin Chambers Brown, came to Los Angeles in 1895. He began to etch in 1914 and was widely exhibited in the East. Brown was apparently the first Los Angeles area etcher to work in color, and he and his brother, Howell, were the earliest etching enthusiasts of the region. His soft-ground color etching *At the Paint-Wharf* is dated 1919.[12] Brown is reported to have devised his own technique for color printing, and he won international acknowledgment when his color etchings were purchased by the British Museum. Writing of Brown in 1924, Edna Gearhart defended the artist for combining color with etching, an indication that traditionalists objected to what the then modernists accepted, namely, color as a completion of line and pattern.

Other Pasadena pioneers in the field of color prints were two sisters from Illinois, Frances Hammel Gearhart and May Gearhart. In 1911 they held an exhibition of their watercolors at the Walker Theatre building in downtown Los Angeles. In 1920 they were both making color prints: Frances, woodcuts; May, etchings. May Gearhart had studied at Columbia University, the Art Institute of Chicago, and the University of California, Berkeley, and was a pupil of Walter Shirlaw and Hans Hofmann; she was also supervisor of art in the Los Angeles city schools from 1903 to 1939. An article about her by Arthur Millier in the *Los Angeles Times,* 1935, reveals that as an educator she held the "advanced" views of her period which encouraged children to study and make art in terms of creation, that is, upon knowledge of basic art and design principles, not according to the rules of imitation.

Not many prints by May Gearhart are readily found, but, as seen in the soft-ground etching *Two Gentlemen of Xochimilco,* she could use color directly and brilliantly. The two sisters' trips to Mexico undoubtedly had a bearing upon their employment of color, but another factor was the stimulation they received from the production of several large motion pictures by the pioneer art director Park French, in which the frames were tinted in an effort to obtain color. In 1923 the Gearharts held an exhibition on their premises in Pasadena of original color compositions resulting from their experience of French's sets for films starring Mary Pickford and Douglas Fairbanks.

The Gearharts were longtime members of the Pasadena-based Print Makers Society of California. Until the Los Angeles County Museum stopped holding the society's international exhibition in 1938, the society was the chief organizing body of and organ for the printmakers of the greater Los Angeles area. The aims and program of the society are preserved in its monthly *Newsletter,* dating from 1922 to 1938; they are significant inasmuch as they undoubtedly reflected the attitude to "modern" art not only of part of that body but of the larger Los Angeles art community. "Modernism" was generally anathema. The *Newsletter* encouraged the acquisition of prints by living artists and proclaimed the need of American artists to free themselves from influences of other countries in order to find their own expression.[13]

Among the most productive etchers of the 1920s in Los Angeles were Wilson Silsby, Arthur Millier, and Loren Barton.[14] Born in Chicago, Silsby was associated with motion picture set design for many years. He began etching in the early 1920s, making a considerable number of prints in Europe. In his book *Etching Methods and Materials,* 1943, Silsby showed himself open to modest experimentation with material and processes, but the masters he suggested as guides to prospective etchers revealed his essential traditionalism.

Like Silsby's, the prime focus of Arthur Millier's etching needle was the landscape. "To many persons," wrote the author of an article on California etchers in 1924, "California appears to be more an etcher's than a painter's paradise. Its stretches are so wide, so panoramic, that mere suggestion of them rather than an attempt to comprehend their expansiveness seems to be fitting."[15] In terms of its physical beauty, its clear, bright light, and its Spanish background, California appeared as probably the most "romantic" state in the Union, and this natural allure led to the proliferation of many views etched to capture its essential character. Millier said of himself that he was "best known for a series of plates done in the Old Plaza Los Angeles."[16] His admiration for the etchings of Rembrandt and Corot was manifest in his prints. It is also of note that Millier was perhaps one of the earliest printmakers—if not in the country, then in California—to include an automobile in an etching. His *Rest on the Flight* shows Mother and Child under a sycamore tree while Joseph works over the engine of the car.

An anomalous figure among Los Angeles etchers of the early 1920s was the Hungarian-born Franz Geritz. In 1922 the Los Angeles County Museum "for the first time in the history of

13. The Print Makers Society of California was not alone in its condemnation of modern art. On the brink of World War II, the art critic Thomas Craven, in his introduction to his *Treasury of American Prints,* 1939, denounced Picasso and "the abortions of surrealism—the culminating rot of European gadget makers . . ." But while Craven hailed the emergence of a native American school of graphic artists, the Print Makers Society of California spokesmen drew the line even against American modernists such as Peggy Bacon and Louis Lozowick, among others.

14. The California etcher who received international recognition in the 1920s was Roi Partridge, who lived and worked in San Francisco and Oakland. James Laver, author of *A History of British and American Etching,* 1929, suggested that Partridge was perhaps the best-known etcher of California.

15. J. A. Selkinghaus, "Etchers of California," *International Studio,* February 1924, p. 383.

16. A. Millier, "Far-Western Print Makers," p. 16.

Southern California"[17] held an exhibition of his woodblock portraits. Geritz was said to be at that time "the only woodblock artist in the United States."[18] He worked in both black and white and color. Curiously enough, however, one of Geritz's more interesting portraits is not a woodcut but his 1922 etching of Margrethe Mather, already mentioned as one of the founding members of the Camera Pictorialists of Los Angeles. In its stark simplicity and theatrical tilt of the head, Geritz's profile portrait captures the self-conscious sophistication of the 1920s.

Trained at the University of Southern California and the Art Students' League of Los Angeles, Loren Barton burst upon the local scene in 1920 like a prodigy, receiving accolades ranking her with Rembrandt, Millet, Whistler, and Zorn. Her best-known and possibly most successful print was the drypoint *Manuel,* 1923, an effective portrait of an early California Spaniard with penetrating gaze and restrained power, based on her painting of the same subject. The influence of Whistler was apparent in her etchings of marine views. At a time when landscape was the primary, predilected subject of Los Angeles etchers, Barton was notable for her efforts at portraiture. She was one of the few Los Angeles printmakers represented by the Associated American Artists Gallery in New York in the 1930s.

Like Barton, Mildred Bryant Brooks is a Los Angeles etcher who studied at the University of Southern California. F. Tolles Chamberlin, the co-founder of Chouinard, was one of her early mentors, but she also learned technique from a Whistler pupil, E. Stetson Crawford. Brooks taught and printed for etchers in the 1930s at the Stickney Art Institute in Pasadena, a professional arts school.[19] It was there that she installed her two-hundred-year-old German press, a gift from a private patron, Mrs. Charles (Josephine) Everett, who had a home and gallery near the old Vista del Arroyo Hotel. A longtime resident of Pasadena and a consummate technician, from 1932 Brooks has devoted her career largely to landscapes, with trees a predominant theme. Brooks's dedicated attachment to such motifs is visible in the precision and delicacy of her plates in which she preferred not even to introduce drypoint. *Companions,* 1937, depicts a gnarled, leafless tree whose grotesquely writhing branches make a stark pattern against the densely foliated tree behind them. The etching won the main prize at the Chicago Society of Etchers, the first time that the international society honored a woman and distributed a print by a Westerner instead of an Easterner or foreign printmaker.

From the 1920s to the 1940s, Los Angeles printmakers fell largely into two categories: those who were members of the Print Makers Society of California or the Los Angeles Print Group, organized in 1928, and those who worked outside of any defined group. Whether the artists were affiliated or not, however, the landscape continued to be the seductive reality as subject, exerting its attraction for traditionalist and modernist alike. Many of the earlier etchers were at a point in their subject matter that could be paralleled by the Dutch artists' absorption in landscape during the seventeenth century. But while there were no major figures among the Southern California lovers of the land, there was diversity of expression and personal interpretation. Orpha Klinker and Harold Doolittle, for example, often worked in aquatint: Klinker approaching the flat effect of the Japanese woodcut, Doolittle combining fine with porous, larger grain in his *Rugged Cliffs.* These works were largely transcripts of nature, but other artists were more personal in their interpretations.

A truly forgotten Los Angeles etcher of this kind of landscape was Willard Nash, whose career was cut short by untimely death. A painter and watercolorist, Nash taught at the Los Angeles Art Center School in 1936 and probably made no more than nine prints in all. In 1921 he was involved in the formation of a group calling itself *Los Cinco Pintores;* two years later, the group was shown at the Los Angeles County Museum. Nash himself exhibited twice in New York in 1935, once at the Whitney Museum in *Abstract Art in America* and again in a show of his watercolors at the Marie Harriman Gallery. Nash's superior design qualities are manifest in the 1927 etching *Landscape.* The flattening of the planes, non-naturalistic perspective, faceted shading, crisp lines, and abstractly decorative treatment of the landscape elements have an individual character free of romanticism yet delicate and fine in the extreme.

Also gifted and individual is the painter and watercolorist Nick Brigante, who in 1930 produced about a dozen etchings of landscape motifs. Chiefly trial proofs, they are now all in the Museum's collection. One of the first abstractionists on the West Coast, Brigante has long been an integral part of the forward-looking art movements in Los Angeles and was responsible for Macdonald-Wright taking over the direction of the Art Students' League in 1923. After his Cubist period in New York, where he exhibited with many leading American painters, Brigante returned to Los Angeles where he executed a monumental watercolor, as a series of nine screens. This work disclosed a profound influence of Chinese painting and also his desire to extend the potentialities of the watercolor medium. Brigante's highly personal etchings showed the atmospheric freedom and lyricism of line that already foretold the dynamic calligraphy and Orientalism of his later work.

Two other Southern California etchers of the 1920s and 1930s who should be mentioned for their effective work in pure aquatint were Charles Keeler and Marian Hebert. In the *Street of Life and Death, Segovia* Keeler combined smoothly toned areas with passages of finely grained aquatint; in her fresh design of *Rose Arrangement,* 1938, Hebert applied a uniformly porous grain for a lively surface. Flower pieces were produced in abundance in Southern California, but Hebert avoided the fairly common, sterotyped formula that characterized many of them.

This brief survey of Los Angeles etchers through the 1930s allows for some conclusions which may be summarized as fol-

---

17. *Los Angeles Times,* July 12, 1922, p. 12.

18. Ibid.

19. Arthur Millier gave classes at the Stickney while Lorser Feitelson made a handful of etchings there, experimenting with the process. Helen Lundeberg Feitelson kindly supplied this information.

lows. An interesting though not totally distinguishing feature of some early Los Angeles etchings was in the use of color, contrasting with the general disuse of color by contemporary printmakers on the Eastern seaboard. While the founder of the Ashcan School, Robert Henri, had an exhibition at the Los Angeles County Museum in 1914, and while a group of Los Angeles artists protested against academism and tradition—although a decade later than their New York counterparts—Southern California etchers did not adopt themes comparable to those of the New York realists such as Sloan, Bellows, Hopper, Marsh, or for that matter to some of the printmakers of the Northwest. Landscape, the natural and the picturesque view of the famous environment, continued as the central motif for etchers, rather than features of the area's developing urbanization, the effects of the Depression, or of the advancing technology.

In the 1920s, the revolutionary work long since accomplished by Picasso, Braque, and Villon in their Cubist etchings and the experimental directions of Hayter's Atelier 17 in Paris disclosed no reverberations or stimuli among Southern California etchers. Although closely in touch with not only English but also continental printmakers, through their International Exhibitions at the Los Angeles County Museum, earlier Los Angeles etchers with few exceptions steered clear of reflections of Cubism, Expressionism, or Abstractionism—in short, of contemporary modernism.

The attitudes of the Print Makers Society of California remained consistent through the many changes taking place in their environment resulting from great real-estate booms and the heavy influx of tourists and new settlers. Nor, as previously mentioned, did the economic distress occasioned by the Depression of 1929 find echo in the work of local etchers. As late as 1934 the editor of the *Print Makers Newsletter* wrote, "It may interest conservatives to know that during many miles of travel in Europe this past summer only a very few modernistic pictures . . . were seen in any country"; and he expressed hope that when the modern art movement reached California it would sink into the ocean.[20] A year later, editor Howell Brown published in full an article, "Art for the Public," from the *Art Digest* in New York in which the author asked, among other arguments defending the public's right to buy what it likes, "Why should a man, interested in the play of a light on a landscape, be told that it is not good art and that he should purchase some gruesome or grotesque picture of New York slum life because it is admired by his [the artist's] colleagues?"[21]

The deathknell for the Print Makers Society exhibitions at the Los Angeles County Museum, which had continued for almost two decades, was probably first publicly sounded in 1936 by the avant-garde book designer and art collector Merle Armitage. In his critical review of the society's Seventeenth International Exhibition he wrote, "My feeling is that virile printmakers will be discouraged from sending to this annual exhibition unless a more liberal jury is selected, and I am perfectly certain that exhibitions of this kind cannot continue to interest the public."[22]

The early and mid-1940s were a fairly fallow period for the art of etching in Los Angeles. With the end of representation of both the Print Makers Society of California International Exhibitions, in which the prevailing technique was etching, and the Camera Pictorialists at the County Museum, a new atmosphere, favorable to the various styles of contemporary art, supplanted the conservative, traditionalist approaches of the previous two decades.

One of the younger Los Angeles etchers of the late 1940s, Ynez Johnston, was attracted to exotic motifs, inspired by pre-Columbian and East Indian art. In 1949 the California Centennials in Art purchased her black-and-white etching *Ship and Storm* for the County Museum. Johnston evinced an engaging freshness and originality in her flat patterning, delicately interweaving lines, and tonal contrasts. More literal than Paul Klee, Johnston nevertheless evoked her own world of fantasy. Later, she introduced brilliant color into her prints, heightening their effectiveness.

The regeneration of the etching process in America was inspired, as it had been earlier in Europe, by Stanley W. Hayter's celebrated Atelier 17, which moved from Paris to New York in 1940. The year 1947 became the watershed in the history of modern American printmaking with the Brooklyn Museum exhibition that provided the first significant forum for work in new experimental graphic media. In the 1950s, Hayter's pupil, the South-American-born Mauricio Lasansky, developed another focal center for intaglio art at the University of Iowa.

Exhibiting at the Felix Landau Gallery in 1950, California-born Leonard Edmondson was something of a pioneer in abstract color etching. The artist conceived his prints as expressions of space and objects or shapes. Edmondson's earlier work presented space as a "deep atmosphere" for the enveloping of shapes entering at different speeds. Later, space was conceived as rather a sheath or web; still later, Edmondson returned to his original figuration of space as a reception for his dynamic, Mirò-esque shapes. Although the artist confesses that themes such as landscape or the human figure are at the base of his designs, his transmutations of them by means of free-floating and swinging shapes is complete as he strives to achieve his goal of visual stimulation and response.

The 1950s continued with a high point in Los Angeles etching, or *intaglio* as it was re-christened in light of its new technical complexities, in which artists combined etching with soft-ground and aquatint. One of the key figures was a transplanted Lasansky pupil from Iowa, John Paul Jones, who completed his first print in 1948. In 1954 intaglios by Jones, then teaching at the University of California, Los Angeles, together with prints by the French etcher Henri-Georges Adam, were exhibited at the Los Angeles County Museum. Originally an abstractionist, Jones turned to elements of Surrealism, then evolved his own

20. October–November, 1934, n.p.

21. May, 1935, n.p.

22. M. Armitage, "The California Print Makers' Show," *Prints*, vol. 4, April 1936, pp. 198–200.

personal expression by structuring his figures and compositions with deep light and shade. Jones approached abstraction from a geometric-Cubist base, pure and austere but without primary sculptural intent, remaining in the domain of the planimetric. In *Landscape #2*, 1950, the artist composed with transparent planes woven through with straight and curved lines to refine the pattern. In his abstract etchings Jones was concerned with the relationships of shifting, darting lines that created a concentrated field of dynamic tensions. Triangles or cones of negative space heighten the contrasts of the compositional structure. In the interaction of forms and the integration of his compositional means, Jones achieved fields of space charged with kinetic action. Through richly graded tonal surfaces and apparitional figures, Jones in later prints achieved a graphic sonority. This can be seen in the diffusive, striated passages of *Double Portrait*, 1957, that appear as though burnished from a black background into a vibrating chiaroscuro.

Other Los Angeles area artists working in intaglio in the 1950s included Ernest B. Freed, the head of graphic arts at Otis Art Institute, and Dick Swift, active in the Long Beach area. Both printmakers were influenced by the resurgence of color intaglio in mixed media, in which etching, engraving, aquatint, soft-ground, and roulette could be combined and were sometimes printed with overlaps of either wood or linoleum cut.

Primarily a painter, muralist, and draftsman, Howard Warshaw made a very small number of prints. After his first exhibition at the Julian Levy Gallery in New York in 1945, Warshaw came to Jepson's School in Los Angeles. An exhibition of the reproduction of Picasso's *Guernica* at the Frank Perls Gallery crystallized Warshaw's direction as an artist, since it infused naturalism and emotion into what had been for him before a Cubist and abstract mode of expression. During a stay as assistant professor at the University of Iowa, when he was twenty-nine, Warshaw began a study of Picasso's work from slides. Unable to have a model, Warshaw used his own hands for the spectacular 1952 etching in green ink, *Hands*, in which a pair of giant, manacled hands become a synecdochical expression of some larger torment of the human species and also a piece of "sculpture" of compelling force. Through the open fingers, Warshaw also intended to project the reality of the shifting nature of space, a concept he appreciated through his study of Cubism.

In 1939 for the first time the Los Angeles County Museum had an art man, Roland McKinney, as its head. In 1945–46, with the reorganization of the Museum's art section under the joint directorship of James H. Breasted, Jr., as administrator, and Dr. William R. Valentiner, as director-consultant for art, new policies were inaugurated for the encouragement and promotion of artists of Los Angeles and vicinity. Under this program, juried exhibitions were held on an annual basis and prints were included in various *Annual*s.

The Museum's last *Annual* of 1961 was devoted to all media except painting. Two hundred and twenty-five prints were submitted, from which the jury selected thirty-five, awarding six prizes. The prizes divided into three intaglios, one lithograph, one serigraph, and one monotype, indicating that even at this time the etching medium was still the most prevalent in the Los Angeles area.

WOODCUT AND WOOD ENGRAVING

One of the earliest printmakers in the field of woodcut in California was the now quite forgotten Bertha Lum who was born in Tipton, Iowa, in 1879 and died in Genoa, Italy, in 1954. After study at the Art Institute of Chicago, Lum went to Japan in 1903, returning there several times afterward to perfect herself in the art of color woodcut. She also resided for a time in Peking. Lum worked in two styles of woodcut: one, an Occidentalized version of the Japanese *nishiki-e* print; the other, more interesting, a still imperfectly understood technique that she developed as the result of experimenting with an old Chinese printing process. She called her work in the second style "raised-line" prints, for the design stands out in strong relief and the color is filled by hand. Lum never disclosed her technical procedures in the raised-line print, but obviously every impression, if colored by hand, would be in a certain sense "unique."

Given her current obscurity and the fact that she was a much traveled person, it has not been ascertained how long Lum lived in Pasadena, but she was exhibiting in Los Angeles and Hollywood from 1920 on for about two decades. She is represented in the exhibition with a raised-line woodcut, *Spinning Goddess*, a well-preserved example of her unusual technique. The exact date of this work is problematical. The same subject in a traditional woodcut medium bears the copyright date of 1936, but the print itself was reproduced in an English-language newspaper, *The Leader*, published in China in the issue of December 2, 1930.[23] Lum's technique in her raised-line prints was essentially that of *gauffrage*, the process of deeply embossed woodcut. It is possible that she pressed a very damp, special paper or paper pulp upon the block, thus obtaining the raised lines or ridges which, after becoming permanent through drying, were then painted over by hand. This would make Lum's technique a curious forerunner of the currently practiced technique of paper casting or molding.

Contemporary with Lum in Southern California was Frances Hammel Gearhart. Born in Illinois, she was an educator in the Los Angeles city school system like her sister, the etcher May Gearhart. Frances was essentially self-taught, although she took lessons from the etcher Charles Henry Woodbury and the painter Henry Varnum Poor. Frances showed little influence of Oriental prints, and her woodcuts were charmingly direct transcripts of nature. Usually employing three blocks, including the key block whose black outline fused her composition together, Gearhart's work was popular, winning prizes and consistent praise for its color.

23. This archival material on Lum is preserved at the Achenbach Foundation, Palace of the Legion of Honor, San Francisco. Thanks are expressed here to Robert Flynn Johnson for making it available.

Another woodcut specialist was the English artist Frank Morley Fletcher, who came to Southern California in 1923 and offered instruction in the medium of woodblock printing. Among his pupils was the well-known local artist Channing Peake, later responsible for bringing Rico Lebrun to Los Angeles. Fletcher is represented in the exhibition by an undated color woodcut redolent of the flat, decorative patterning of Art Nouveau with its merging, flowing rhythms.

Such Southern California pioneers in the medium of color woodcut were largely without followers, for few other color woodcuts of this period have survived in the Los Angeles area. Woodcut, however, was not the widely preferred technique that etching was at this time, although a few other printmakers in the field are known. Those active in the 1920s included the Swedish-born artist Carl Oscar Borg and Stephen de Hospodar, born in Hungary.

Arriving in San Francisco in 1904, Borg, who had already studied in France, attracted the attention of Phoebe Apperson Hearst who gave him the opportunity to live and work among the Southwest Indians and also to travel abroad. An accomplished painter, Borg's Southwestern subjects were as popular in Europe as they were in America. He also worked as an art director for films and is known for his part in the 1926 motion picture *The Black Pirate,* starring Douglas Fairbanks. Borg's searching portrait *Navajo Chief* exemplifies his sympathetic powers of observation and excellent technique.

Another set designer for films, Stephen de Hospodar, exhibited his starkly delineated woodcuts in the Los Angeles area for a decade from the second half of the 1920s.

In 1928, having made some linoleum cuts the previous year, the Russian émigré painter and sculptor Peter Krasnow (also discussed in the following section on lithography) was moved to try wood engraving. He picked up the rudiments from a fellow printmaker and made several blocks. Becoming dissatisfied with the results, he gave up the traditional tools and turned to his own wood-carving instruments, including the chisel.[24] With these means he was able to achieve the distinctive design quality seen in the wood engraving *The Family I,* where profiled figures with dense interior modeling and shallow planar overlapping parallel the low relief of his distinguished wood sculpture.

A long-forgotten woodcut printmaker active in the 1930s in Los Angeles was Seattle-born Prescott Chaplin, a pupil of Chase, Bellows, and Max Bori. Chaplin's informal "diary" of impressions as he traveled in Mexico, California, and Alaska was published in Los Angeles by Print Guild International in 1932. *To What Green Altar?* recalls the intellectual atmosphere of the post-World War I era as Chaplin records his clicking vignettes of figures who were influential as thinkers, artists, and culture-carriers in the late 1920s and early 1930s, from the Indian philosopher and poet Rabindranath Tagore to the anarchist Emma Goldman. Secretive, or at least evasive, as he appears to have been in personality, Chaplin affected the life of a "tramp," although he had a productive career as screenwriter, set designer, and puppeteer; he also established an art school bearing his name.

Mexican themes and motifs played a large part in Chaplin's graphic work. His bold black-and-white woodcuts reflected his knowledge of German Expressionism and formed an approach opposite to that of the beautifully crafted, "popular" color lithographs of Charlot. Chaplin's *Market Day, Mexico* is a multicolored woodcut whose black masses and silhouettes merge harmoniously with the reds, yellow, green, blue, and orange of the decorative composition.

Also occupied with figurative subjects, Colorado-born Fletcher Martin was termed a "proletarian" artist when he won the main prize for his painting *Rural Family* at the Los Angeles County Museum in 1935. A one-time sailor and boxer, the self-taught Martin was one of the strongest Los Angeles Social Realist painters of the 1930s and 1940s. His most successful expression was found in themes drawn from the world of work and sport. In 1931 Martin won a full-time scholarship to the productive Stickney School of Art in Pasadena. A few years later he became acquainted with the great Mexican artist David Siquieros and worked with him as a muralist.

About the same time, in 1933, Martin had his first one-man exhibition at the Dalzell Hatfield Gallery, then located on West Seventh Street. The show consisted wholly of woodcuts. A brief brochure with statements by Hatfield and Merle Armitage and containing two illustrations, issued for the exhibition, has become as rare as the prints themselves. Armitage admired Martin's technique in which careful scraping resulted in atmospheric effects such as those seen in the print *Showers.* By lightly rasping over the entire block with a rain of fine white lines, Martin worked at the opposite pole of traditional woodcut with its sharp and often static contrasts of line and mass. A Japanese flavor was lent to his woodcuts by his pictorial diffusiveness, his simplified, semi-abstract figures emerging from the dark by means of scraped white contours.

After Rockwell Kent, who is reputed to have considered Landacre the leading wood engraver in the United States, Paul Landacre was probably the most gifted American artist in that field of his period. He differed completely from Kent in subject matter and technique. A frequent prizewinner in print competitions, Landacre was one of the very few Los Angeles printmakers to receive mention in Carl Zigrosser's *Prints and Their Creators.*

Born and educated in Ohio, Landacre came to California in 1922 and never left. Working initially with linoleum blocks, he also experimented with lithography and etching until he found his preferred technique in wood engraving about 1928. Landacre prepared his prints carefully—often with preliminary drawings, although at times initially as woodcuts—and he carried the engravings through trial proofs. Between the early 1930s and the 1940s, the artist changed his style of engraving from rather

24. *Los Angeles Times,* Sept. 14, 1930, part 3, p. 1.

wide, irregular lines to a system of very closely laid ones, achieving greater fluency and integration of light and form. But from the beginning of his career he showed his undeniable talent for conveying the solidity of the massed forms of rolling hills by the most economical means. His simplification of form, meticulously fine, white-line crosshatching, and solid blacks created some of the most memorable prints of the period. In a style that was quiet yet lyrical, Landacre strove not so much to expand the frontiers of his craft as to achieve purity and precision in composition and technique. As a result, his has become perhaps the best-known name among earlier Los Angeles printmakers.

Landacre worked with relatively limited tools. By his own account, ninety percent of his work was done with two types of gravers in addition to a chisel that was shaped for routing. His aesthetic goals were the simplest and most demanding. "The blacks," he declared, "should be black, the whites white, and every line or dot engraved on the block should show clean in the proof." With his pristine technique, Landacre eschewed "story and . . . profound significance unless," he wrote, "one realizes that there is more significance in any aspect of nature than mere words can impart."[25]

In his best engravings, Landacre's crisp, sharp line had a concentrated, almost abstract quality, as though he had cut through to the essential forms of his landscapes and uncovered their basic configuration without the addition of literal or passing elements. By 1945 the artist had made about 150 engravings and 300 illustrations, book plates, commercial designs, and other graphic works. Of the thirty-five or so books he illustrated, several were printed at the Ward Ritchie Press in Pasadena, others by Jake Zeitlin's Primavera Press in Los Angeles. Among the illustrations were the engravings of twelve great composers for the concert programs of KECA in 1936; the surety of design and execution resulted in an outstanding series. In 1939 the well-known print critic and connoisseur Carl Zigrosser came to Los Angeles on a study trip of American printmaking. His meeting with Landacre and the subsequent events are described in Ward Ritchie's bibliography of Landacre's book illustrations.

After World War II the relief print began to lose favor to the intaglio processes which were stimulated by the presence of S. W. Hayter and his Atelier 17 in New York. Paul Landacre's silent, restrained world, often conveyed by white line screens against solid black space, can be said to have emblemed the containment and close of an age of relative social serenity in Los Angeles. Here, as elsewhere in the country, artistic foundations and responses, rocked and revolutionized by world events, were to be radically reshaped by the hands of other artists.

LITHOGRAPHY Lithography was practiced only desultorily in Los Angeles during the early 1920s, and it did not find much reception until the mid-1950s. In 1923 a plea was made in an issue of the Print Makers Society of California *Newsletter* for increased activity in lithography, a plaint regularly repeated. Public apathy toward the medium was blamed on the popularization of chromolithography, considered destructive of lithography as a fine art. The editor also noted the practical problems inherent in printing lithographs: the need for stones and the cost of presses. Four years later, public lack of interest was still deplored; yet for those who did do lithography, the large size of their prints was criticized.

But in the late 1920s, incursions into the field of lithography were beginning in Los Angeles. There were commercial lithographers who undertook the printing of artists' lithographs. Among such early artists pioneering in lithography was the Russian émigré artist Peter Krasnow. After living in the East, Krasnow moved to Los Angeles in 1922. Following a sojourn of about four years in the south of France, Krasnow returned to Los Angeles where he continued to live until his death in 1979. Primarily known as a sculptor and painter, Krasnow also engaged in printmaking for a period from 1927 to 1929.

With his youthful experience as an interior decorator in southern Russia as his father's apprentice, it is not surprising that Krasnow's work was permeated by a strong decorative quality enlivened by a pervasive rhythm. Krasnow executed about seventeen lithographs from zinc plates in 1928. They were printed by a commercial printer, whose name the artist did not recall, and issued in an edition of twenty-five.

Unlike Chagall, whose fantasy was often edged with wit, Krasnow's poetic nature was more sombre, as seen in the imaginative and imposing lithograph *Glory* in the exhibition with its enigmatic symbolism and sculptural form. *The Slave*, on the other hand, in the abrupt truncation of the upper part of the head and the left leg, seems like a precursor of the nude studies by the contemporary realist painter, draftsman, and printmaker Philip Pearlstein.

While Krasnow was working in lithography, the twenty-two-year-old Millard Sheets had the experience of making a lithograph in Paris, and in Los Angeles itself an enterprising young printer, Lynton R. Kistler, together with his father, Will, became interested in lithography as a viable printing process.

Historically, Lynton Kistler must be regarded as the pivotal figure in the development of lithography in Los Angeles, as his early involvement in the medium opened up the means for its progress. Kistler, born in the city in 1897, with his father converted their letterpress plant into an offset lithographic printing shop in 1928, thus closing the gap that had existed between lithography and commercial printing. Kistler's interest in lithography coincided with the development of advertising art in Los Angeles, and in due course he attracted the attention of the remarkable Los Angeles book designer, impresario, and collector of modern art Merle Armitage. Armitage was a prime mover in music, opera, and the fine arts in the city. He enriched the Los Angeles County Museum's collection with his gifts of prints

25. P. Landacre, "Wood Engraving Technique," *The Relief Print*, ed. E. W. Watson and N. Kent, New York, 1945, p. 25.

and illustrated books and collaborated with Kistler on many publications. Written and designed by Armitage, they were printed by Kistler and published by the New York book and print dealer E. Weyhe. Through this association the work of several local artists and printmakers were diffused in limited editions of two hundred.

Among the first of the printmakers featured in these publications were Richard Day and Henrietta Shore. Day was a gifted motion picture set designer who collaborated with Erich Von Stroheim in all of the latter's films, not always receiving screen credit. It was not unusual in 1932 for a distinguished print connoisseur in the East to sound a slightly patronizing note concerning graphic art in Los Angeles, as Carl Zigrosser wrote in his foreword to the *Lithographs of Richard Day:*

One does not expect much from dwellers in Paradise; existence itself ... seems sufficient; why worry about thinking... or doing things? California has always seemed such a paradise to me, and thus it happens I do not look for much from California in the Graphic Arts.

Yet Day's lithograph *Boat on the Ways,* in the exhibition, compares favorably with prints by Charles Sheeler.

For the publication on Henrietta Shore, dedicated to the early Los Angeles art collector and Museum patron Ruth Maitland, texts were provided by Reginald Poland, Edward Weston, and Armitage. The frontispiece by Jean Charlot is a color portrait from a zinc plate of the amazing-looking Shore herself, whose prints were exhibited for the first time in Los Angeles in 1928 at the Jake Zeitlin Book Shop and Gallery at Sixth and Hope streets in downtown Los Angeles. Born in Canada, Shore had studied in England, Holland, and New York with Henri, Chase, and Kenneth Hayes Miller. It was John Singer Sargent who influenced her to go directly to nature. One of the founders of the New York Society of Women Artists and the Los Angeles Modern Art Society, Shore was a competent graphic artist who characteristically, for her time, reflected the ideal of significant form by means of her emphasis upon design. Reduced to basic outlines and rhythms as filtered through the artist's dreamlike vision—in some instances hills and rocks appeared as biomorphic forms—nature lost its physical elements. Shore's feeling for the human figure, exemplified in her undated lithograph in the exhibition, *Gypsy Encampment,* is conveyed by a technique that is basically that of crayon drawing and close in manner to that of Diego Rivera.

The earliest color lithograph in the exhibition is *Beach Figures,* 1930, by the Santa Barbara painter Douglass Parshall, probably one of the most successful of the area's academicians. He studied at the Art Students' League in New York and later with Frank Morley Fletcher. Although the figures in Parshall's print are stationary, their arrested positions form a rhythmic composition about one of Southern California's most popular pastimes. The unusual, low-keyed, muted brown colors, instead of the Pacific Coast blues and white that might be expected, may point to technical difficulties with color lithography at the time. This print was Parshall's only lithograph; twenty impressions were issued in color, ten in black and white.

In 1933 Lynton Kistler, who had come to know the French-born artist Jean Charlot through Merle Armitage, printed his first color lithograph from stone, Charlot's *Mother with Child on Back.* It was a monumental image and testimony to the printer's skill in a difficult undertaking since, in his own words, "the image spread very fast... and... we got only about thirteen good proofs."[26] Because of his experience in both commercial and hand printing, Kistler was prepared to use an offset press for fine lithographs, thus demonstrating his consistently pragmatic approach to his craft. Says Kistler, "I was so attracted to offset printing because it provided an opportunity for competent artists to make their work available on a large scale."[27] The veteran printer is still laboring to make the practice of offset acceptable to the philosophy of the market and to collectors who tend to prefer limited editions of fifty to a hundred and twenty-five as compared to the edition of one thousand that Kistler proposes.

Through Armitage, Kistler also came to know Stanton Macdonald-Wright, who together with Lorser Feitelson was one of the most articulate and effective proponents of modern art in Los Angeles. Macdonald-Wright informed local artists of Kistler's eagerness to have them make lithographs for him, and Helen Lundeberg recalls that the printer himself brought the zinc plates to their studios in his assiduous efforts to engage them in the medium.

Among the earliest artists to work with Kistler in this undertaking in the mid-1930s were Conrad Buff and Palmer Schoppe. This was the time of the WPA art project, and several Los Angeles artists became involved with the lithography shop created by the project. Not eligible to work for the WPA because of his self-employment, Kistler printed independently in his "studio" garage. Conrad Buff's *American Pioneers,* a composition in reverse of his painting *Westward* (collection of the Los Angeles County Museum of Art), typifies the graphic style of this Swiss-born painter of the Southwest landscape. Although some of his contemporary critics decried them as literal transcriptions of this rugged, picturesque terrain, his lithographs are now perceived as almost abstract designs created by undulant forms rendered unsubstantial by cast shadows.

Buff was also something of a pioneer in lithography in the city. He turned to the medium during the Depression, working with Kistler and with a highly skilled German-American printer, Paul Roeher, using zinc plates and experimenting with color. Buff acquired a press himself but found it more profitable to transfer his hand-printed lithographs to the offset process which could yield about three thousand impressions an hour.

26. P. Morse, *Jean Charlot's Prints,* Honolulu, 1976, p. 77.

27. C. Adams, "Lynton R. Kistler and the Development of Lithography in Los Angeles," *Tamarind Technical Papers,* no. 8, winter 1977–78, p. 108.

Buff preferred offset to hand-printed lithographs because he felt that offset preserved textures better than original printing.

In 1935 Kistler printed the portfolio of a young Los Angeles lithographer, Palmer Schoppe, a group of scenes from black life entitled *Caroline Low Country.* But after making only about fifteen prints, Schoppe discontinued lithography. His rugged, stylized *Head of a Negro* in the exhibition was printed in an edition of twenty-five; it is undated and may have been done before 1935. Schoppe later turned to mural painting.

Beginning in 1927, Fletcher Martin (see also reference in the section on woodcut) worked for several years in the shop of Earl Hays, a commercial printer who made motion picture inserts. In the 1930s Martin undertook printmaking himself, but the extent of his work in the field is not well known and after this initial activity in the field the artist discontinued printmaking. His best-known print is probably *Trouble in Frisco.* According to his artist brother, Kirk, the print antedated the 1938 painting of the same subject in the Museum of Modern Art. *Trouble in Frisco,* printed by Earl Hays, was shown in the first exhibition of Martin's lithographs at the Jake Zeitlin Gallery on South Carondelet in 1935–36. Signed and titled by Martin, it bears no date or edition number.

Fletcher Martin was at his strongest in themes drawn directly from contemporary American life. With such subjects his vigor, rhythmic design, and sensitive realism combined most successfully. The subject of *Trouble in Frisco* was the strife of local longshoremen. In contrast to the painting which apparently developed from the lithograph, as from a preliminary drawing, the view of the action in the print is not seen through a porthole but takes place on a pier. Martin, however, was obviously already thinking of a telescopic view, and the roundel format allowed him a design in which the figures and their movement flow with the circularity of the setting, accentuating the rhythmic interplay of their bodies. This work was undoubtedly the most complex composition that the artist had undertaken at that period.

Among important Los Angeles artists whom Kistler encouraged to make lithographs in the late 1930s were Lorser Feitelson and Helen Lundeberg. But in 1938 the pair were working with the WPA project.

Through the WPA project and its lithographic printer, Carl Winter, Feitelson and Lundeberg undertook to make prints which reflected these noted artists' achievements in Post-Surrealist Abstraction, which they pioneered in Southern California. Two Lundeberg prints in the exhibition are translations into crayon lithography of the artist's poetically surreal paintings, *The Red Planet* (in reverse to the canvas) of 1934 and *The Mirror (#1);* the latter print is in an edition of only five. Feitelson's major print of this period was titled *Post-Surrealist Configuration: Biological Symphony.* This striking work of 1939, from an edition of twelve, exemplifies the artist's classically virile drawing style; the structure of the composition adds reality to the Surrealist conception.

Also in this period, Boris Deutsch, the Lithuanian émigré artist who settled in Los Angeles in 1920, made a rare lithograph, *Mother and Children,* printed by Carl Winter. One of the principal organizers of the Group of Independent Artists in Los Angeles, Deutsch had struggled many years for recognition. The WPA brought him into the limelight; as a result he received various mural commissions. In 1946 his painting *What Atomic War Will Do to You* won first prize in the Pepsi-Cola Annual Competition.[28] *Mother and Children,* Deutsch's vivid print of a young mother, ranks with the best graphic work produced at the time on the subject of blacks. With a deep purple-black crayon, the immediacy and pictorialism of the artist's handling of light and modeling resulted in one of the more vital figurative lithographs created in the area in the late 1930s.

Ranking equally as a superior, richly executed stone lithograph of the period is *The Laundresses,* 1939, by the Vienna-born painter Oscar Van Young, who has lived in Los Angeles for more than forty years. Here the shimmering, vibrating coloristic background captures the weary figures in its unifying pattern of light and shadow, transforming the directness of the melancholy subject into a strikingly orchestrated and formally restrained composition. Like many of the painters under discussion here, Van Young produced a very restricted number of lithographs. He prepared several drawings for *The Laundresses* and also used the lithograph itself as a stage in the development of a painting.

In this same period, the internationally noted Los Angeles painter Stanton Macdonald-Wright made what was probably his only lithograph for his good friend Lynton Kistler, *Clump of Trees,* printed by Kistler in an edition of twenty-eight; it was an example of an artist's drawing, executed simply as a lithograph, that resulted in a gray "echo" of the original.

Meanwhile, in the course of the Depression, Kistler, driven by his all-consuming absorption in lithography, used his garage for printing on weekends. Between 1937 and 1940 his press was located in the candy factory operated by the well-known art dealer Earl Stendahl. Among prints issued by Kistler at this period were works by Millard Sheets, then head of the art department at Scripps College, teacher at Chouinard, and art director of the Los Angeles County Fair. Sheet's stylized image *Horse Frightened by Lightning* was printed in 1939. A historic figure in the development of Southern California design—including mosaics, murals, sculpture, and tapestry—Sheets now declares that if he had had a cause as strong as that of his Mexican muralist contemporaries, it might have improved his work.

One of the few Los Angeles artists who responded to social and political concerns in the 1930s and 1940s was Edward Biberman. A Philadelphian who held his first exhibitions of painting in Paris and Berlin in the late 1920s, Biberman came to Los Angeles in 1936. By that time, as he later wrote in his book *Time and Circumstances,* "all of us looked with fear and forebod-

28. *Southern California Artists 1890–1940.* Laguna Beach Museum of Art, 1979, p. 68.

ing at a world which was careening toward a holocaust." In the late 1930s, Biberman's lithograph *Pietà*, based on his painting of the same subject, was printed by Kistler; Biberman made his message more explicit by adding the words on the fallen placard. His work reflected an influence of contemporary Mexican graphic artists, not only in his themes of current socioeconomic and political issues but also in the careful crayon drawing, reminiscent of the dense strokes of Rivera and Orozco.

As the WPA project continued, turning many artists to more realistic themes, artists produced lithographs printed by Carl Winter. Among them was *The Pitchman* by Benjamin Newton Messick, a kind of John Sloan of Los Angeles lithography. Born in Missouri, Messick received his training at Chouinard Art School under F. Tolles Chamberlin, Clarence Hinkle, and the illustrator Pruett Carter. *The Pitchman*, after the artist's painting of 1940, stands out for its subject matter in a period when comparatively few artists in Los Angeles chose to make prints that were realistic in character.

Sometime after the end of World War II, Kistler reopened his lithography shop. Among artists whose work he printed were the painter, muralist, and mosaicist Richard Haines, whose 1948 prize-winning print *Bus Stop* shows the artist's coloristic handling of black and white. Another talent printed by Kistler that year was the Swiss-born abstract painter Hans Burkhardt, who had studied with Arshile Gorky in New York. Burkhardt came to Los Angeles in 1937 and made his living for many years as a furniture decorator. The two printer's proofs of 1948 on blue paper exhibited here exemplify Burkhardt's style in, respectively, Biomorphic Cubism and Abstract Surrealism. In this same year Kistler succeeded in getting Lorser Feitelson and Helen Lundeberg to make one print each for him. Feitelson's lithograph entitled *Reading*, here shown in a delicate impression from a proof edition of twelve, was printed in yellow-brown from stone. The final edition numbering fifty was printed in black and carried Kistler's chop. Lundeberg's sensitively romantic, atmospheric *Moonrise*, from an edition of seventeen, related to paintings of trees which occupied the artist during this period when she and her husband, Lorser Feitelson, were living in Westwood.[29]

Among the best of the internationally known artists of the period who worked with Kistler in Los Angeles was the Russian-born Neo-Romantic Eugene Berman. Brought from Paris to New York by the dealer Julien Levy in 1936, Berman came to California four years later. He painted murals for the home of the noted Santa Barbara collector Wright Ludington and worked in the Hollywood-Los Angeles area for five years. Berman was introduced to Kistler by Jean Charlot. Along with Max Ernst and Man Ray, Berman had exhibited at the William Copley Galleries in Beverly Hills, the leading avant-garde art gallery in Southern California until it closed in 1949. Despite his excessive, if not unreasonable, demands upon the technique, Berman made several lithographs with Kistler, among them the 1951 *Pisan Fantasy* shown here in a black-and-white printer's proof before the addition of color. Dissatisfied with the result, Berman insisted upon pressing a sheet of corrugated paper upon the stone to gain an additional effect for the print. The original stone with an impression made with the corrugated sheet is also included in the exhibition.

The second historic year for the development of lithography in Los Angeles must be regarded as 1948; it was two decades after Kistler went into lithographic printing. In that year, two artists who were to be of the greatest significance for the future of lithography came into Kistler's plant. The first was California-born Clinton Adams, then teaching at the University of California, Los Angeles; he was soon followed by Chicago-born June Wayne, who had come to Los Angeles for her health. Adams had learned about Kistler from Stanton Macdonald-Wright; Wayne had sought Kistler out on her own and came to know Adams at the shop.

America's first great lithographer, George Bellows, as well as other significant American artists in the medium through the mid-1940s, worked in the traditional black-and-white crayon method. Although color had come into general use in French lithography in the last decade of the nineteenth century, it was infrequently found in American work during the first half of the present century. And it was the French artist Jean Charlot who pioneered it in Los Angeles with the always open, experimentally minded Kistler.

The crayon method, in which the image was drawn on a stone or a zinc plate (or transferred from a special paper to the stone or plate), was obviously the most direct and simple. Often the lithograph was merely the reverse composition of an artist's painting or drawing. The stimulus to extend the frontiers of crayon lithography and explore other methods for making lithographs arose in part from the entrance of Picasso into the field in 1945 at Mourlot's in Paris. Other artists—among them Man Ray, for example—also initiated new lithographic techniques. In 1948 he suggested the "rainbow roll," the blending of separate inks on the rolling slab, to Kistler when they worked on the artist's print *Le Roman Noir*. The print consisted of a white-line composition made by means of a stylus drawn against a black background and printed in four colors.[30]

Kistler recalls that while Clinton Adams was able to develop the crayon technique to the point of its potential, other artists were unable to advance beyond the fundamental use of crayon or tusche (greasy ink). But among local artists who worked successfully in extending lithographic techniques by the use of washes and abrasives, the one who was to revitalize the medium and make the initial nationwide impact was the heroic June Wayne, who established the Tamarind Lithography Workshop on the street of the same name in Los Angeles in 1960.

Unlike many Los Angeles artists of the period, June Wayne

29. Information kindly provided by the artist.

30. C. Adams, "Kistler," p. 105, n. 15.

was absorbed by symbolism rather than direct representation; in this way her work has always been close to Surrealism. The themes of her earliest lithographs, printed by Kistler, dealt with justice and were based on the writings of Franz Kafka; while her illustrated book, *Songs and Sonets,* of a decade later, was inspired by the poetry of John Donne. With her literary culture, occupation with psychology, interest in the impact of space exploration, and continual technical investigations, Wayne created an intriguing mix of poetic images transmuted from physics, optics, and other sciences to express the alterations taking place in man's conception of and attitude toward the unfolding vastness of the cosmos. In terms of synthesizing these universal themes of nature, science, and art, Wayne is probably unique in the field of contemporary printmaking.

Wayne started working with Kistler in the early summer of 1948. He commented:

June was very demanding, right from the beginning. She came in periodically for two or three years and worked with me. Later she became intensely interested in lithography. She was a meticulous worker. It took her a long time to do a stone; she didn't just rattle them off. All of her subjects were intellectual, and she was insistent that the meat of her ideas should be reflected in the competence of her work. Sometimes it would take her three or four months to get something out of the stone that she was willing to accept. . . . Gradually, she worked on larger and larger stones. It took two men to get the heavy stones into her studio.[31]

Size for the printer was an important factor, since the cost of printing from large stones, those exceeding Kistler's preference for sixteen by twenty inches, was in his words "prohibitive." As for the use of color, "no one could afford it."

Wayne printed with Kistler for eight years. The lithographs from that period shown in this exhibition reveal the artist's use of a highly personal symbolism in a dynamic, pictographic style. The early prints were done chiefly in the crayon method, amplified by pen work and sprayed tusche; but already in one of the most brilliantly original and dynamic of lithographs of the 1950s, *The Witnesses,* the artist employed other materials. She introduced components such as string and small objects such as wood and seeds to effectively distribute the tonal notes of her symbolic configurations. Wayne's fascination with the "crystalline module" culminated in the extraordinary imbricated patterning of the 1958 diptych *Adam and Eve.* In the *John Donne* suite, completed in Paris in 1959, her highly skilled technique with washes and with salt on zinc appeared for the first time. This technique resulted in the wrinkled "toadskin" appearance that later became a hallmark of the work done at Tamarind. In France, where she did the book, Wayne was able to explore color more extensively than she had been able to in the United States and to have the advantage of printing on handmade papers.

"Without Kistler's pioneering efforts, neither June Wayne nor I would have had the initial opportunity to become so deeply committed to the art of the lithograph," wrote Clinton Adams, associate director of Tamarind in 1960–61.[32] Adams is represented in the first part of the exhibition by *Silver Bottle,* a crayon lithograph in green and black, printed by Kistler in 1950; it was a heroic undertaking at the time, given the cost of color printing. Always a controlled, meticulous worker, Adams composed here a well-balanced, harmonious still life whose tonal gradations, reflected light, and silhouetted vessels were carefully modulated to make the silver bottle the focus of the composition. Kistler rightly considered that the print demonstrated a high degree of proficiency.

Among the leading Los Angeles artists of the 1950s who worked with Kistler was Howard Warshaw (also discussed in the section on etching). As with etching, Warshaw stayed with lithography only briefly. He made two prints on the subject of traffic victims. The *Head of Traffic Victim* in the exhibition was printed in a limited edition of twenty-five; it shows the painter experimenting with the technique of scratching and scraping to attain the highlights of his dramatic theme.

Unlike Warshaw, his close friend and painting colleague Rico Lebrun was active in lithography for many years. His first prints in the exhibition are also the earliest color lithographs after the Parshall and Charlot shown here. Lebrun's three lithographs, from his suite *Villon's Ballad,* date from spring 1945 when the artist was teaching at the Fine Arts Center of Colorado Springs on a brief leave from the University of California, Santa Barbara, where he was artist-in-residence. His printer was Lawrence Barrett.

The Neapolitan-born Lebrun came to Los Angeles in 1938. He was, together with Lorser Feitelson, one of the most influential artists in the area from the late 1940s to the early 1950s. In 1949, he exhibited at the Venice Biennale with Gorky, de Kooning, and Pollock. Lebrun introduced tragic themes and the elements of classical Italian drawing to a city whose art and culture were, with several significant exceptions, still striving to arrive at vital and meaningful expression. Lebrun quickly found fruitful ground for his teaching and example, through which he stimulated awareness of the historical and cultural nature of art. Renewed appreciation for the drawn line, expressive content, and the human condition began to emerge in the work of many Southern California artists seeking to create modern forms by means other than pure abstraction. Among artists in the present exhibition who were influenced by Rico Lebrun are Howard Warshaw and John Paul Jones.

In 1944–45 the Julien Levy Gallery in New York showed the work of Rico Lebrun. The contemporaneous color lithographs of the *Villon* suite reflected Lebrun's study of the Spanish masters. The figures in these dramatic compositions, which were included in the first Biennal of color lithography held at the Cincinnati Museum in 1950, retain their formal wholeness, while in Lebrun's later work at Tamarind the figures become more expression-

31. Ibid., p. 105.

32. Ibid., p. 109.

istically exaggerated and abstract.

Toward the close of the 1950s significant events took place that were to initiate important developments in the art of lithography in Los Angeles. After seeing a lithograph by Mario Avati, printed in Paris, June Wayne, dissatisfied with the technical range of her Kistler oeuvre, went to the French capital in 1957 and began to work with the master printer Marcel Durassier. The result was the *John Donne: Songs and Sonets.* Returned to Los Angeles, in 1959 she acquired the now historic Tamarind site, and that same year she proposed a plan for the restoration of lithography to the Ford Foundation's Program in Humanities and the Arts.

Independently in New York that year, California-born Sam Francis prepared his first stone which was printed at Universal Limited Art Editions in West Islip, New York. The following year, Tamarind Lithography Workshop, Inc., opened in Los Angeles; at the same time, Francis was printing color lithographs with Emil Matthieu in Zürich for Eberhard Kornfeld. Two Los Angeles artists thus had taken major steps toward the propulsion of lithography as one of the most vital and pervasive print processes of modern times.

SILKSCREEN Silkscreen, or serigraphy, has been a recognized and popular print process since 1940 when the National Serigraph Society was formed under the direction of Anthony Velonis during the Federal Art Project. Serigraphy was pioneered in Los Angeles by Guy Maccoy and his wife, Geno Pettit. They made the first creative silkscreens in 1932 and held the first all-serigraph exhibition in 1939. In the early 1950s the Western Serigraph Institute was formed in Los Angeles with the Viennese-born art dealer and collector Oscar Salzer as representative. This active group of more than thirty serigraphers circulated exhibitions designed to serve museums and art centers as well as communities, schools, and universities. An exhibition culled from the work of the members was shown at the Los Angeles County Museum in 1953 and later circulated by the Smithsonian Institution. Among the artists represented in the show were Dorothy Bowman, Howard Bradford, Jack Otterson, Leonard Edmondson, Ralph Peplow, Richards Rueben, and Sister Mary Corita.

Mary Corita became a focal point of serigraphy in Los Angeles after her print *The Lord Is with Thee* won first prize at the Annual of Artists of Los Angeles and Vicinity at the Los Angeles County Museum in 1951. Working at the Convent of the Immaculate Heart, which she entered in 1936, Mary Corita studied printmaking at the University of Southern California but was taught serigraphy by the widow of the Mexican painter and muralist Alfred Martinez. Professionals in other fields who influenced her included the German art historian Alois Schardt, the Immaculate Heart instructor Paul LaPorte, and the designer Charles Eames. Corita's early prints were, in her own words, "extremely derivative . . . very Byzantine."[33] The artist depended considerably on medieval art in her beginnings. Both silkscreens in the current exhibition were inspired by prototypes of that era, sculpture as well as illuminated manuscripts. For example, Mary Corita used the closely arranged, rowlike figures of late Roman/early Christian art in her first brush stencil serigraph *The Lord Is with Thee.* The subject was originally *The Assumption,* but the artist found her work to be so bad that she began to add colors for improvement and ended by transforming it into the vibrant color composition which first won her fame. In *This Beginning of Miracles,* the impastolike colors, rather than achieving the deep intensity of the former silkscreen, were more jewellike, taking their cue from illuminated manuscripts but still incorporating the hieratical figures of the Byzantine.

Around Sister Corita and the staff of Immaculate Heart there developed a kind of joyous unorthodoxy of art expression which attracted national attention. Mary Corita herself, more in sympathy with the untrammeling effect of Abstract Expressionism than with a modernism of traditional religious art, began to create silkscreens in the late 1950s and early 1960s. She used the freedom of abstraction increasingly to universalize her texts and statements. The number of her early prints is actually small in comparison to the work she later produced, when many of her prints were intended to speak as "signs" or "advertisements" in her continuing effort to communicate to the fullest with all people. Her first silkscreens remain like "primitives" in the body of her work, charmingly beguiling evocations of medieval icons, glowing like stained glass.

Silkscreen can be said to have come fully into its own in Los Angeles as elsewhere in the 1960s, particularly with the advent of Pop Art and multiples. Its character was then exploited for its surface quality of absolutely flat color. It also was a process that could easily be combined with photography, photolithography, collage, multiples, and other processes, creating new printing methods and techniques which could transmit the interests and aesthetic values of contemporary artists.

---

33. *Los Angeles Art Community: Group Portrait/Corita Kent.* Oral History Program, University of California, Los Angeles, 1977, p. 129.

INTRODUCTION The 1960s were a period of profound, even revolutionary change, both socially and culturally, in American society. Southern California felt the impact of these changes as much as any sector of America, and in many respects it was at the vanguard of social and cultural upheavals. The birth of a radically new period in the history of printmaking in Los Angeles can be pinpointed with astonishing accuracy: July 1, 1960. On that date, June Wayne's Tamarind Lithography Workshop officially opened and ushered in a printmaking renaissance in Los Angeles. Although Tamarind was concerned exclusively with lithography, its spirit of experimentation permeated all sectors of printmaking. And for the first time, Los Angeles became a center of international renown and importance in the arts.

"When, in 1959, I designed the Tamarind project," wrote June Wayne in the preface to the *Tamarind Book of Lithography*, "the art of lithography had gone into a grave decline in both Europe and the United States." This decline became very clear to Wayne in the late 1950s when she decided that Lynton Kistler, who had served as her printer for most of her earlier lithographs, could no longer service her increasingly ambitious desires for exploiting lithography. In Paris, where she printed the suite *John Donne: Songs and Sonets* with Marcel Durassier, she found a more suitable artistic ambience. But the impracticality of traveling to Europe to print underscored the desperate future of lithography in the United States.

Consequently, in 1960 with the first of several grants from the Ford Foundation, Wayne inaugurated the Tamarind Lithography Workshop. Kistler was first recruited as the shop's head printer, but his heavy involvement in offset printing precluded his participation. Bohuslav Horak, a Czech master printer from Paris, was thus installed in this position. Tamarind could not claim to be the first important workshop responsible for the revival of interest in lithography. That honor must probably go to Tatyana Grosman's Universal Limited Art Editions, established in West Islip on Long Island in 1957, where Jasper Johns and Robert Rauschenberg were first introduced to lithography. Tamarind's purpose, however, was different from Universal's. Its primary *raison d'être* was the training of a new generation of master printers. Instead of the relaxed and intimate atmosphere prevalent at Universal, intense and highly concentrated activity was the rule at Tamarind. Artist-fellows were invited for only two-month periods, during which they were essentially asked to create on demand. A number of artists were not accustomed to such working procedures, and the artistic results occasionally were dismal. Others thrived in this atmosphere.

All aspects of lithography were explored at Tamarind, with a special emphasis on the collaborative relationship between artist and printer. For many of the artists, this experience in printmaking represented their first exposure to lithography. As pointed out by Clinton Adams, Tamarind's first associate director, "While few American artists made lithographs in the 1950s, there are few in the 1960s who have not done so, either at Tamarind or at the workshops established as a consequence of the Tamarind program."[1] Tamarind offered the opportunity to print with special inks on the most luxurious papers, producing impeccable impressions in editions strictly limited to twenty. The meticulous documentation of each print produced at Tamarind set a high standard that eventually became the norm in contemporary printmaking. During the course of its existence, from 1960 to 1970, Tamarind produced more than 2,500 editions from the hands of 152 artists working with 68 printers.

The roster of artists who worked at Tamarind was international in scope; it included Josef Albers, Jacques Lipschitz, Masuo Ikeda, Rufino Tamayo, Jose Luis Cuevas, Allen Jones, and David Hockney. As might be expected, a large contingent of Southern California artists participated in the program, including John Paul Jones, Rico Lebrun, Sam Francis, Richard Diebenkorn, Ed Ruscha, Billy Al Bengston, Ken Price, Ed Moses, James Strombotne, Jules Engel, William Brice, Connor Everts, John McLaughlin, Emerson Woelffer, Robert Cremean, and, of course, June Wayne herself.

The Tamarind program exerted considerable influence on the graphic arts, not only in Los Angeles but also throughout the world. This influence spread widely as a number of workshops opened that were manned by printers trained at Tamarind. These include Kanthos Press in Los Angeles, the first offspring, founded in 1963 by Joe Funk; the Hollander Workshop in New York, begun in 1965 by Irwin Hollander; Gemini Ltd. in Los Angeles, started in 1965 by Kenneth Tyler, and to become Gemini G.E.L. in 1966 with the participation of Stanley Grinstein and Sidney Felsen; Collectors Press in San Francisco, begun by Ernest de Soto in 1967; and Cirrus Editions Ltd. in Los Angeles, the creation of Jean Milant in 1970.

Probably the most successful and influential offshoot of Tamarind has been Gemini G.E.L. Founded in 1965 as Gemini Ltd., it has helped elevate contemporary printmaking to the heights of technical sophistication. From its very inception, however, Gemini was based on a fundamentally different premise than Tamarind was. Whereas the latter was a non-profit organization supported by grants from the Ford Foundation, Ken Tyler's purpose was to make money, while at the same time making great prints. As Gemini developed, furthermore, it was not strictly a lithography workshop; it also produced silkscreens, multiples, and most recently etchings. As did Tamarind, however, Tyler believed that the artist had to be attracted to the medium. As he has stated, "Great artists make great prints—that is, *if* and *when* they get around to it." Gemini has been successful in attracting to its workshop some of the greatest names in American art. These include Jasper Johns, Robert Rauschenberg, Frank Stella (who made his first lithographs at Gemini), Roy Lichtenstein, Claes Oldenburg, and a number of others. The roster of names tends toward those artists with firmly established

1. G. Z. Antreasian and C. Adams, *The Tamarind Book of Lithography: Art and Techniques*, New York, 1971.

reputations, rather than up-and-coming talents.

As Gemini Ltd., the workshop's first prints were outside commissions. These included Gemini's first print, a lithograph by Nicholas Krushenick for the Art Museum Council of the then-new Los Angeles County Museum of Art, and Alberto Giacometti's *Nude in Studio*, the Museum's Graphic Arts Council's first commissioned print as well as the artist's last. Prints included in the exhibition that were printed at Gemini during these fledgling days are David Hockney's *Picture of Melrose Avenue*, printed at Gemini for Editions Alecto, Charles White's *Exodus II*, and John Altoon's *Untitled*.

In 1966, Tyler acquired two business partners, Sidney Felsen and Stanley Grinstein, who provided the capital for the expansion toward a more ambitious program, and the enterprise became known as Gemini G.E.L. With Josef Alber's *White Line Squares* of 1966, Gemini's first commissioned prints, there was another fundamental difference from the Tamarind program: the definition of an original print. Part of the philosophy of the older shop was the necessary collaborative process between artist and printer in the making of a print. With Gemini, however, Albers was never physically present at the shop; instead, he directed the entire operation by mail and telephone.

At Tamarind in 1968, Ed Moses created a series of lithographs that violated the conventional two-dimensional quality of prints by expanding into the third dimension. The traditional vocabulary, even definition of prints would be questioned, explored, and given new meaning at Gemini. The idea of prints as works on paper was immediately challenged by Man Ray's 1966 screenprints printed on Lucite. Artists like Robert Rauschenberg, Donald Judd, John Chamberlain, and Ed Kienholz have created works at Gemini that are three-dimensional objects and are more easily classified as multiples rather than prints. This expansion of the concept and technology of printmaking has been one of the trademarks of Gemini's productions. Another development has been an increase in the size of prints, as they have begun to challenge painting in monumentality. One of the first of these monumental prints was Rauschenberg's *Booster* of 1967, which required considerable research into larger presses and paper. Gemini's success was such that large-scale prints are no longer anomalies.

Compared to those who worked at Tamarind, the number of Los Angeles artists that have worked at Gemini is small, although the charge that Gemini neglects local artists is probably not justified. In keeping with Gemini's policy of working with established artists, local printmakers who have worked at Gemini represent the cream of local talent: Sam Francis, Joe Goode, Ed Ruscha, Ken Price, Ron Davis, Bruce Nauman, and a few others.

The most recent addition to the great triad of Los Angeles print workshops is Cirrus Editions Ltd., founded in 1970 by Jean Milant, a former Tamarind master-printer. Just as Gemini's philosophy differed from Tamarind's, Cirrus provides a strong contrast to Gemini. Instead of the international stars such as Johns, Rauschenberg, and Lichtenstein who have printed at Gemini, at Cirrus one finds an emphasis on and a commitment to California, and specifically to Los Angeles artists. Cirrus functions not only as a print workshop and publisher, but also as an art gallery, featuring exhibitions of paintings and sculptures as well as prints by its artists.

Innovative ideas and materials in printmaking are as prevalent at Cirrus as at Gemini. One may cite Joe Goode's double-layered torn lithographs executed at Cirrus, an idea he explored further at Gemini using cloth and tissue; or Greg Card's screenprint on Plexiglas of 1972 exhibited here, where actual light and shadow are an integral part of the viewer's perception of the work; or multiples such as Eric Orr's lead reliefs and Jay Willis's wire sculptures. Technical innovation, however, is not necessarily the ultimate goal at Cirrus. Milant states, "I believe that good prints may benefit from innovation but do not have to depend on technical novelty for their importance."[2] He goes on to cite Bruce Nauman's lithograph of 1971, exhibited here as an example of conventional techniques that contribute to an important contemporary statement. Nauman's corpus of graphic work at Cirrus is a perfect example of the variety found at the workshop. Using lithography, etching, drypoint, or aquatint, Nauman has created a number of powerful and provocative images. Photolithography and silkscreen—techniques perhaps condemned by "pure" printmakers as too commercial—are frequently used at Cirrus, as in the works by Ron Cooper and the Los Angeles Fine Arts Squad. The philosophy is that how, and to what end, the techniques are used is more important than the techniques themselves.

It is extremely difficult to summarize the stylistic developments of the twenty years covered by this section of the exhibition. The variety is such that one cannot speak of a succession of movements. Instead, Pop or Pop-inspired works stand next to Expressionist images, which abut Minimal works, in proximity to prints that seem to defy all categorization. It is probably still too soon to sort out definitively what was happening in the 1960s, much less the 1970s. This essay will only attempt to find some common ground for often disparate works that defy classification. Purely non-objective forms were rarely encountered before 1960, least of all in printmaking, which seems to have been more resistant to new ideas than painting or sculpture. In the 1960s, however, some of the breakthroughs introduced by Abstract Expressionism made themselves felt in printmaking, particularly in subject, scale, and color. Tamarind and, later, Gemini provided the impetus for these changes because they were able to develop the necessary technical means to implement them; for example, the equivalent to the increased scale of avant-garde painting could not be achieved before the technical problems of producing large-scale prints were first solved. These problems were broached by Ken Tyler at Gemini with the execution of Robert Rauschenberg's monumental *Booster* in 1967. The usual intimacy of prints was eventually sac-

2. J. E. Young, *Cirrus*, Cirrus Editions Ltd., Los Angeles, 1972, p. 1.

rificed for a sense of monumentality, thus challenging a quality formerly reserved for painting. Consequently, the heroic gesture of Abstract Expressionist painting could be effected in printmaking as well, in the works of artist such as June Wayne, Jules Engel, and Tom Fricano. Such monumentality, however, was not restricted to non-objective imagery. In the hands of artists like Rico Lebrun, Connor Everts, and Charles White, figurative forms took on a new sense of power, further accentuating their humanistic and sometimes tragic messages.

Before 1960, among the most notable practitioners of non-objective painting were Karl Benjamin, Lorser Feitelson, Frederick Hammersley, and John McLaughlin, all of whom were featured in a 1959 exhibition entitled *Four Abstract Classicists,* organized by Peter Selz and Jules Langsner at the Los Angeles County Museum.

The clean and immaculate forms introduced by McLaughlin, Feitelson, and others led seemingly and inevitably to the so-called "L.A. Look" and "finish fetish" of the 1960s. Whether or not these artistic developments can be tied to the mushrooming aerospace industry or to the Southern Californian obsession with the automobile, a number of artists experimented with new materials and new techniques in printmaking. During its ten-year existence, Tamarind stayed mostly within the conventional parameters of the print as a two-dimensional image on paper, with the important exception of Ed Moses's 1968 suite of eight lithographs that moved into the third dimension. These lithographs represented an important innovation, signaling a first blurring of the line of demarcation between the print and the sculptural multiple, a tendency that would increase. In 1973 an exhibition organized by Joseph Young at the Los Angeles County Museum of Art entitled *Dimensional Prints* explored some of these directions in Los Angeles printmaking.

Much of the experimentation in new materials has been in the area of three-dimensional multiples, such as those by Larry Bell and Ed Kienholz; their categorization as prints or graphic arts, even allowing for considerable leeway in definition, still remains somewhat problematic. This spirit of experimentation in new materials can be seen nevertheless in a number of works by local artists. Joe Goode's torn fabrics, Greg Card's and Gene Gill's use of Plexiglas and Mylar, physical erosion employed by Charles Christopher Hill, Ed Ruscha's printing with foodstuffs, David Hammons's body prints, Joel Bass's lead sheets, Timothy Washington's etched aluminum plates—all represent a search for new aesthetic effects undreamed of twenty years ago.

These often spectacular technological experiments have occasionally been characterized as cold and sterile by-products of a technological environment. Close examination of the works belies this notion. McLaughlin's 1962 lithograph is a perfect example. While the composition exhibits a rigorous austerity worthy of Piero della Francesca or Nicolas Poussin, the contrasting tones of black ink reveal a marvelous, velvety, even sensuous surface unknown in McLaughlin's paintings. Similarly, Moses' 1968 lithograph's architectonic, almost industrial structure is contrasted with a soft and lyrical use of color.

Alongside these works customarily associated with the archetypal "L.A. Look" were created prints reflecting the infusion of Abstract Expressionist ideas into Southern California. Although conventional wisdom purports that Abstract Expressionism "died" with the 1950s, it asserted itself relatively late in Southern California. With some exceptions, before 1960 much abstract art was still rooted in some manner to the Cubist forms of the middle and late periods of Picasso. In the late 1950s, however, a new generation of artists spearheaded by John Altoon emerged to challenge the old forms. Furthermore, immigrants such as Sam Francis, whose style developed in Paris in the attempt "to make the late Monet pure," and Matsumi Kanemitsu, who absorbed the lessons of deKooning in New York, brought a cosmopolitan and original vision to the area.

In spite of the new dominance of abstraction in Los Angeles printmaking, figurative art continued to be a viable form of expression, although with new twists. The Expressionist style of Rico Lebrun and his followers, a style that dominated the local art scene for much of the 1940s and 1950s, continued into the early 1960s, although Lebrun's influence appears to have diminished after his death in 1964. As evident from the title, Lebrun's *Grünewald Study II,* executed at Tamarind in 1961, is based on the central panel of Matthias Grünewald's Isenheim altarpiece, the subject enhanced and transformed through Lebrun's Cubo-Expressionist treatment and his interest in Baroque movement. William Brice had studied, along with Howard Warshaw, with Lebrun at the Jepson Art Institute in the 1940s; but Brice's Tamarind lithograph of 1961, *Striped Robe,* shows the artist abandoning both the Picasso-inspired forms and the agonized subjects of Lebrun for a more straightforward and elegant, though still expressively delineated, portrayal of the sitter. Closer in spirit to the tradition of Lebrun and Warshaw is Connor Everts's *Execution,* a Tamarind lithograph of 1960.

Although Richard Diebenkorn did not move permanently to Southern California until 1966, he spent 1961–62 in the area as a guest professor at the University of California, Los Angeles, and as an artist-in-residence at Tamarind. During that period he executed a series of lithographs at Tamarind. His 1961 lithograph, although a figurative work depicting a woman looking pensively off into space, displays Diebenkorn's ongoing concern with formal structure, particularly in the spatial juxtapositions of large areas of black and white. These formal elements dominate the image to the extent that the female figure is not immediately recognizable. Diebenkorn combined Abstract Expressionist principles with a figurative subject more successfully than any of the artists in the Lebrun camp.

Los Angeles figurative artists, in general, did not adopt the Photo-Realist attitude prevalent in New York in the 1960s and

1970s. Some, in fact, such as James Strombotne, viewed the Eastern figurative movement with suspicion, as "the Establishment's alternative to minimal art . . . the minimal version of figurative art."[3] Instead, Strombotne viewed his art as "symbolic realism" and banded together with other artists, including Shiro Ikegawa, with similar ideas. In Robert Cremean's sculpture as well as in his suite of lithographs *Fourteen Stations of the Cross*, done at Tamarind in 1966–67, Surrealist overtones are present as the figure is often subtly transformed from solid to void.

In contrast to the sometimes purely aesthetic and hermetic concerns of much abstract and even figurative art, a number of artists, particularly minority ones, were more interested in socially relevant themes.

The late 1960s saw increased activity on the part of black artists in Los Angeles. Charles White, the doyen of American black artists, came to California in 1956 and began to teach at Otis Art Institute in 1965; the following year he was invited to make the lithograph *Exodus II* at Gemini G.E.L. Unlike his earlier Tamarind lithographs, which integrated background and figure in a manner reminiscent of Analytical Cubism, White's *Exodus II* presents a single monumental figure dominating the space with a sense of heroic dignity.

In fact, much of the art produced by black and other minority artists dealt with specific social themes, a message made clear in 1971, when the work of White and two younger contemporaries, David Hammons and Timothy Washington, was presented at the Los Angeles County Museum of Art, the first exhibition of this kind ever held in the city.

Both Hammons and Washington explored new graphic techniques to present powerful social statements. Hammons's *Injustice Case* of 1970 was undoubtedly inspired by the case of Black Panther Bobby Seale at the trial of the Chicago Eight. The gripping sense of realism and immediacy is achieved by Hammons's use of his own body as the printing "plate," as it were. He covered himself, including his clothes, with margarine, and pressed his body against an illustration board. He then covered the greasy print with powdered pigments and sprayed the image with a fixative; the result is a brilliantly colored and deeply moving image. Hammons's use of his body is a particularly dramatic example of an artist's sense of self-revelation in his work. His monoprints stand halfway between Jasper Johns's lithographs from the early 1960s, such as *Hand* and *Skin with O'Hara Poem*, and George Segal's *Blue Jeans Series* of soft-ground etchings of 1975. But Hammons's work is considerably different in both technique and intention.

Like Hammons, Washington combines an unusual medium and a powerful message in his *One Nation Under God* of 1970. The aluminum sheet is coated with enamel, and the image is scratched on the surface with an etching needle. The technique is essentially that of drypoint, but instead of subsequently inking the plate and producing a paper impression, Washington presents the plate itself as the finished work. The cold and hard aluminum is contrasted with the warmth and emotion of the subject, a dichotomy that Washington purposefully exploits.[4] Washington, furthermore, believes that the large, simple shapes and round, staring eyes produce a direct and lasting impact on the spectator.

Betye Saar's graphic works are reminiscent in their structure of Joseph Cornell's assemblages, but with a particularly personal twist. Her prints are incorporated into three-dimensional structures recalling doors and windows. *Black Girl's Window* of 1969 is undoubtedly her masterpiece in this mixed-media technique. The images are drawn from the realm of astrology, phrenology, and other aspects of black folk culture. According to Saar, "The window is a symbolic structure which allows the viewer to gain insight and to traverse the threshold of the mystic world. My graphic interpretation is to create an occult atmosphere which will leave a strong impression of the vague and unexplained."[5]

The landscape of Southern California had provided almost unlimited subject material for artists through much of the first half of the twentieth century. It continued to be a potent attraction in the 1960s and 1970s, although its depiction was hardly as sentimental and bucolic as before. As the landscape itself changed, so did the artists' attitudes and responses. Ed Ruscha and David Hockney often selected the most mundane, even tacky elements in their environment as subjects.

Ruscha's *Standard Station* of 1966 is part of a long series of works in which the artist explored the image of the gas station, a ubiquitous fixture of the Southern California landscape. The image first appeared in 1962 in Ruscha's *Twenty-Six Gas Stations*, a book of deadpan, documentary views of various gas stations, as though snapped from a passing car in a trip across the country. The image was then carried through up to 1969 in a series of paintings and silkscreens, in which the gas station becomes almost iconic, a temple serving America's and particularly Southern California's obsession with mobility.

The inclusion of David Hockney in this exhibition of Los Angeles printmakers might raise some eyebrows: after all, he is not even an American citizen. He has been included, nevertheless, because he lives most of the year in Los Angeles, a second home (if such an inveterate traveler may have one) from the time of his first visit here in 1963. Even more importantly, Los Angeles and its environs have proved to be the source of much of Hockney's inspiration. With perhaps the exception of Ruscha, no other artist has responded to the Southern California landscape with such obvious relish and enthusiasm as Hockney.

Hockney's 1965 lithograph *Picture of Melrose Avenue with an Ornate Gold Frame* is part of a series entitled *A Hollywood Collection*, one of Kenneth Tyler's first productions at Gemini Ltd. At that time, Tyler's workshop on Melrose Avenue shared a building with Jerry Solomon's frame shop, and Hockney was inspired by the various frames he saw in the window. The resulting suite

---

3. Statement of the artist, in *Graphic Arts Council Newsletter*, Los Angeles County Museum of Art, vol. 5, no. 7, 1970, p. 4.

4. J. E. Young, *Three Graphic Artists: Charles White, David Hammons, Timothy Washington*, Los Angeles County Museum of Art, 1971, p. 9.

5. R. Castellon, *Marie Johnson/Betye Saar*, San Francisco Museum of Modern Art, 1977, unpaginated.

of lithographs forms a sort of ready-made art collection, all pre-framed and representing all the standard subjects: still life, portrait, landscape, even a "pointless abstraction under glass." The *Picture of Melrose Avenue* continues a theme Hockney had earlier explored in a number of paintings from 1964. The lithograph is particularly close in composition, though considerably looser in technique, to *Wilshire Blvd., Los Angeles.*[6]

Other examples of popular imagery appear in the Los Angeles Fine Arts Squad's 1973 lithograph *Isle of California,* depicting Vic Henderson's and Terry Schoonhoven's famous mural in Venice. The mural itself is one of the Squad's most renowned examples of trompe l'oeil effects and represents a modern revival of public art in Southern California. Unlike the heroic idealism usually represented in the New Deal projects in the 1930s, however, the *Isle of California* apotheosizes the habitual fear, particularly prevalent among visitors, of California's cataclysmic demise by an earthquake. Rather than reproduce the finished mural, the lithograph documents the work in its unfinished state, a condition that renders even more surreal the shattered freeway as it towers above the schematically outlined landscape. A more whimsical view of humanity's use and misuse of technology is provided by the work of William Crutchfield. His delicately and meticulously rendered machines of absurd incongruity, such as his *Tamarind-Tanic* of 1970, are monuments to Crutchfield's wildly creative imagination and often have a certain sympathetic pathos.

Perhaps reflective of a 1970s sensibility is the depiction by a number of artists of what might be considered "inner landscapes." Though based on objective reality, the works transcend their ostensible subjects to reveal more cosmic and mystic meanings. A prime example is the graphic work of Vija Celmins. Her drawings and lithographs are works of time-consuming and painstaking precision. Although obviously admirable, Celmins's virtuosity is not the main point of her art. Her numerous and familiar variants on views of the ocean, as well as the 1971 lithograph printed at Cirrus and exhibited here, are depicted without any indication of human scale or presence, as well as without foreground or horizon. As a result, her works appear to be removed from the world of nature, and they become abstract patterns. Again, such purely formal qualities are not the primary intention; instead, these abstracted views seem to be only microcosms in a larger infinity, which could extend without end in all directions. Man becomes almost depressingly small and insignificant in the face of this cosmic vastness.

In its source of imagery, Craig Kauffman's series of four lithographs executed at Cirrus in 1971 is diametrically opposed to Celmins's prints. His works are based on photographs of microscopic blood cells that appeared in *Scientific American;* Kauffman even retained the grid pattern of the photographs. Brilliantly colored, glowing luminously from the black paper, and removed from their original setting, Kauffman's images, like Celmins's, become abstract patterns. Through the distortion in scale, the images appear to be transformed into surreal lunar landscapes.

Ann McCoy's *The Night Sea,* a two-paneled, hand-colored lithograph of 1978, is a reflection of what McCoy considers the dark side of her psyche. Her earlier, more light-filled works, such as the large 1972 drawing *Mt. Maurice* in the collection of the Los Angeles County Museum of Art, were superseded by a darker naturalistic vision. As McCoy has explained, "My own notions of spirituality at that time were lofty and inflated. I had forgotten Jung's words that to know heaven one must have one's feet planted in hell."[7] The reference to Jung is appropriate because McCoy's work is concerned with the collective unconscious, "the primordial images [that] evolve through us and exist in every period and culture."[8] In *The Night Sea,* Jules Verne's Nautilus and the story of Jonah and the Whale become McCoy's metaphors for her journey into the unconscious and her transformation upon emerging. Her imagery is a magical, highly personal vision, combining strange and beautiful creatures and forms from the depths of the ocean and extraterrestrial space.

One of the most mysterious and innovative prints in the exhibition is Jerry McMillan's "photo-sculpture." A color offset lithograph is mounted inside a handcrafted paper bag. A hole is torn away to reveal the lithograph within. The image—here the exterior of a modest house—suddenly takes on a mysterious and evocative power through McMillan's skillful and inventive manipulation of its setting and presentation.

LITHOGRAPHY The story of lithography in Los Angeles since 1960 begins, of course, with the Tamarind Lithography Workshop whose history has been recounted earlier. Although chronologically not the earliest of the Tamarind lithographs exhibited, June Wayne's *At Last a Thousand II* of 1965 is the appropriate work with which to begin a discussion of lithography.

This print, whose title refers to the creation of the one-thousandth lithograph at Tamarind, epitomizes the technical developments pursued at the workshop. The complex textural effects of the tusche, in particular, are one of the hallmarks and great achievements of Tamarind. Salt particles were allowed to oxidize on the plate, and then the water-tusche washes were sprayed over, rather than directly onto, the plate. The results resemble a craggy and desolate volcanic landscape, an ideal setting for Wayne's rather pessimistic imagery. The lithograph is part of a series of works dealing with the idea of lemmings as a personal metaphor for her views on the human condition.

Equally concerned with textural effects, but without Wayne's allusion to natural landscapes, is Matsumi Kanemitsu's Tamarind lithograph *Number Six State II* of 1970. Although born in the United States, Kanemitsu lived in Japan during most of his childhood. In this lithograph, the ink is applied in a way that brings to mind Oriental calligraphy, as well as the gestural emotionalism he undoubtedly absorbed during his years in New York

6. *David Hockney: Paintings, Prints and Drawings, 1960–1970,* Whitechapel Art Gallery, London, 1970, p. 43, cat. no. 64.10.

7. In *Ann McCoy: The Red Sea and The Night Sea,* The Arts Club of Chicago, 1970, unpaginated.

8. Ibid.

from 1946 until his move to Los Angeles in 1961 at the invitation of Wayne. A marvelous tension between the flat and the sculptural is achieved through the varying degrees of transparency of the lithographic ink, as well as by the carefully controlled directions of the gestural marks.

Part of Tamarind's program was to push the limits of lithography to suit the requirements and ideas of the artist. Included among these tours de force are Norman Zammitt's lithograph of 1967 and William Pettet's of 1970. Zammitt's print required painstaking effort in the registration of color in order to achieve the subtle shifting optical effects. Working with a master image of repeated hexagonal shapes, Zammitt created the lithographs by slightly shifting the grid for each color run. Pettet's work is one of six lithographs printed simultaneously on the same sheet of paper, then cut to produce prints ranging in size from the one exhibited here to one measuring three inches square, the smallest lithograph produced at Tamarind. Through a complicated method called the Polymer Drawing Process, Pettet was able to interlock without overlapping the different areas of color.

Also related to Tamarind's experimentation with new techniques and materials is Billy Al Bengston's *Mecca Dracula* of 1968. The "iris" image is one of Bengston's familiar symbols, along with the chevron and the valentine. Bengston's work has tenuous links with Pop Art, although he straddles the border between abstract and figurative art. The use of polymer and lacquer in his paintings can be traced to his work as an automobile painter, a significant fact for Southern California where the "customized" car was elevated to a peculiarly local and popular art form. Although the sheen and translucency of lacquer could not be reproduced in lithography, in *Mecca Dracula* Bengston achieved a parallel glossy effect by mixing gold powder with the lithographic ink and air-brushing the image on the stone. The other link with Pop is provided by Bengston's use of signature motifs drawn from mass culture. In the case of the "iris," the image was not suggested by the flower, but from the moment in Dracula movies when the bat is transformed into the figure of the count. The connection with motion pictures is accentuated by the use of titles like *Big Duke, Busby,* and *Bela* in his paintings of the early 1960s.

Sam Francis has been particularly prolific in lithography since his introduction to the medium by Tatyana Grosman in 1959: he has created an oeuvre of more than 200 editions in the last twenty years. Those first stones, however, were not actually printed until 1968; therefore, his first published lithographs were those commissioned in 1960 by Kornfeld and Klipstein and executed in collaboration with the printer Emil Matthieu. After spending most of the 1950s in Paris as well as traveling around the world in 1957–58, Francis settled in Los Angeles in 1962. While in Paris, Francis's paintings owed a debt to American Abstract Expressionism, in the all-over patches of dripping transparent color, as well as to his study of Monet's late paintings of water lilies. In the late 1950s, however, undoubtedly due to his exposure in Japan to a different kind of aesthetic and mode of composition, Francis loosened his painterly structure, allowing the white of the canvas to play an increasingly important role in the composition. *The White Line* is a particularly impressive example of this phase, as the colored shapes appear to have split apart and moved toward the edges of the paper, creating a dynamic void at the center.

After settling in Los Angeles, Francis worked as an artist-in-residence at Tamarind in 1963 and again in 1969. Perhaps as a result of this last residency, he established The Litho Shop in 1970 in Santa Monica, for the purpose of printing and publishing his own editions. In contrast to the intense collective working environment at Tamarind, The Litho Shop provided Francis with the opportunity to work on his prints at a leisurely and continuous pace.[9] There he has worked in a close collaborative relationship with his printers, first with Hitoshi Takatsuki, and since 1973 with George Page. The Litho Shop, however, has not been the exclusive outlet for Francis's printing energies. In 1971 he made his first prints at Gemini, where he has done a number of large-scale screenprints. In 1973 he expanded his printmaking activities even further. At Studio 2RC in Rome, he made his first series of aquatints; and with Garner Tullis at the Institute of Experimental Printmaking in San Francisco, he began working in monotype, an activity to which he has turned increasingly in recent years.

Bruce Nauman's prints at Cirrus are mostly very traditional in his use of the classic techniques of lithography, drypoint, and aquatint. The imagery of his prints falls into two general categories. One group is drawn from his neon word pieces and takes the form of sometimes witty, sometimes scathing, anagrammatic messages. With a few exceptions, such as the *Perfect* triptych, these lithographs are powerful and painterly in execution, with rich and darkly atmospheric tusche washes. The second group is more abstract in form and is based on his video and environmental works. The untitled lithograph of 1971 exhibited here is related to the video-environmental piece *Spinning Spheres* performed earlier that year at Leo Castelli in New York. Nauman also explored these ideas in drypoints at Cirrus. Another set of drypoints and aquatints executed at Cirrus are related to his piece *The Floating Room.* Among Los Angeles artists Nauman has shown considerable range in both technique and subject and has been particularly successful in translating non-static or non-visual aesthetic ideas into powerful and original forms. In the lithograph exhibited here, nothing is so literal as the representation of the spheres themselves. Instead, Nauman employs radiating razor-cut lines, overlapping and entwined circular forms, and broad strokes of gray and orange to suggest the notion of speed and movement.

Like Nauman's lithograph, Ron Cooper's 1972 *Tri-Axial Rotation of a Floating Volume of Light,* also executed at Cirrus, is related to his neon light environments. Cooper's lithograph,

9. From an interview by Brooke Alexander with the artist, in *Sam Francis: The Litho Shop, 1970–1979,* Brooke Alexander, Inc., New York, 1979, unpaginated.

however, based on an actual photograph, is as literal as Nauman's is imaginative, but it is no less evocative. The rather mundane image of wall and door is transformed by the mysterious blue light into a highly charged and slightly foreboding environment. While the effect is real, the source of this illumination—the "floating volume of light"—appears only conceptually as the diagrammatic notation on the wall.

Cooper's use of offset lithography is positive proof that any medium—in this case one often spurned by purists as too commercial—is acceptable as long as the resultant image is eloquent. Jerry McMillan's *Porch Bag* has been discussed earlier. Another moody example is Peter Alexander's series done at Cirrus in 1972, based on images taken directly from television commercials. Perhaps the most surreal and disturbing, because of the image and Alexander's manipulation of color, are *Anacin I* and *Anacin II,* where the man's head is detached literally and coloristically from his body. Photographic plates were also employed for Tony DeLap's *Karnak* series printed at Cirrus in 1972. The halftone plates used for the lines of simulated wood grain produce a softer and more atmospheric effect than could be achieved with lines drawn directly on the stone.

SILKSCREEN Lithography was not the only graphic technique that experienced a renaissance in the 1960s. The use of silkscreen boomed as well, and the principal impetus may be related to the aesthetics of Pop Art. To artists like Warhol and Lichtenstein, the commercial, industrial look of the silkscreen was beguiling, as was its ability to use and manipulate ready-made imagery for artistic purpose. These and other aspects were explored by Southern California artists in their use of silkscreen. Ed Ruscha's *Hollywood* silkscreen of 1968 does not entail the literal re-use of a given image, but the transformation of the famous hillside sign into a Pop icon. Ruscha moved the sign to the crest of the Hollywood Hills, where it stands as a symbol and beacon to the thousands lured to California for riches and fame. Similar to the *Standard Station* of two years earlier, *Hollywood* combines areas of opaque flatness inherent in the medium, with the dense and rich coloration, created by the split-fountain technique, of the evening sky in Los Angeles. Also similar to the *Standard Station, Hollywood* of 1968 is only one of several explorations of the theme by Ruscha. At Tamarind in 1969, he executed a number of lithographs on the subject, generally in a very elongated format. And at Cirrus in 1971 the sign was printed "organically," using fruit-flavored Metrecal rather than conventional inks.

Silkscreen has been practiced as much outside the major workshops as within. It was not part of the Tamarind program, of course, though it has found increasing use at Gemini and Cirrus. One explanation for its independent stature is that silkscreen does not generally require the same elaborate set-up and equipment as lithography. In addition, screenprinting could be put to new uses for which lithography was not adaptable. At Gemini, for example, Ron Davis has printed on Mylar and Joe Goode on fabric and tissue; at Cirrus, Greg Card has printed on Plexiglas. Independently, Gene Gill, the printer for Lorser Feitelson and Helen Lundeberg, printed on superimposed layers of plastic sheets, which were then set against a backdrop of brushed aluminum.

Feitelson and Lundeberg had not made any prints since the late 1940s, when they were introduced to silkscreen in 1971 by Joseph Young, the former assistant curator of prints and drawings at the Los Angeles County Museum of Art. Silkscreen was the ideal medium for the translation into prints of the crystalline precision in their paintings. In Feitelson's untitled silkscreen, the white element can be read perceptually in two ways: as a now swelling, now tapering form moving across the red field; or as a void created by the dynamic relationship between two dynamic red masses. This ambiguous figure-ground relationship serves to emphasize the non-literal, flat character of Feitelson's work. Lundeberg shared her husband's predilection for hard-edge forms. Her color is softer, however, tending toward pale blues and cool grays, and the large, rounded shapes do not have the electric tension inherent in Feitelson's; nevertheless, the shapes are juxtaposed, as though about to collide, against a creamy white background that expands and contracts in a particularly dynamic fashion.

One of the attractions of the silkscreen technique for some artists, including Feitelson and Lundeberg, was the ability to produce hard, clean, and precise edges, as well as flat, unmodulated color. Gill screenprinted his linear forms on sheets of plastic, with this superimposition resulting in a kinetic and vibrant visual effect. Gill's works are among the closest to Op Art that one will find in Los Angeles. Local artists certainly have shown considerable interest in optical effects, particularly in the uses of plastics, resins, and related materials. Gill's employment of plastic and aluminum sheets places him in this circle. The kinetic effects produced by the spectator's physical movement and physiological response, however, relates Gill's works equally to those by Agam and Bridget Riley.

One contribution of Pop Art to contemporary printmaking was the incorporation of photographic or photographic-based images in prints. Photolithography and photo-silkscreen lost their commercial stigma because the ends to which artists like Rauschenberg, Warhol, and Johns used these processes transcended the means. In Los Angeles, Ken Price used photographic images in striking and novel ways in two series of prints done at Gemini, the *Figurine Cups* of 1970 and the *Interior Series* of 1971. In the *Figurine Cups,* Price constructed a giant plaster cup (similar to his ceramics), posed a nude model in a variety of positions, and photographed the images to be transferred to aluminum plates.[10] These photolithographic forms were then combined and contrasted with the flat color of the silkscreened settings. A similar procedure occurs in the *Interior Series,* except

10. B. Rose, *Figurine Cups by Ken Price,* Gemini G.E.L., Los Angeles, 1970.

on a much larger scale. Based on more painterly studies in acrylics, the silkscreens themselves are flat, hard-edged, and almost mechanized in their impersonal finish. These qualities, however, are countered by the whimsical intrusion of Price's cups into the vacant interiors.

In the 1970s a number of artists appear to have reacted against the often cool perfection provided by technical innovations in contemporary lithography and silkscreen. Some turned to etching and monotype as a more personal medium. Others, such as Charles Christopher Hill and Ann McCoy, used the printed image as a sort of under-drawing, with color applied by hand, making each print a unique object. Eugene Sturman's *Quadrant #4*, printed at Cirrus in 1977, undergoes a similar transformation in which the screenprinting is only the beginning of the process. The paper was hand-torn, folded, waxed, and gilded. The resulting print, with its rich surface recalling the opulence of Byzantine icons, seems to be the very antithesis of traditional silkscreens.

ETCHING Regenerated and given new forms by the innovations of Hayter and Lasansky, intaglio printing may be said to have experienced its heyday in the 1950s. In the 1960s it was mostly eclipsed by the great revival of lithography as well as by silkscreen. Certainly artists such as Ernest Freed, Leonard Edmondson, Dick Swift, and Ynez Johnston continued to work in intaglio, but they were clearly in the minority. Printmaking in Los Angeles was dominated by the twin shadows of Tamarind and Gemini. Either by definition or preference, intaglio was excluded from their range of interests, although drypoints by Michael Heizer have been done recently at Gemini. Consequently, it did not have the same organized impetus as lithography or silkscreen for creativity and innovation.

Intaglio did not disappear completely from the scene, nevertheless, as woodcut and wood-engraving essentially did; instead, the last decade has witnessed a marked revival in intaglio, particularly in etching. Certainly, Jim Dine has emerged as one of the premier printmakers today, outranked perhaps only by Jasper Johns, and his primary mode of expression is etching. One possible explanation for the etching revival is the dissatisfaction by artists with the increased technical demands required by lithography. That medium had always been one of collaboration between artist and printer. While the innovations introduced at Tamarind, Gemini, and elsewhere certainly produced marvelous and occasionally astonishing works, the results were sometimes more the result of technical wizardry by the printers than of creative inspiration by the artists. A backlash in favor of more intimate participation by the artist may have resulted in the resurgence of etching.

Perhaps equally important has been the emergence of workshops as dedicated to intaglio as Tamarind was to lithography. Without such organized impetus many artists would undoubtedly never have experimented with this "new" medium, particularly since a number of them had not previously done etchings. Foremost among these workshops is Kathan Brown's Crown Point Press in Oakland. A number of artists not otherwise known as printmakers, such as Sol LeWitt, Dan Flavin, Brice Marden, and Robert Mangold—incidentally all attracted from New York—produced etchings at Crown Point. Part of the attraction was the atmosphere of freedom and creativity prevalent at Crown Point. As Brown has stated, these visiting artists encountered a special attitude toward etching "as an adventure, as a pleasure, as a way of being outside one's familiar territory."[11] It is a tribute to this creative and adventurous environment that a number of artists, such as Flavin or Chris Burden, could make meaningful and provocative artistic statements in a medium that at first glance would seem alien to their customary aesthetic. The two prints from Crown Point exhibited here represent polar opposites in the oeuvres of their creators. Richard Diebenkorn was the first artist published by Crown Point, a long association dating back to the early 1960s, while Joel Bass only recently made his first (and so far only) prints at Crown Point. At first glance, etching would appear to be the least likely printmaking medium for two artists whose painted works are so rich in color and sensuous painterly surfaces. In spite of this apparent contradiction, both Diebenkorn and Bass have successfully transmuted their aesthetics into the terms of the new medium. The stark black and white, as well as the inherent linearity of etching, enable them to focus on the formal structure of their works, but the results far surpass the notion that the prints are simply diagrams of their paintings because of the sensitivity of their handling of the medium. Neither artist would consider himself a printmaker, since painting remains their overriding means of expression. Diebenkorn has referred to his printmaking as "a way of drawing" and "just horsing around."[12] The works produced at Crown Point by him and Bass indicate, nevertheless, that both artists were able to produce serious and successful works in an unfamiliar medium

Diebenkorn's *Untitled #5*, a 1978 drypoint and acquatint, relates to his *Ocean Park* paintings, a series that has occupied him since shortly after his move to Los Angeles in 1966. The vertical format, the linear structure, and the careful balance of horizontal, vertical, and diagonal elements are found in both the paintings and prints. Even the variations in the thickness of the lines and opacity of the aquatint suggest the re-workings and *pentimenti* in his paintings. The print, however, also serves as a departure from and a commentary on the *Ocean Park* series, in that the angular, geometric structure is counterbalanced by more fluid and organic shapes that hark back to his abstract paintings of the early 1950s.

Bass's etching with lead collage of 1974 appears deceptively simple at first glance, but is visually rich on closer inspection. A complex series of spatial relationships is set up by the interaction of a number of overlapping planes. These planes are both literal

---

11. P. Plous and K. Brown, *Richard Diebenkorn: Intaglio Prints 1961–1978*, University of California, Santa Barbara, 1979, p. 13.

12. Ibid, p. 13.

and concrete in the forms of the lead sheets and suggestive and illusionary in those created by the etched lines.

In Los Angeles, printer Robert Aull has worked with a number of local artists, including Chuck Arnoldi and Eleanore Lazarof, whose prints are included in the exhibition. Arnoldi's untitled color etching of 1979 displays a dense network of crossing and overlapping lines. Deep etching produces a sense of volume and relief to the surface and relates the printed imagery to Arnoldi's "stick paintings" and, even more, to his recent pastels. Lazarof's color intaglio *Dos Lados de la Mañana* of 1979 is also related to pastel drawings. She achieves a remarkable degree of transparency with the rhythmically spaced planes of overlapping color.

Like Lazarof, Ray Brown employs aquatint in his *Alice N.S.* of 1975 for remarkable coloristic effects. Rather than the usual linear conventions for constructive form, a more painterly use of color etching builds the figure like a watercolor. Similarly, Stephen Anaya, who studied with Brown at the University of California, Los Angeles, makes considerable use of aquatint in *Kuraje* of 1971 to create his fantastic, visionary seascape which is particularly effective in its massive, billowing clouds.

An offshoot of intaglio printmaking is the inkless embossed print. Created through essentially the same process as conventional intaglios, the image is the result of the unique interaction between the printing element, the damp paper, and the tremendous pressure exerted by the etching press. The prints are, in a sense, paper reliefs, with the raised images created by forcing the paper into a mold. Shiro Ikegawa's *Issa* of 1966 combines deep embossing with color intaglio printing. The sculptural effect is so pronounced that the print seems to resemble a wall relief more than a conventional intaglio print.

Claire Falkenstein has termed her prints "Struttura Grafica," and they are especially related to her sculpture. In fact, the printing element employed is not a metal plate at all, but a heavy wire structure that can be appreciated on its own merits as a fine piece of sculpture. When subjected to the pressure of the press, the damp paper molds itself around the metal frame. Falkenstein's embossed prints are exceptional because the quality of relief is significantly greater than in most. Consequently, she had to experiment with a variety of papers in order to find one of the particular strength and resiliency to take and retain the embossing. Because of the nature of her unusual printing element, either the embossed or the recessed side of the print can be chosen as the print, depending on the artist's response to the result. In the case of Falkenstein's *Struttura Grafica* of 1972, commissioned by the Graphic Arts Council of the Los Angeles County Museum of Art, she elected to employ the depressed side. With the addition of pale gray coloring, the print successfully combines a vigorous and sculptural presence with the delicacy of a snowflake.

RELIEF PRINTS The print processes that fell out of favor after the 1950s were woodcut and wood-engraving. The simplest and most direct of techniques, the material and tools could not compete with the potential of the intaglio and planographic media for experimentation. With the death of Paul Landacre in 1963, the day of the straightforward relief print, not only in its traditional technique but even as an expanded expression, was over in Los Angeles. Perhaps as a portent of revived interest, however, Gemini has recently produced its first woodcuts, a suite by Roy Lichtenstein, although the choice of medium was partly dictated by the artist's use of German Expressionist motifs.

An example of expanded expression of the relief process is Tom Fricano's cardboard cut of 1961, *Umbria #1*, a purchase award at the first National Annual Print Invitation Exhibition at Otis Art Institute in 1962. The cardboard cut's large slashing forms and heavily textured surface clearly call to mind the principles of gestural abstraction which have been successfully transferred by Fricano into printmaking.

Jay McCafferty's combination of woodblock printing and silkscreen represents an even more radical departure from traditional woodblock relief printing, primarily in the creation of the woodblock design. For a number of years McCafferty has employed "solar burns," using the heat produced by the sun through a magnifying glass, to create his dramatically original images. In the case of *#1 Alive* of 1977, printed at Cirrus, McCafferty "cut" the wood veneer block by burning holes in the surface. However, the figure-ground relationship between the inked surface and the white of the paper found in most relief prints is negated by printing the block over the silkscreened black background, reinforcing the flatness of the image. In the precarious control over the burning of the holes, McCafferty's unusual technique involves a degree of chance that is not customarily found in conventional woodblock printing.

INDEX OF ARTISTS

Numbers refer to illustrations beginning on page 33 and to catalog entries.

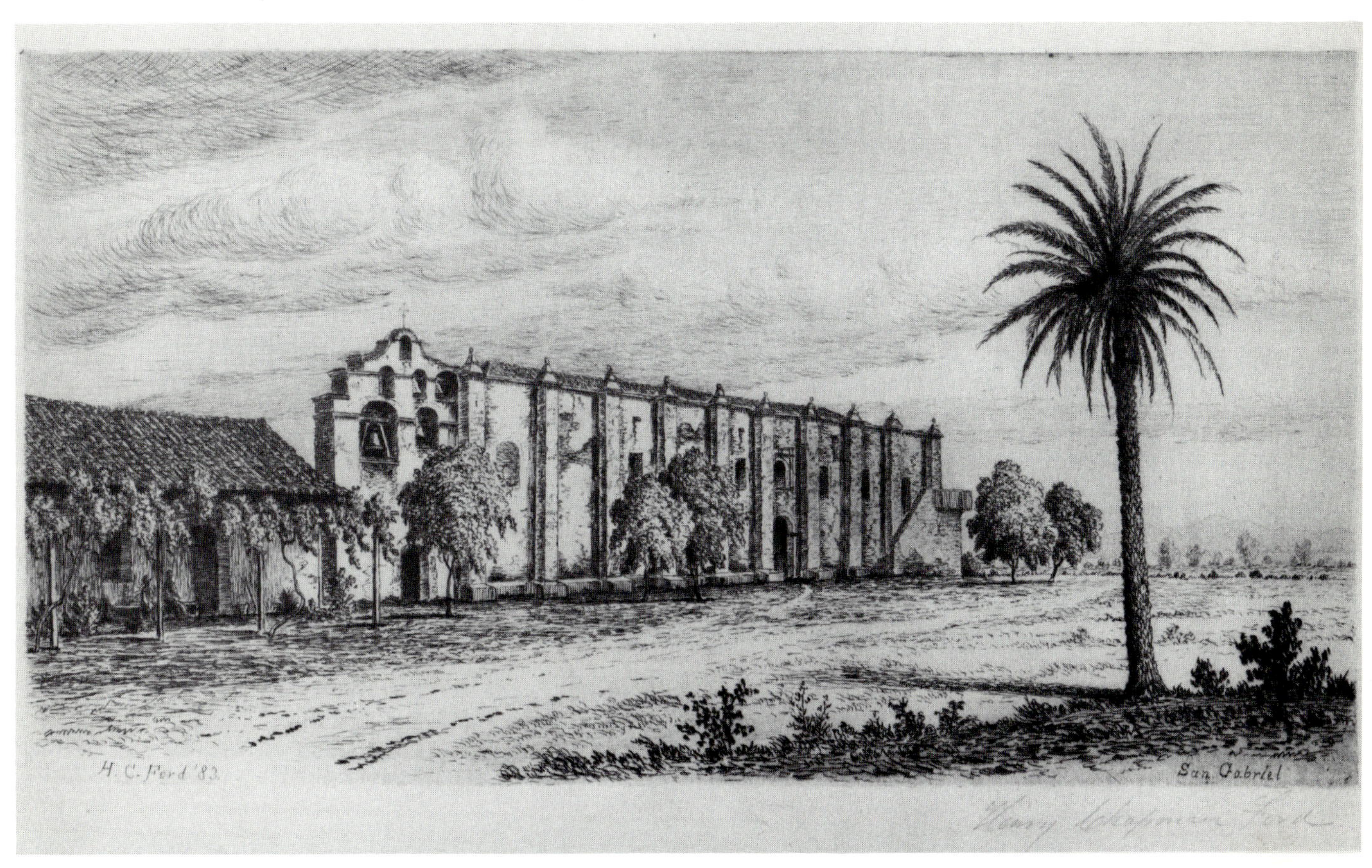

1. Henry Chapman Ford, *Mission San Gabriel*

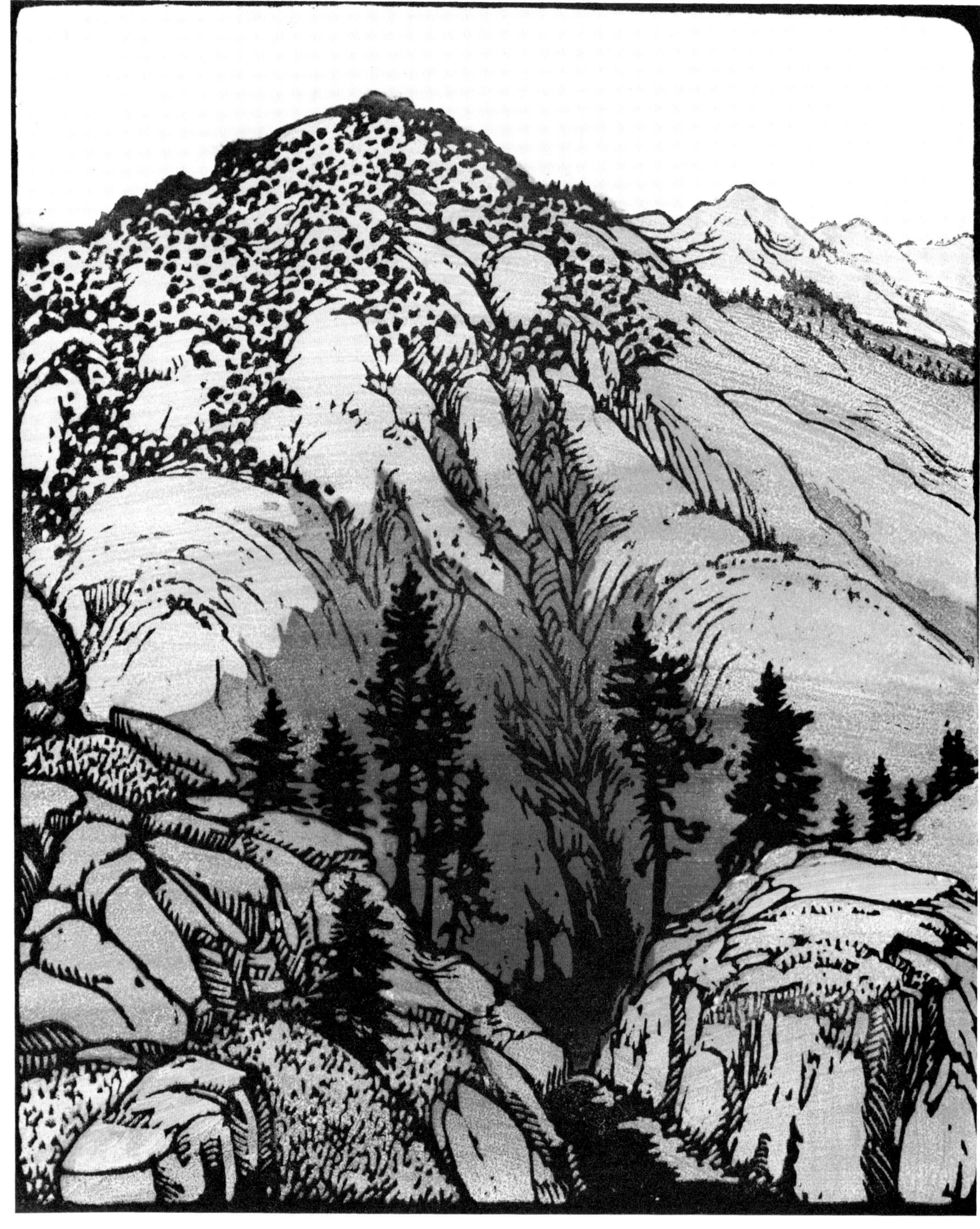

2. Frances Gearhart, *When Summer Comes,* c. 1925–30

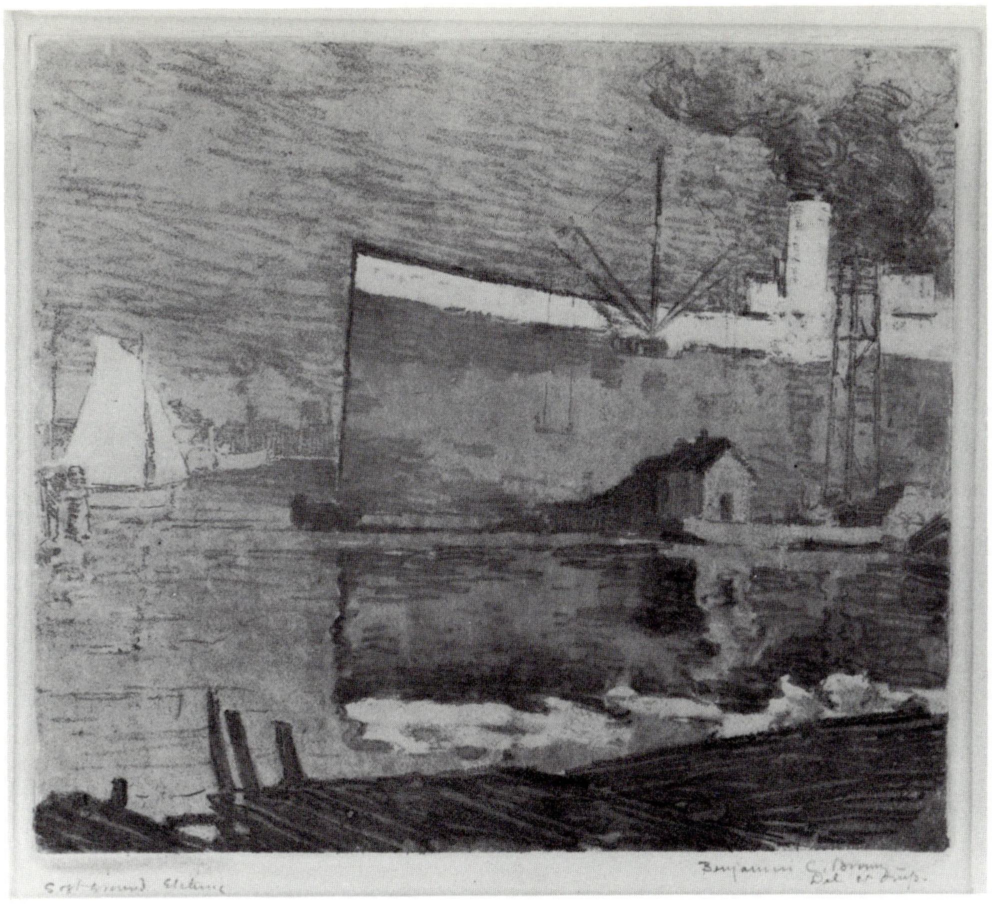

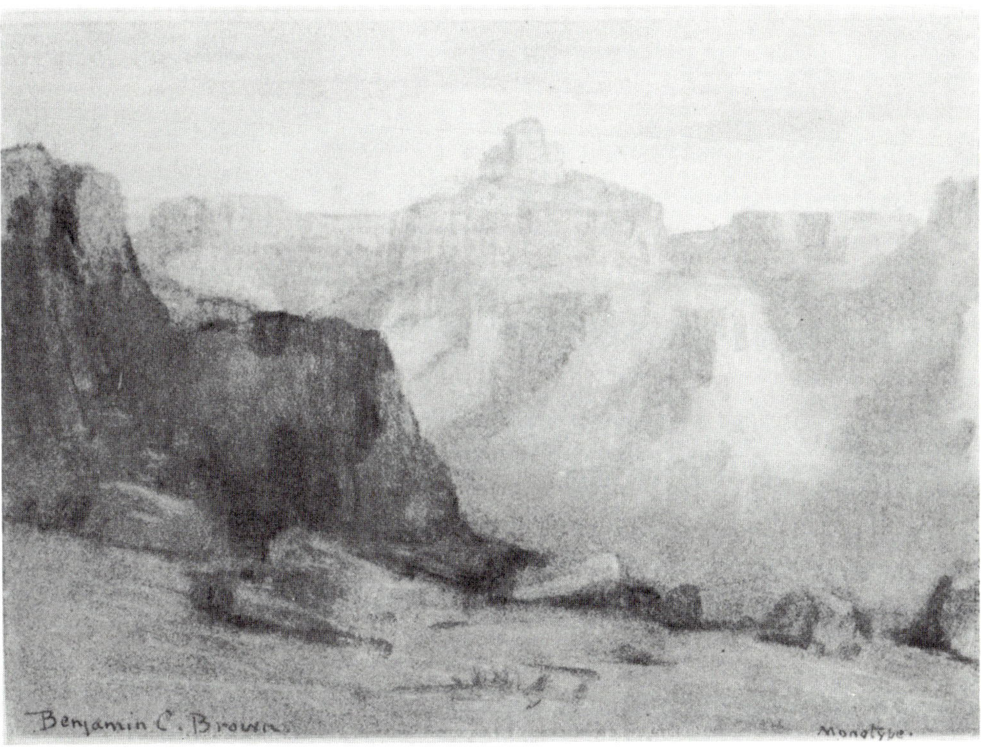

3. Benjamin Chambers Brown, *At the Paint-Wharf,* 1919

4. Benjamin Chambers Brown, *Grand Canyon,* c. 1915–20

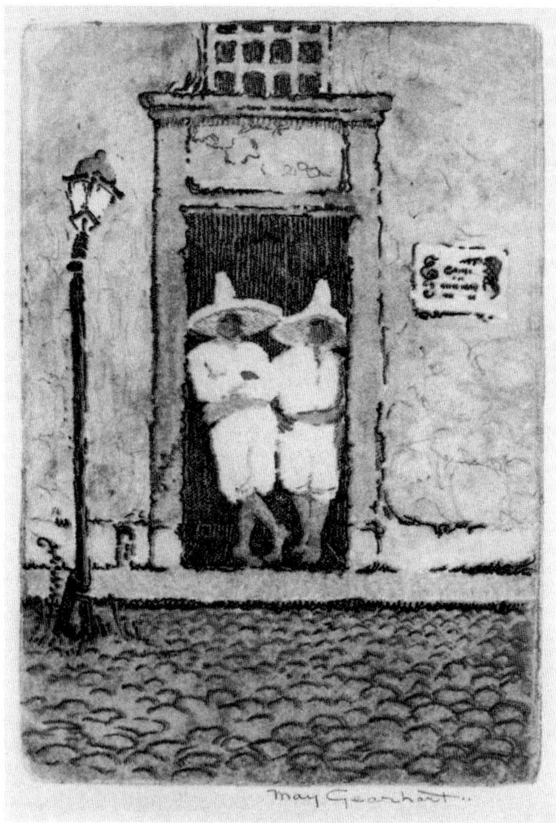

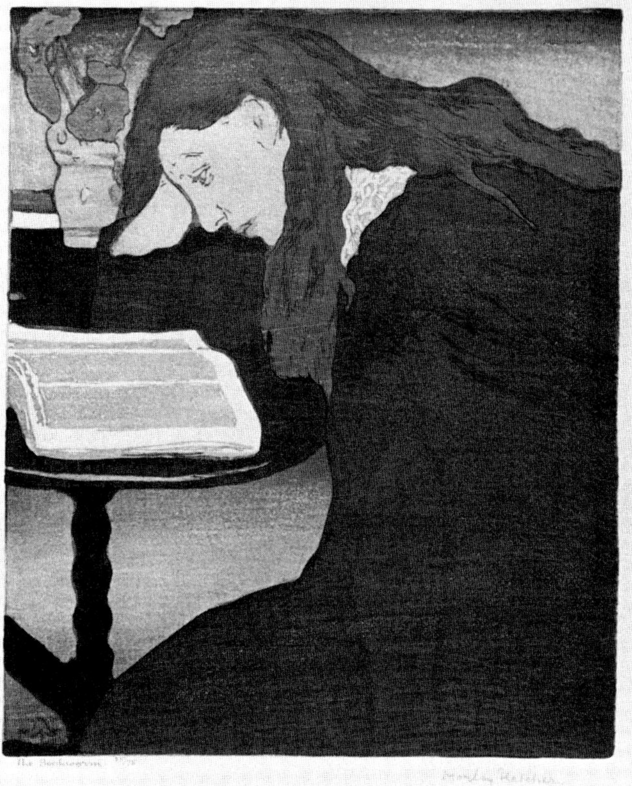

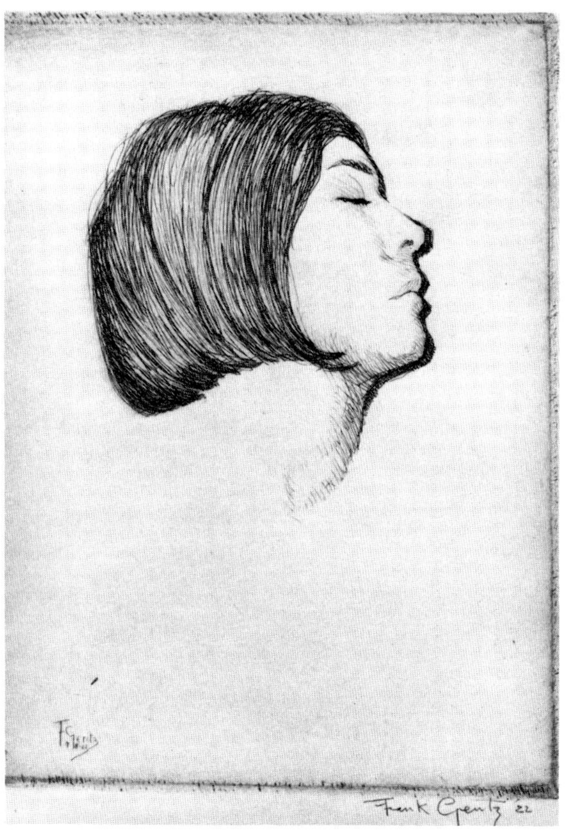

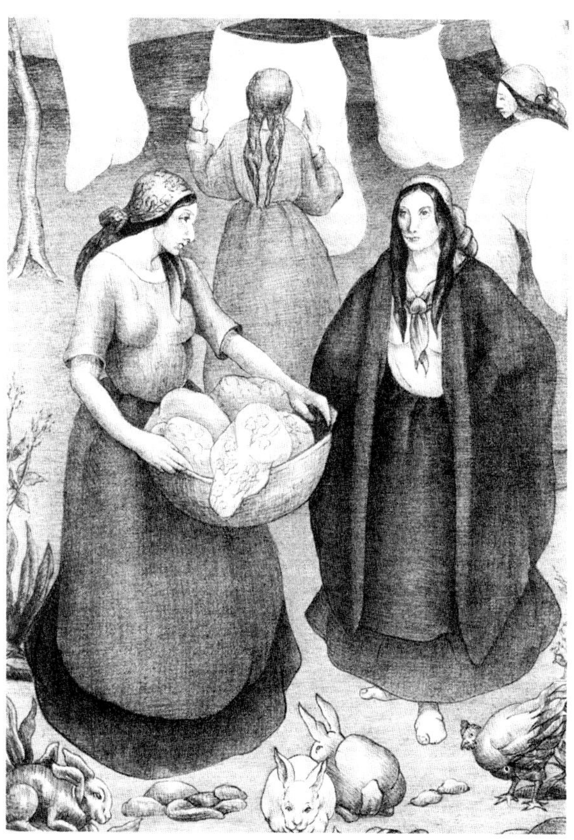

6. May Gearhart, *Two Gentlemen of Xochimilco,* c. 1915–20

7. Franz Geritz, *Margrethe Mather,* 1922

8. Frank Morley Fletcher, *The Bookworm,* c. 1920–25

9. Henrietta Shore, *Gypsy Encampment,* c. 1925–30

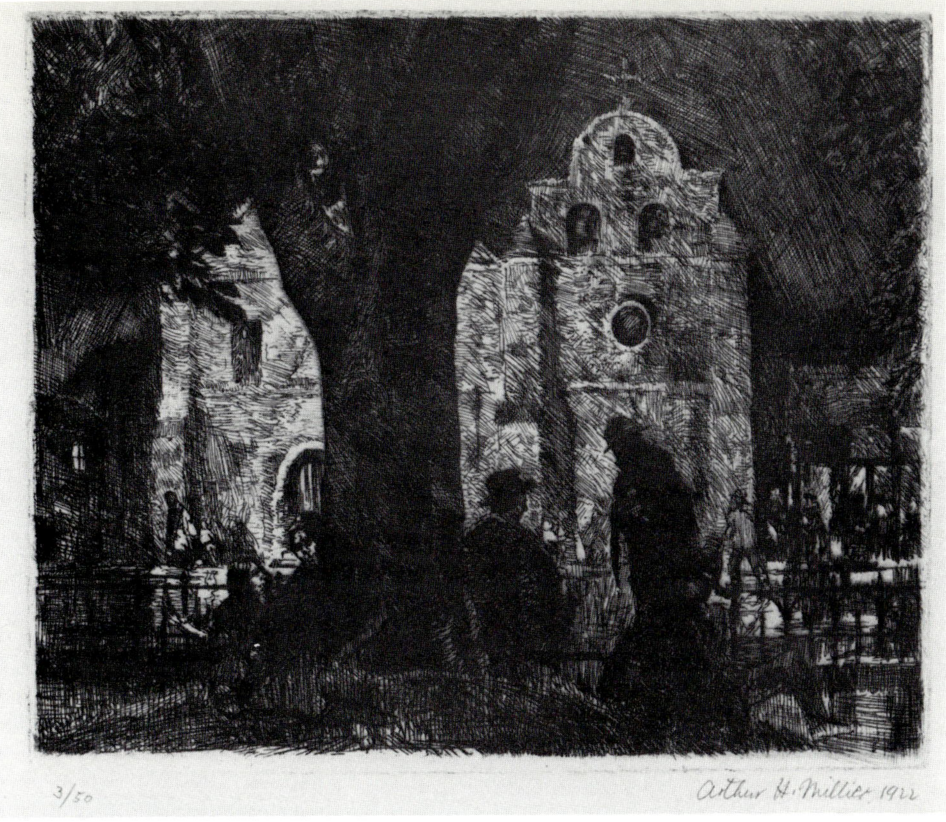

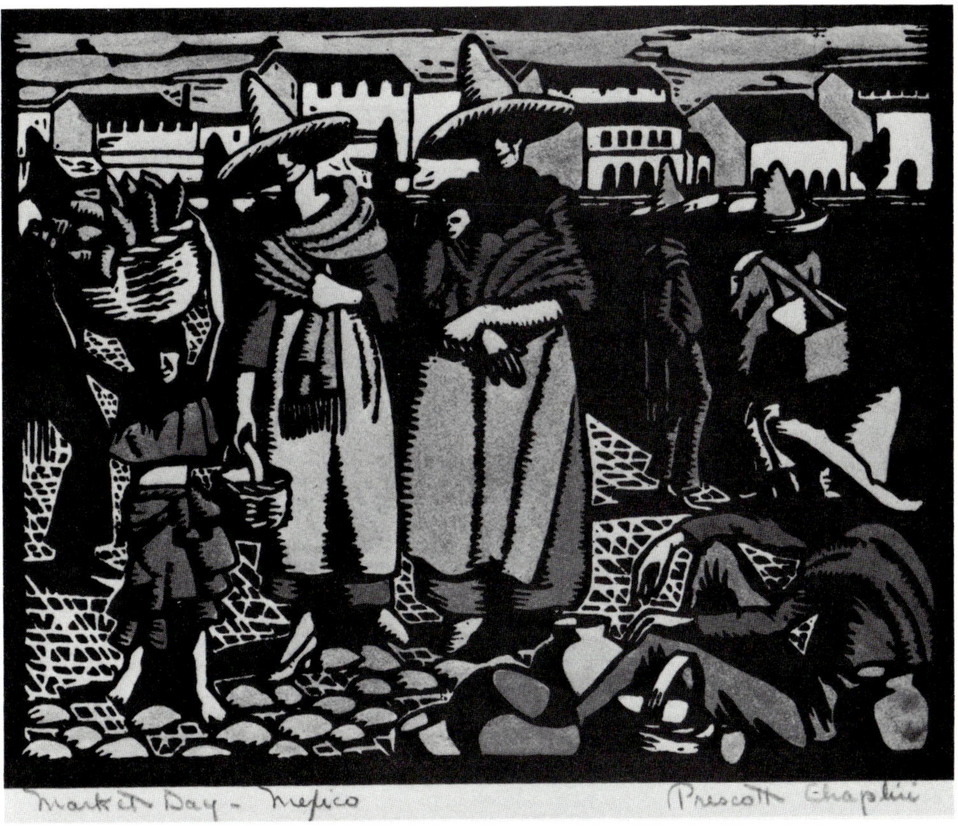

11. Arthur Millier, *Plaza Night,* 1922

12. Prescott Chaplin, *Market Day, Mexico,* 1926–27

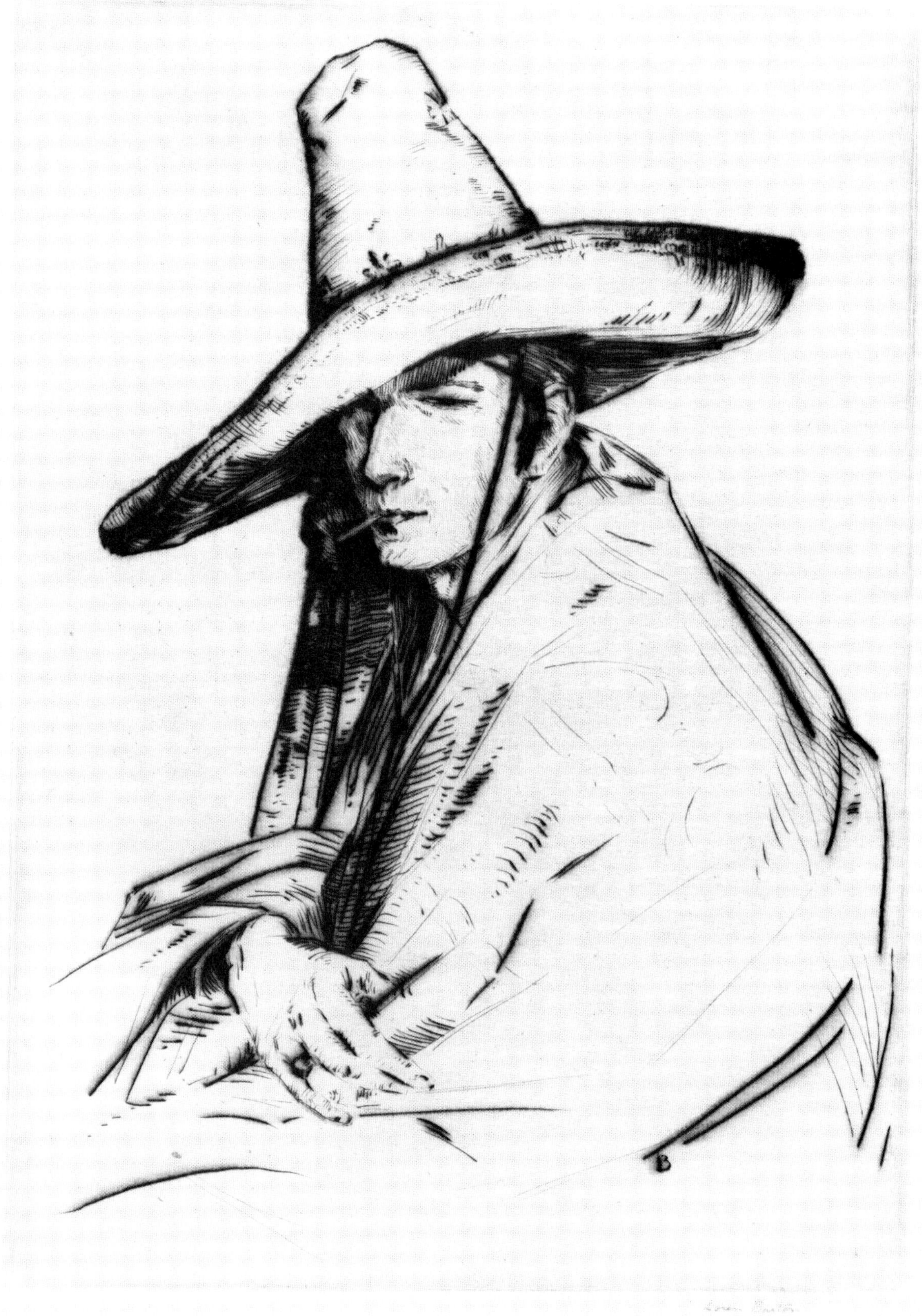

14. Loren Roberta Barton, *Manuel,* 1923

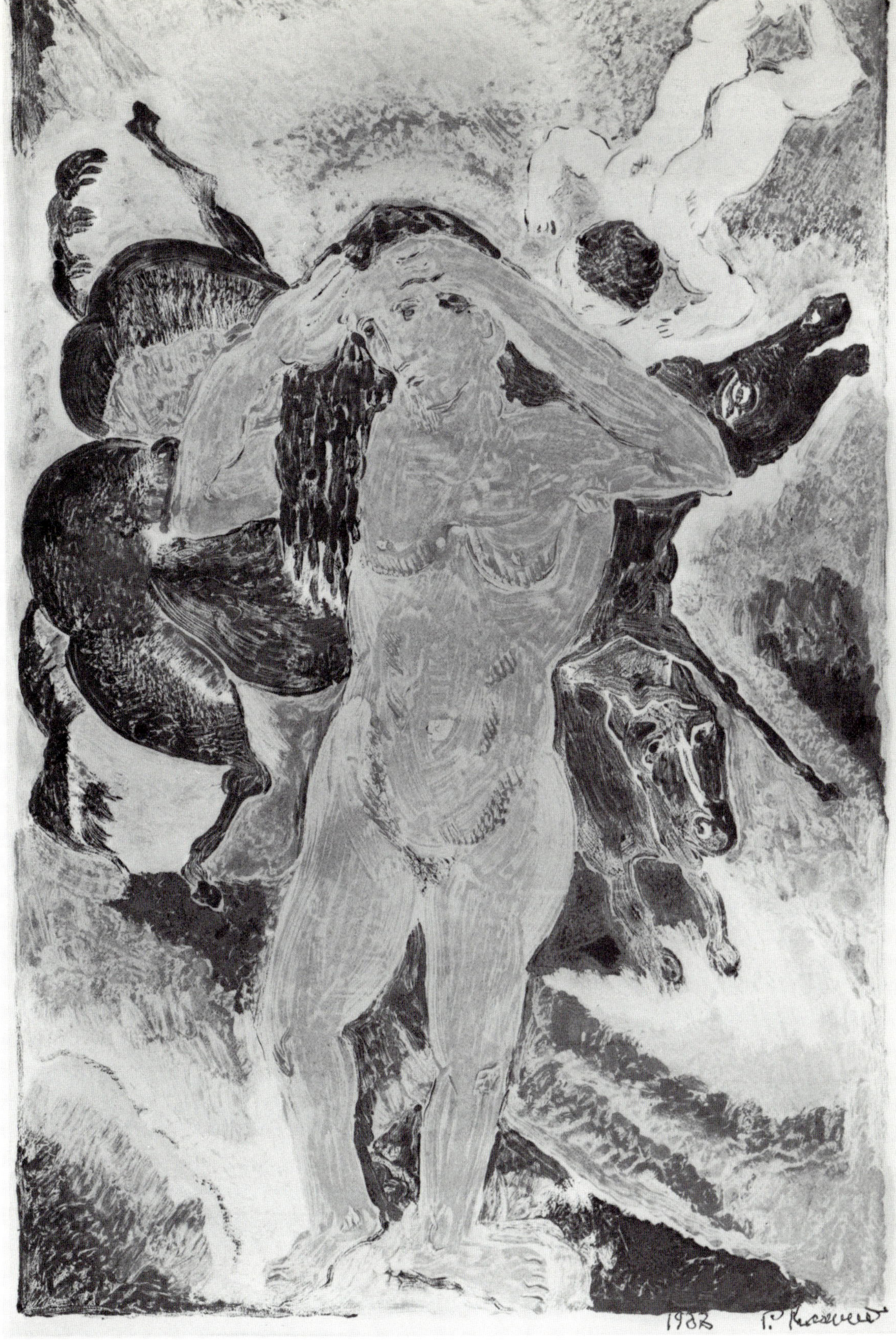

15. Peter Krasnow, *Untitled,* 1928

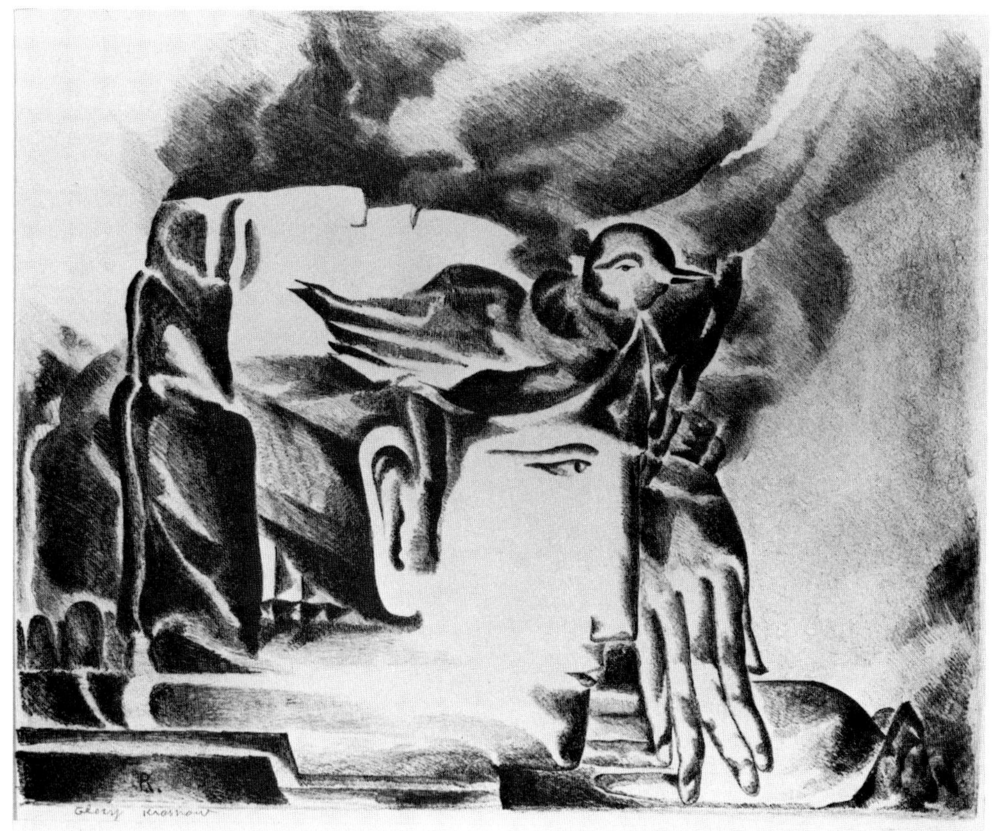

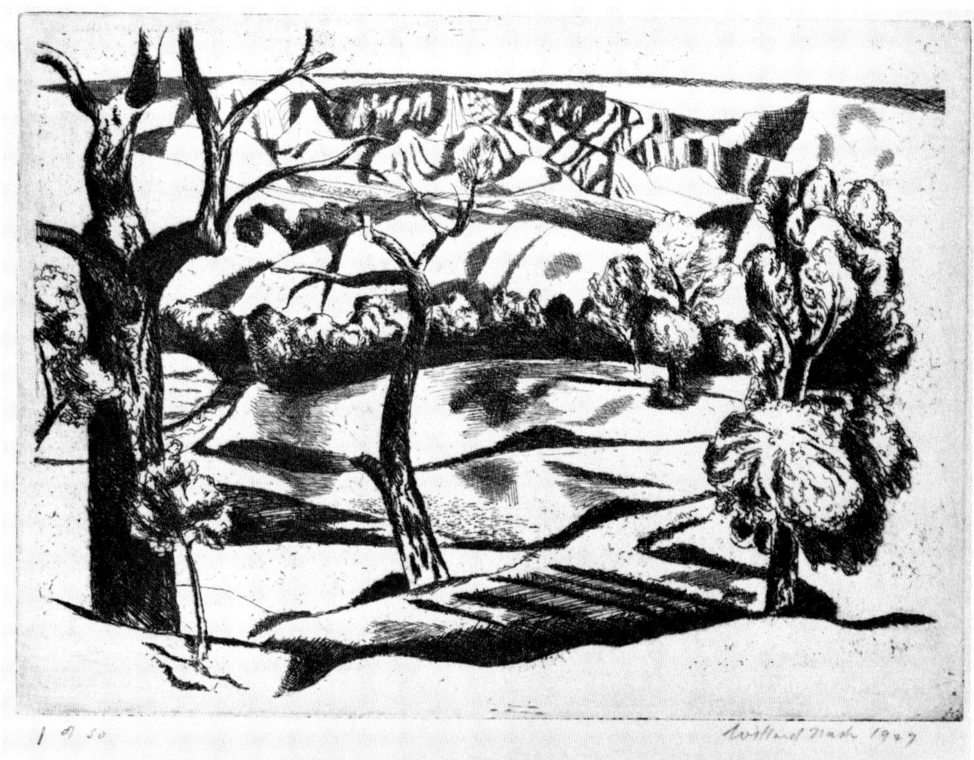

17. Peter Krasnow, *Glory,* c. 1927–29

19. Willard Ayer Nash, *Landscape,* 1927

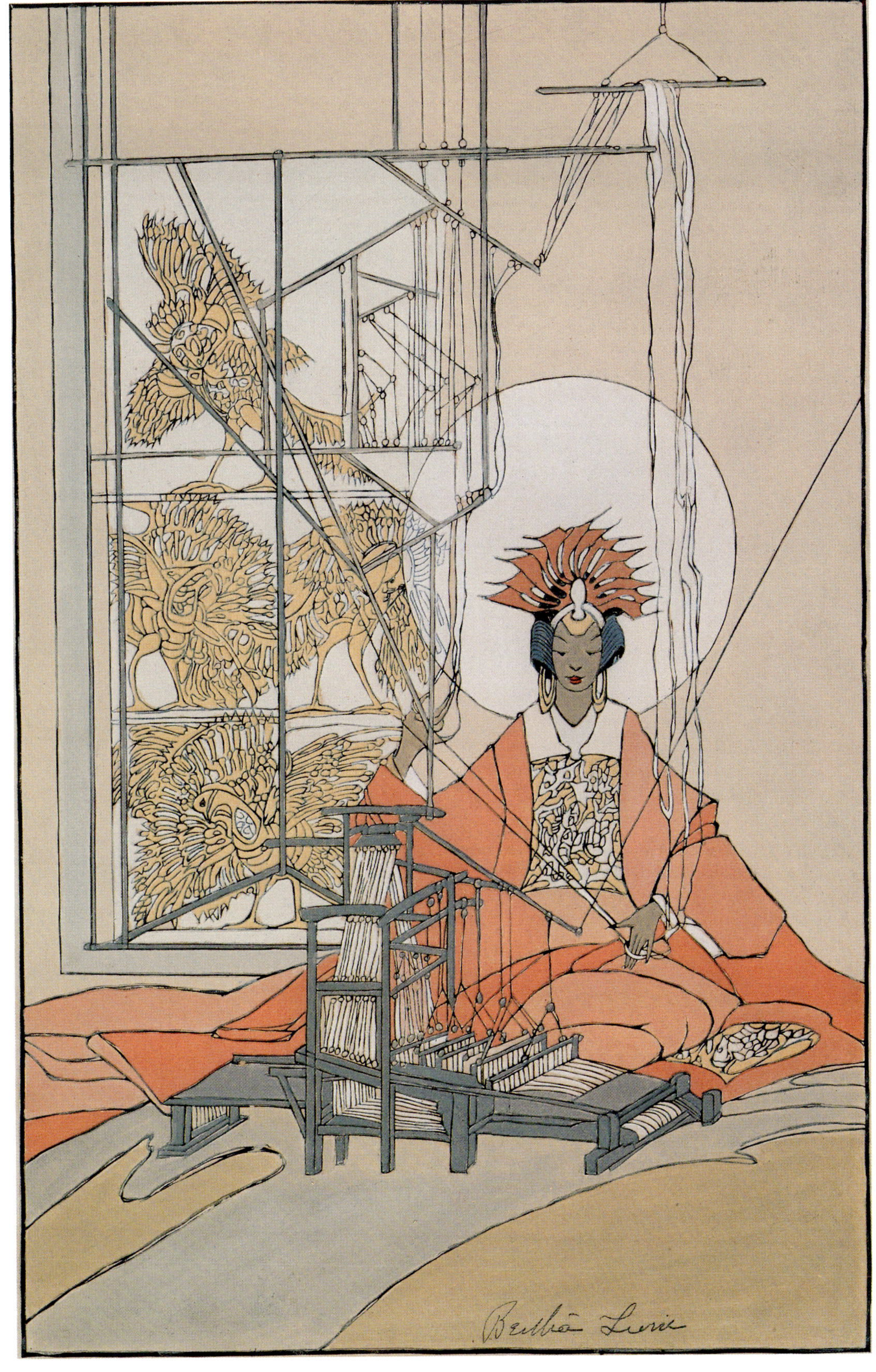

20. Bertha Lum, *Spinning Goddess,* c. 1930–35

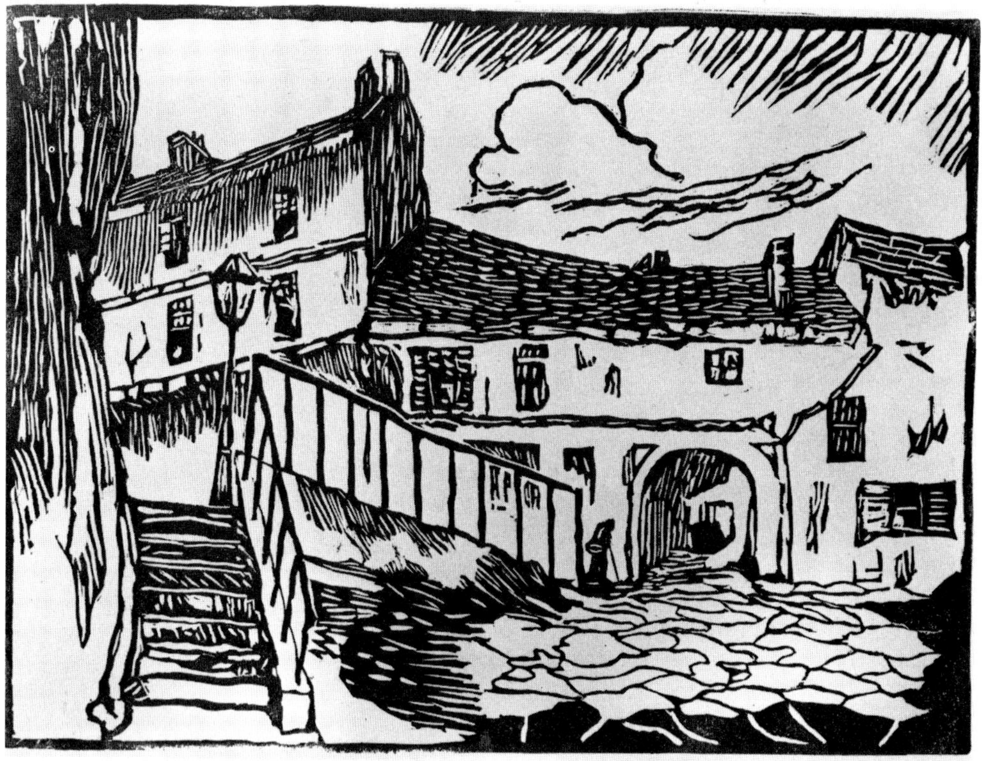

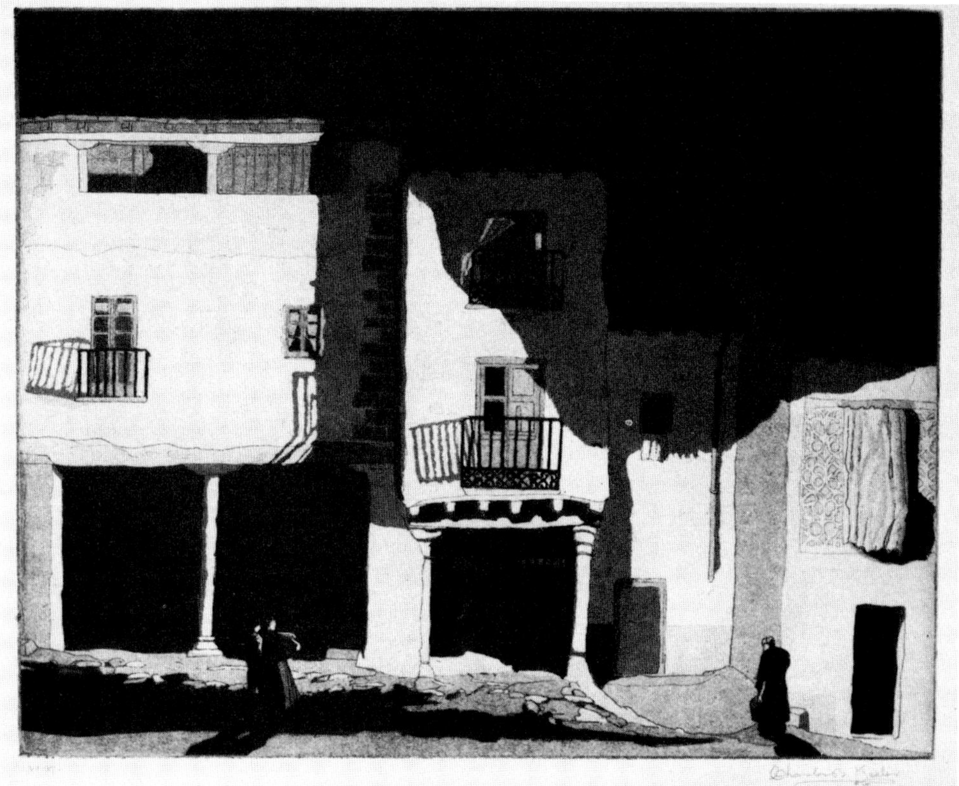

21. Wilson Silsby, *Stairway in Meudon, France,* c. 1930

22. Charles Keeler, *In the Street of Life and Death, Segovia,* c. 1929

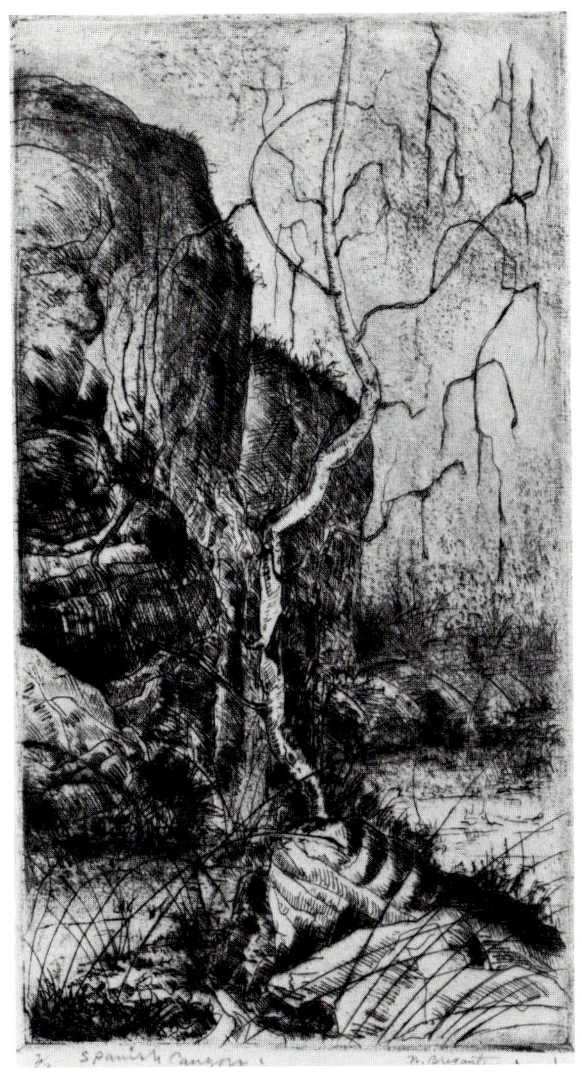

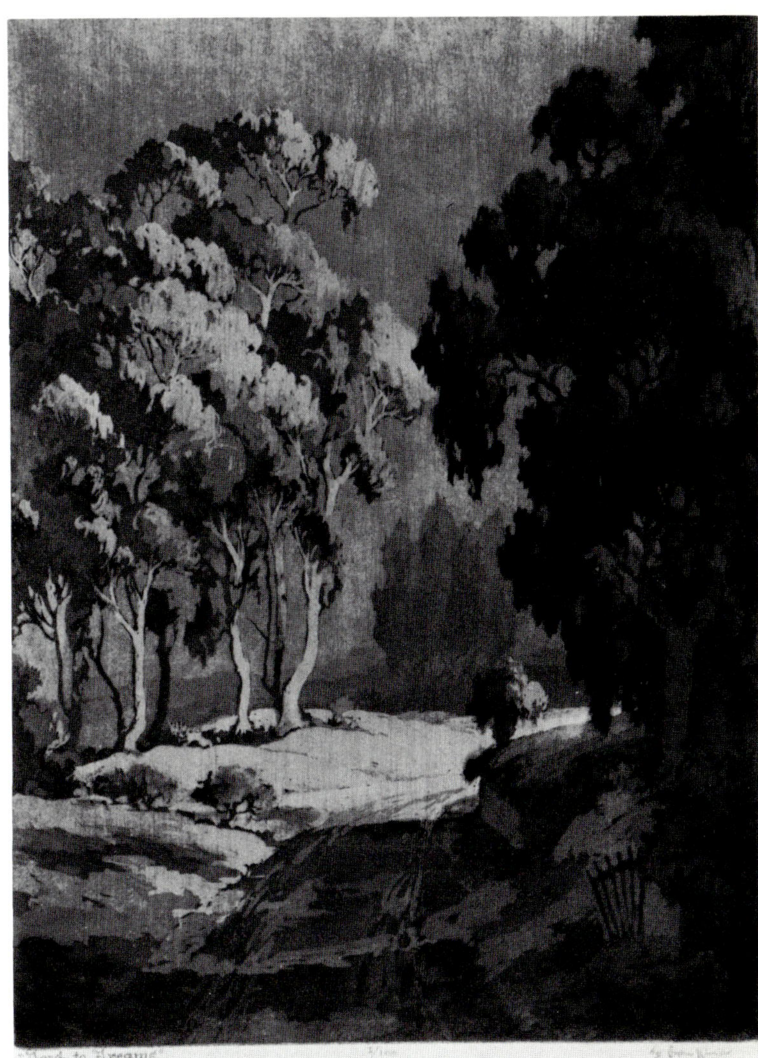

3. Nicholas Brigante, *Spanish Canyon,* 1930

24. Orpha Klinker, *Road to Dreams,* c. 1930–35

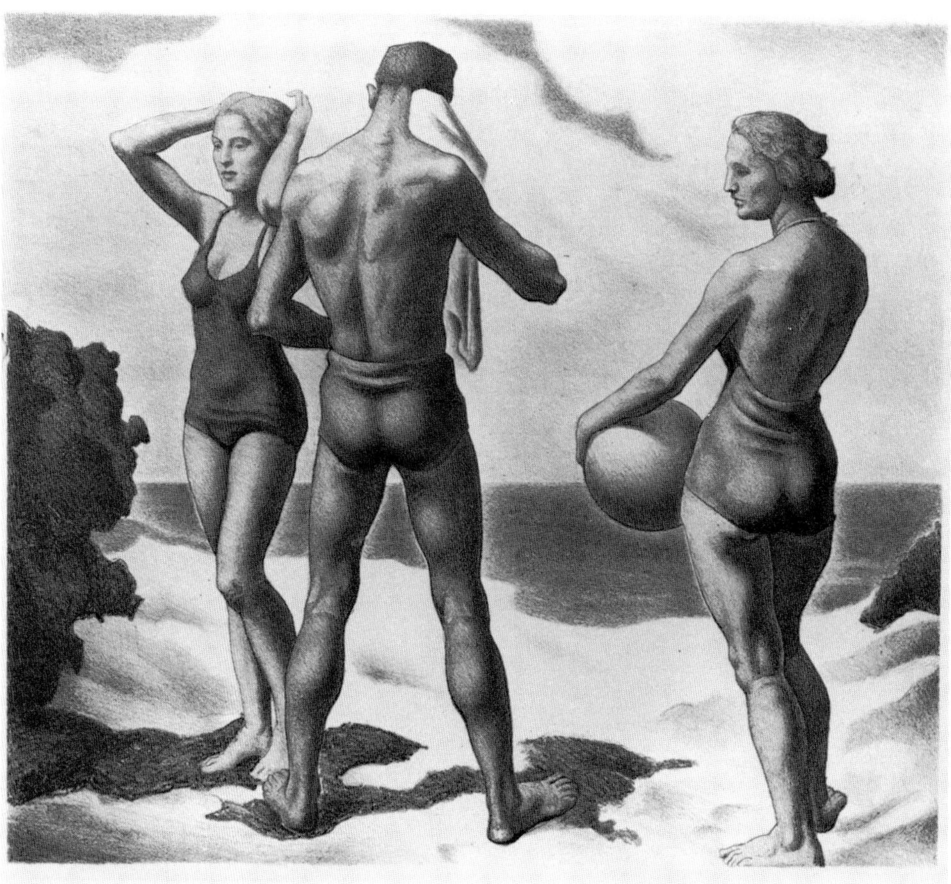

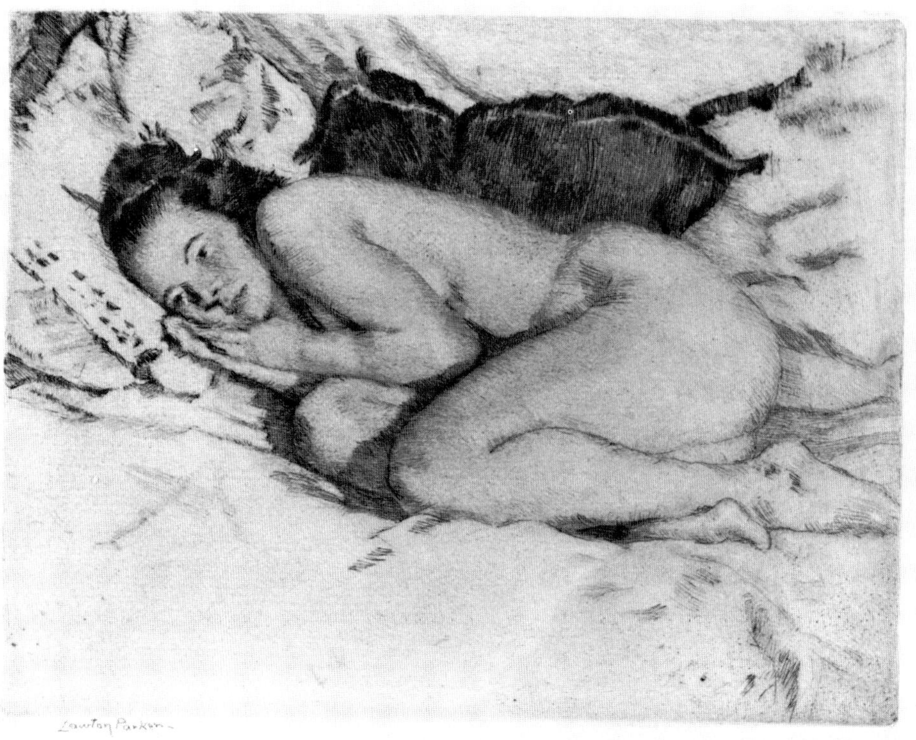

25. Douglas Parshall, *Bathers,* 1930

26. Lawton Parker, *Reclining Nude,* c. 1930

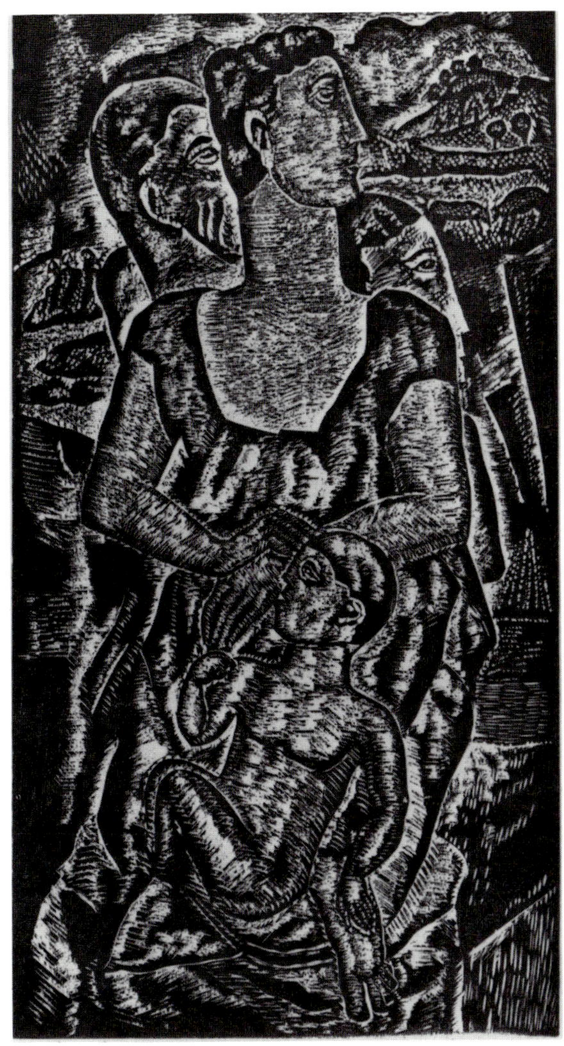

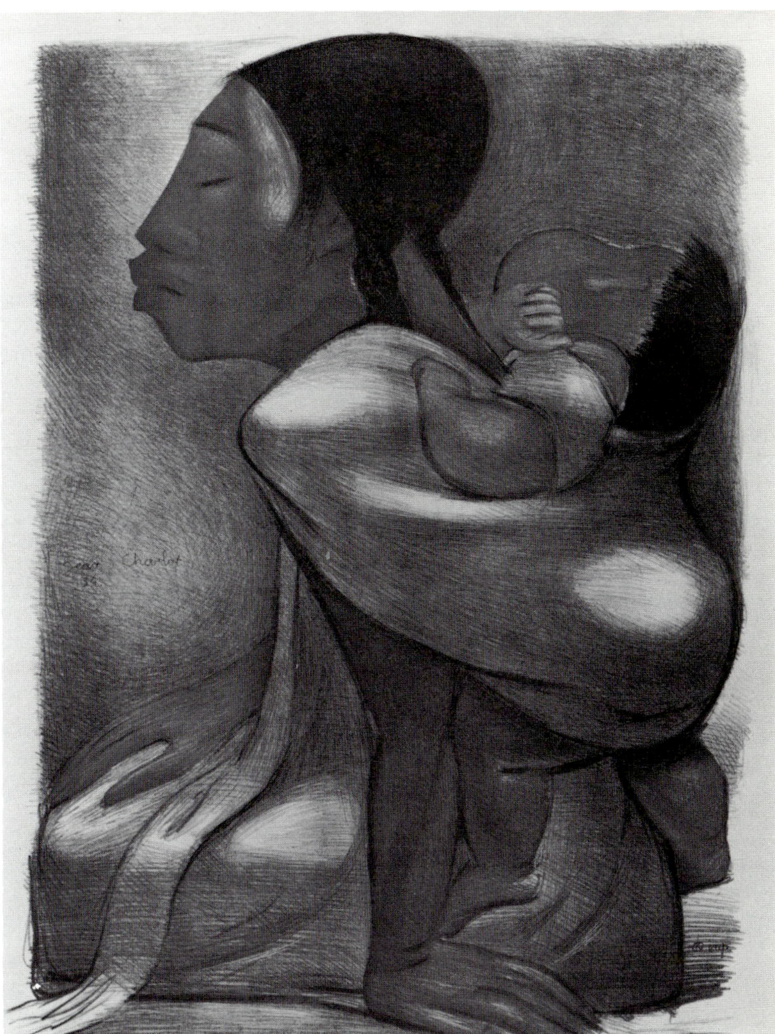

. Peter Krasnow, *The Family,* c. 1927–29

27. Jean Charlot, *Woman Standing, Child on Back,* 1934

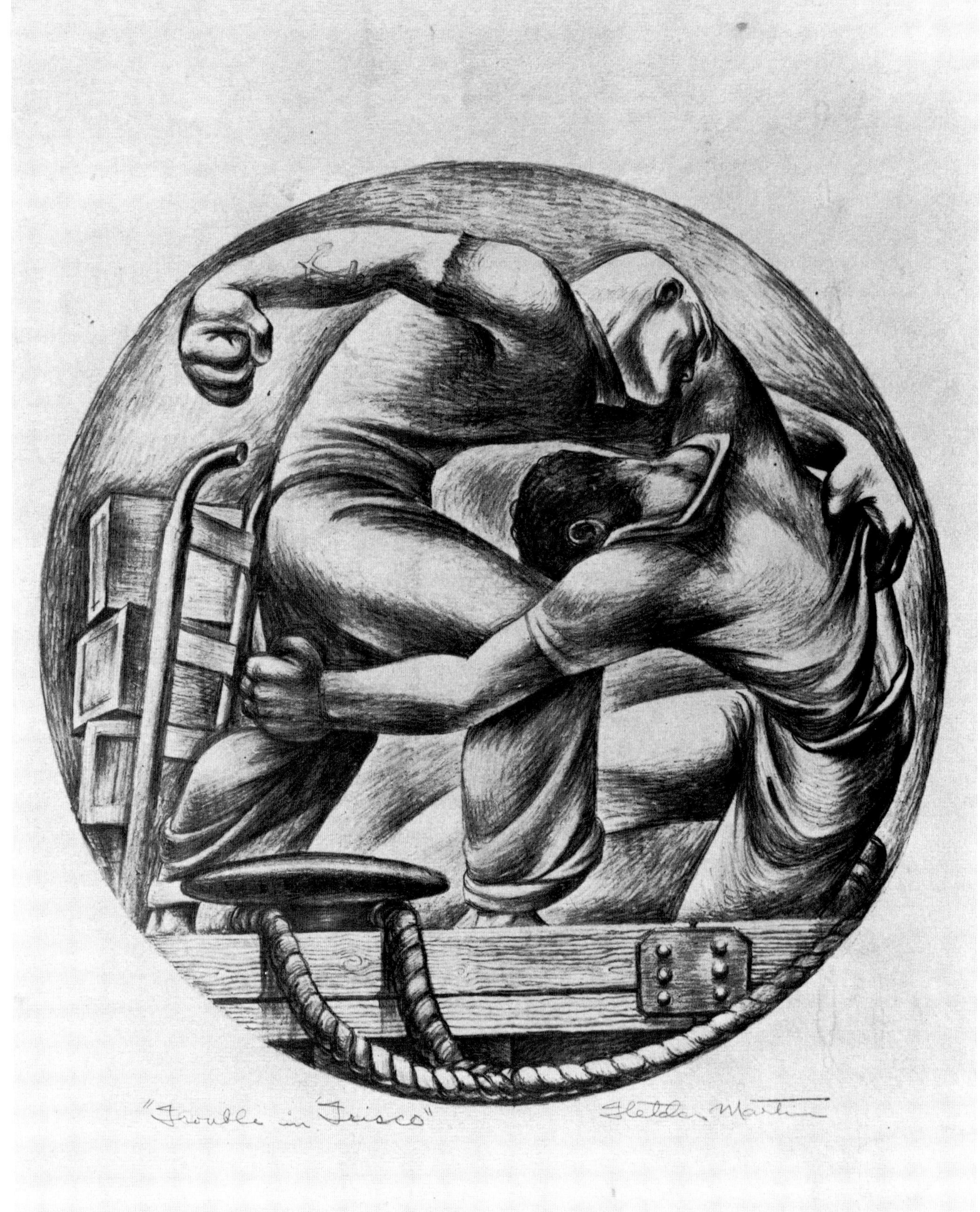

28. Fletcher Martin, *Trouble in Frisco,* c. 1935

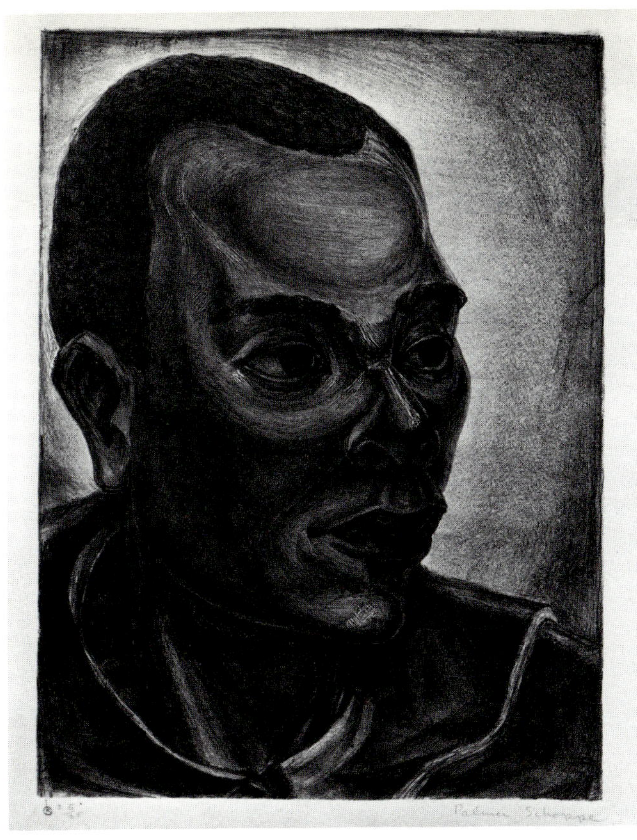

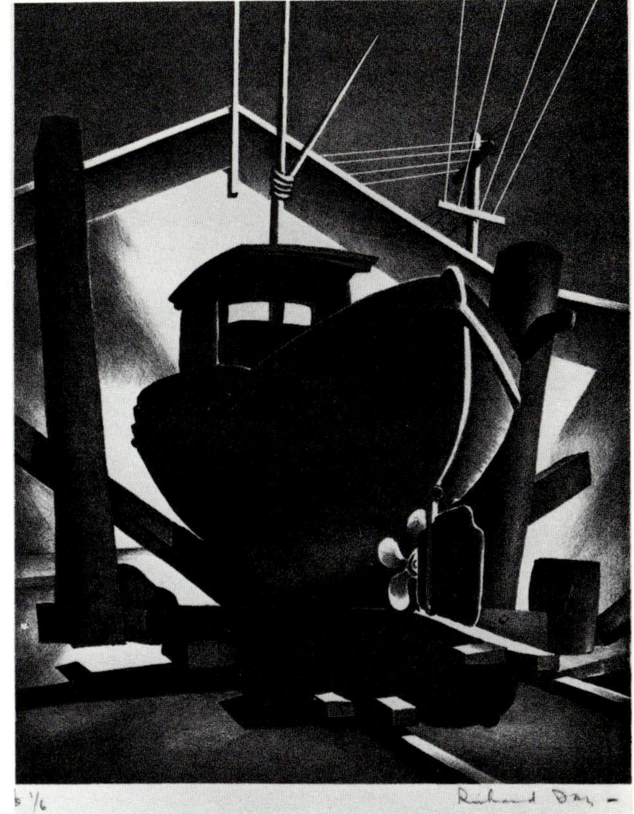

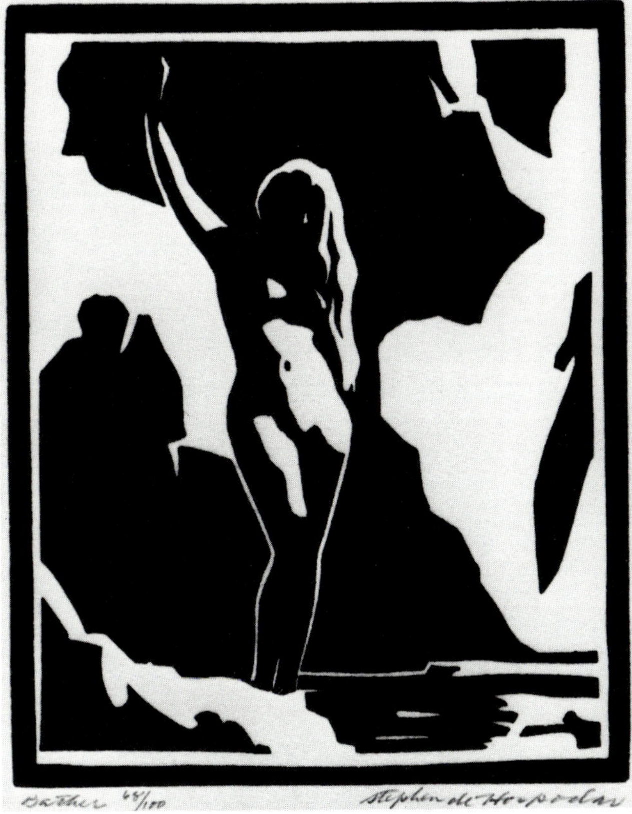

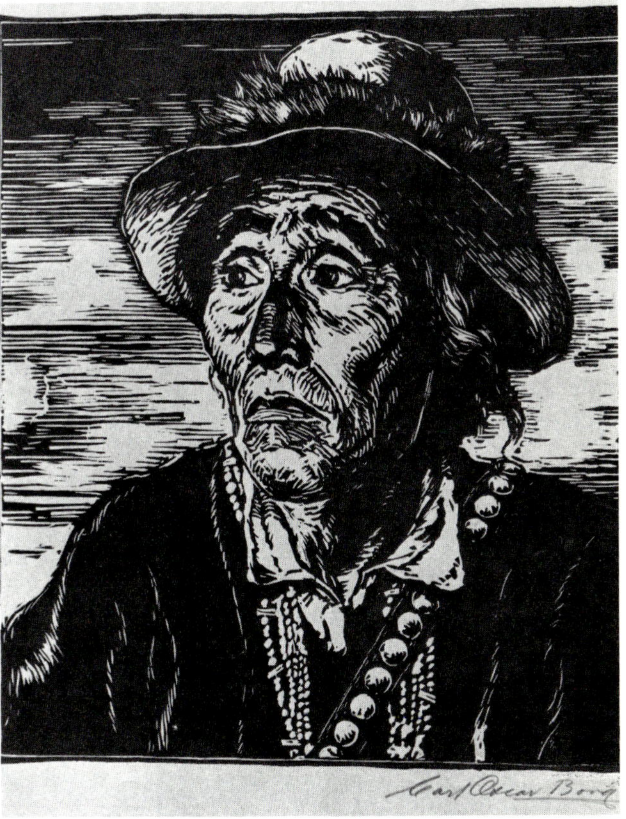

29. Palmer Schoppe, *Head of a Negro,* 1935

30. Stephen de Hospodar, *Bather,* c. 1930

31. Richard Day, *Boats in the Ways,* c. 1931

32. Carl Oscar Borg, *Navajo Chief,* c. 1930–35

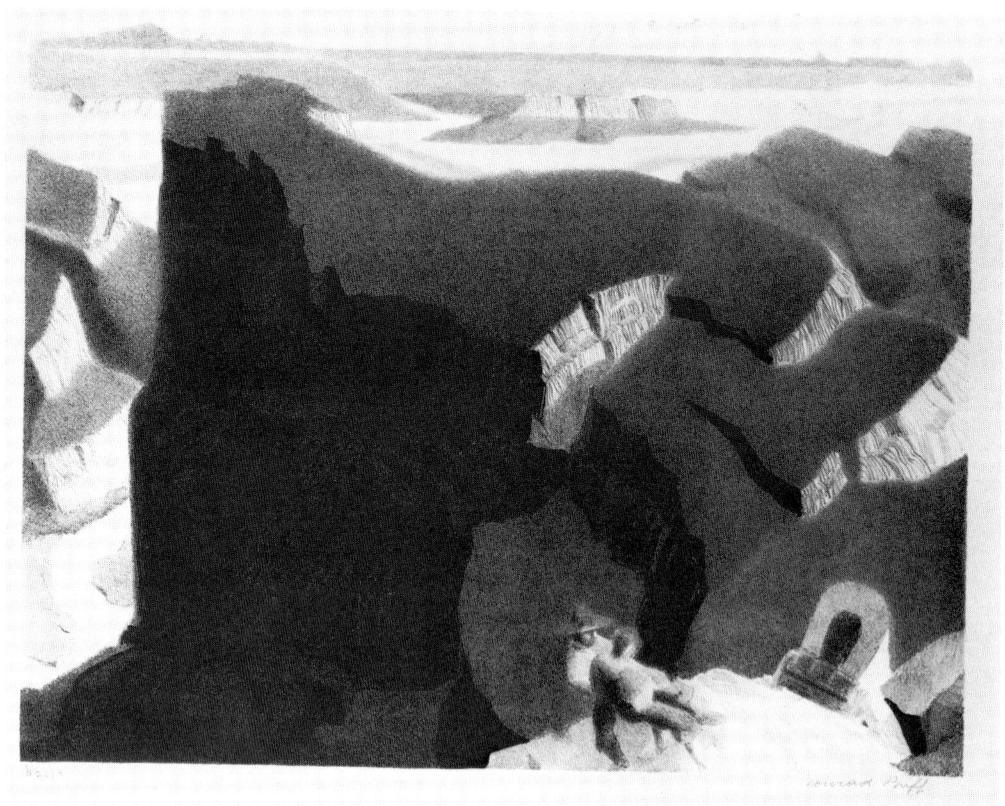

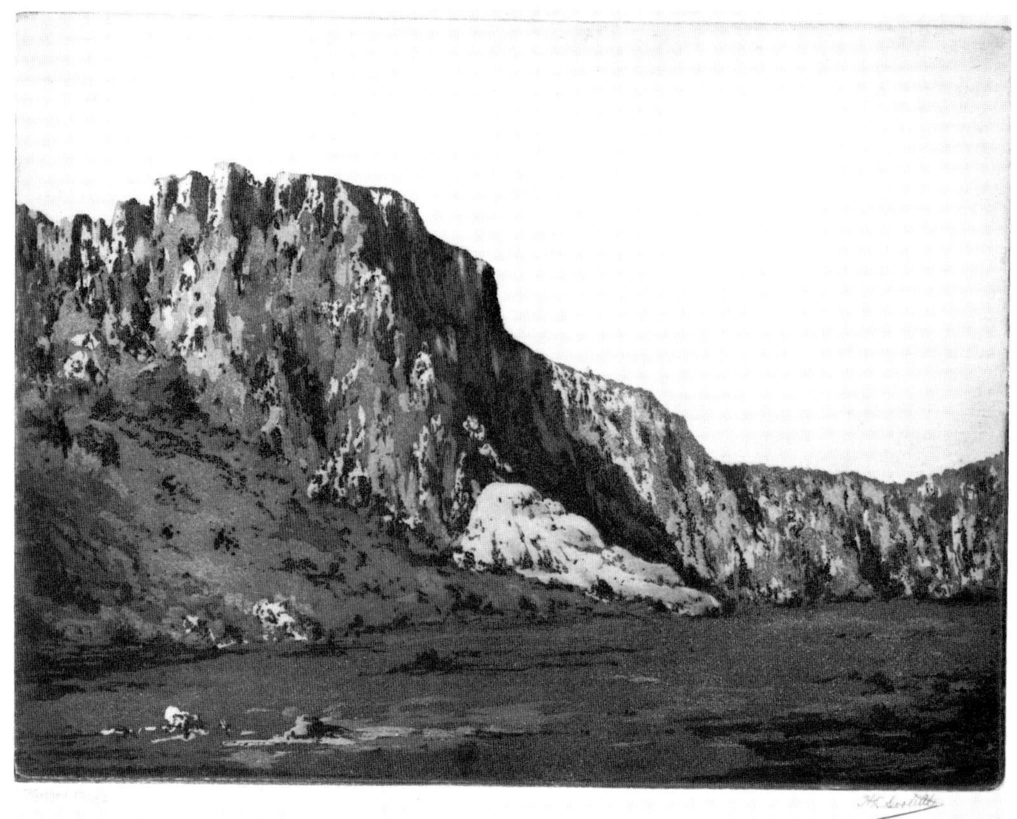

33. Conrad Buff, *American Pioneers,* c. 1935

34. Harold Doolittle, *Rugged Cliffs,* c. 1935

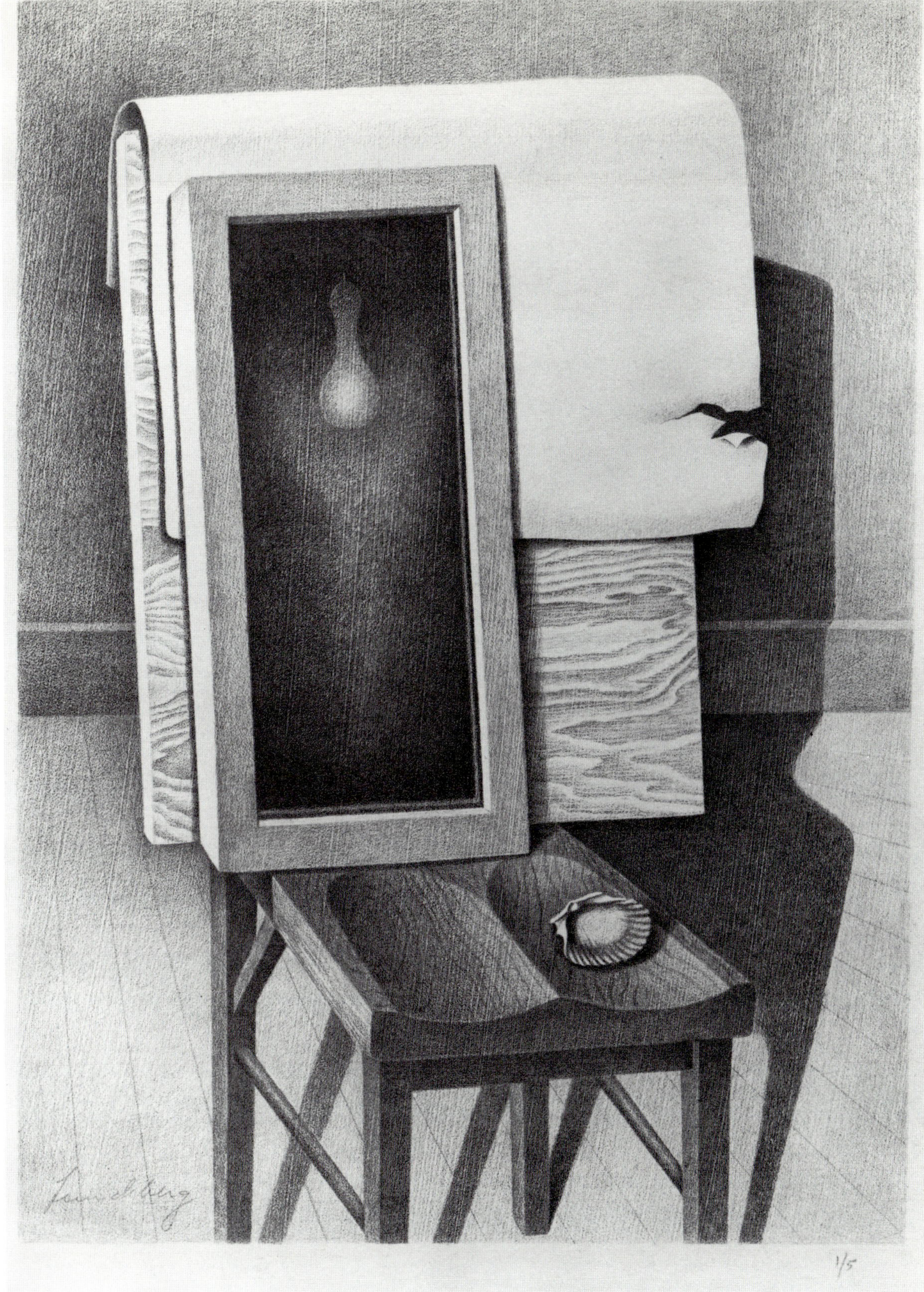

35. Helen Lundeberg, *The Mirror,* 1937

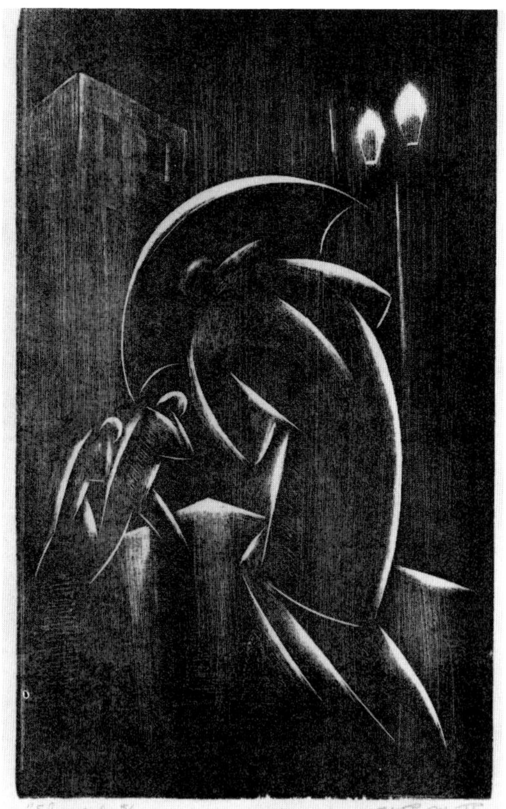

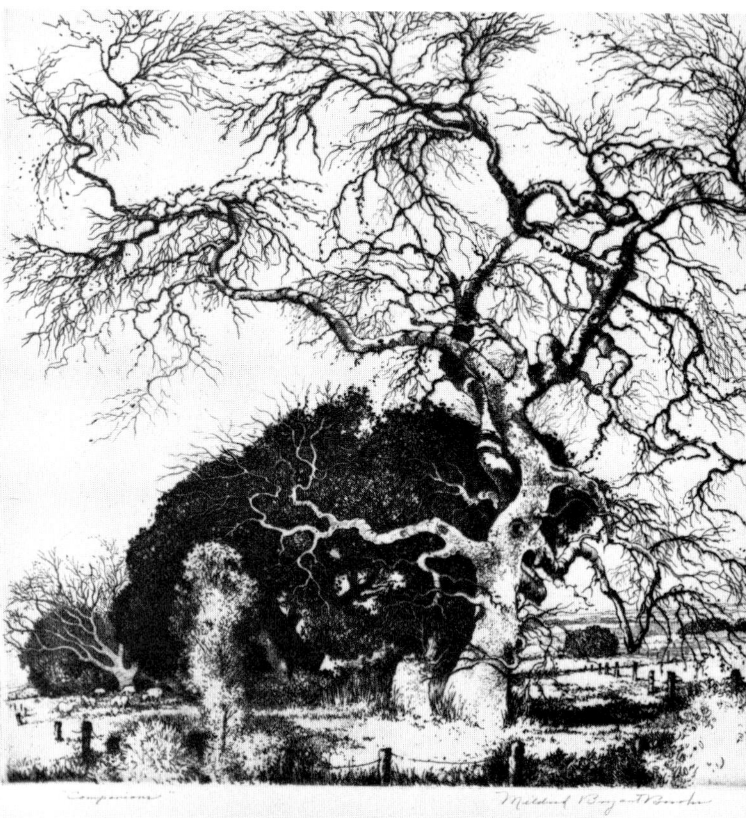

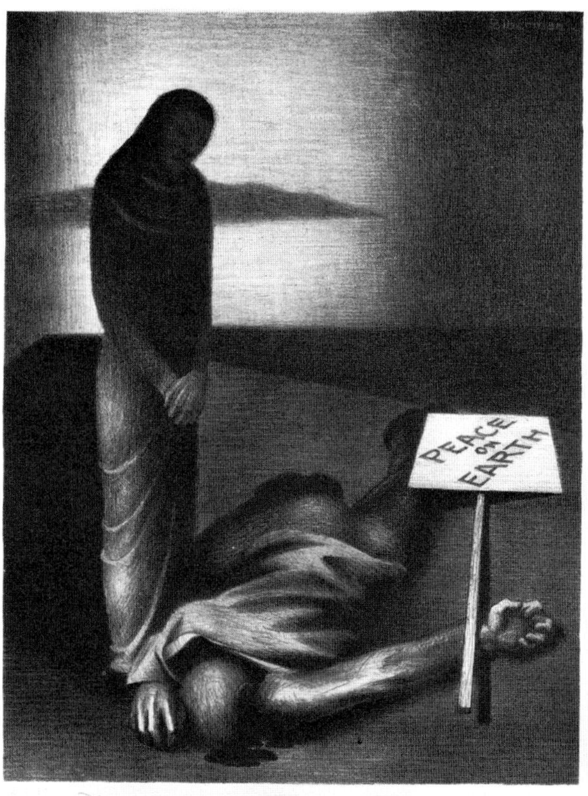

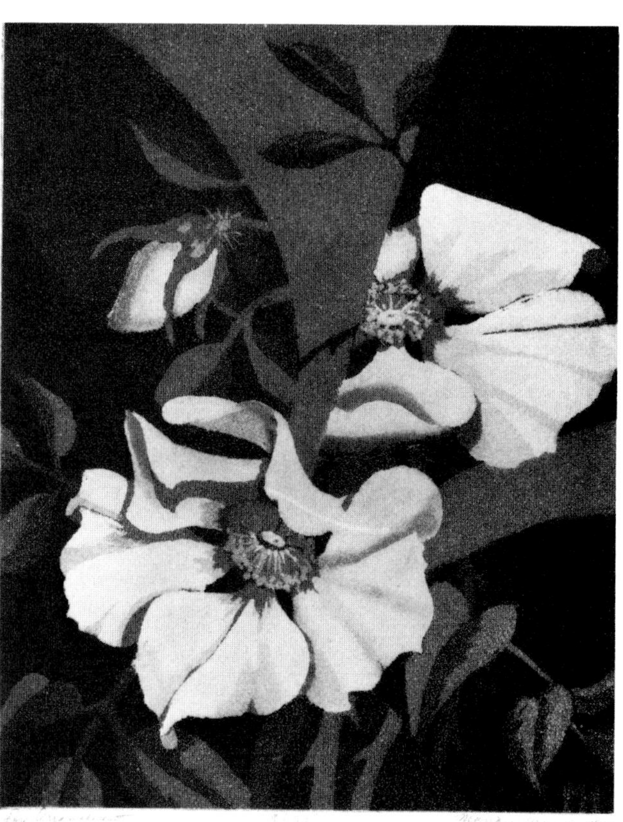

37. Fletcher Martin, *Shower,* c. 1930–32

39. Edward Biberman, *Pietà,* c. 1936–40

40. Mildred Bryant Brooks, *Companions,* 1937

41. Marion Hebert, *Rose Arrangement,* 1938

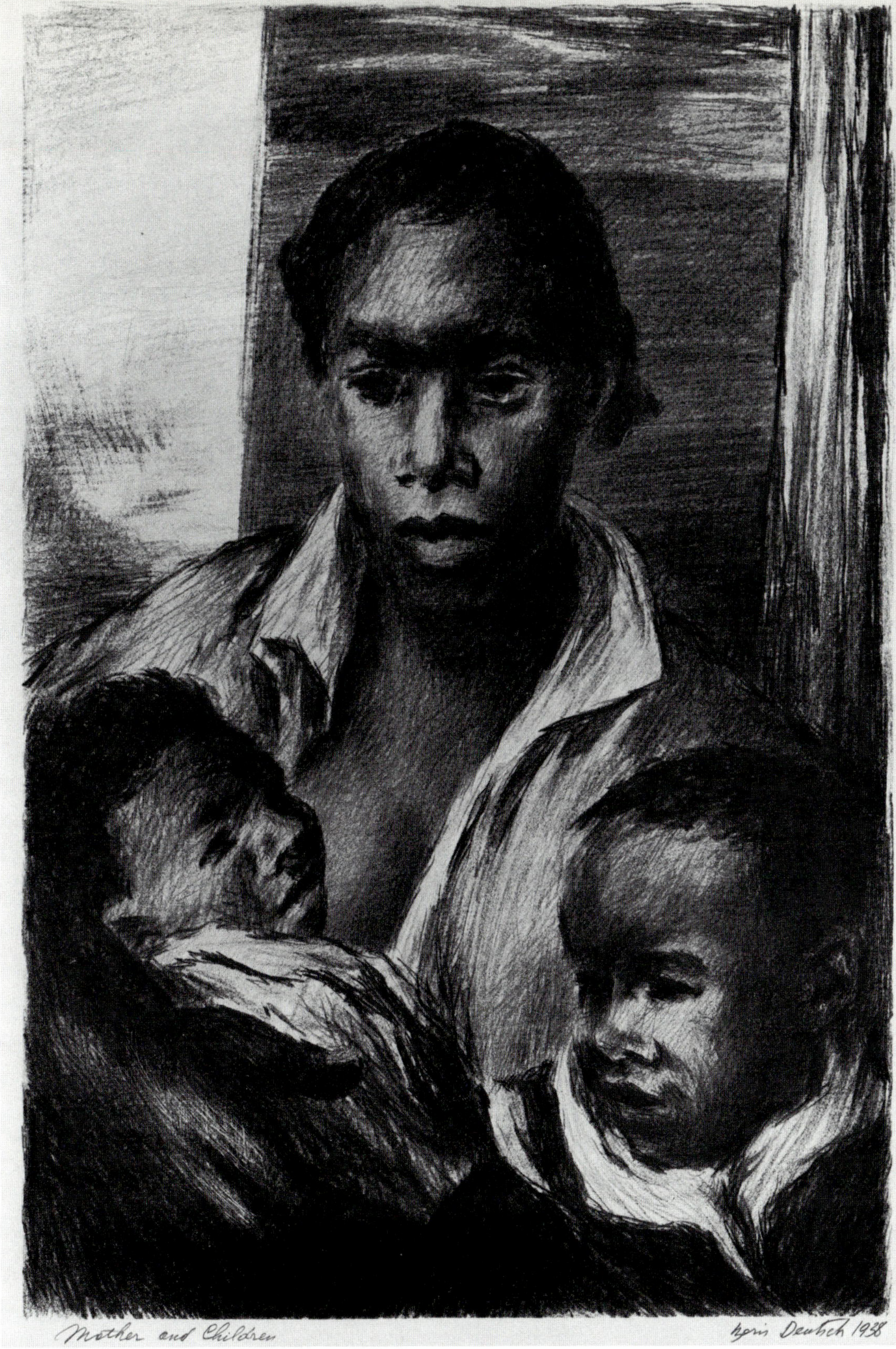

42. Boris Deutsch, *Mother and Child,* 1938

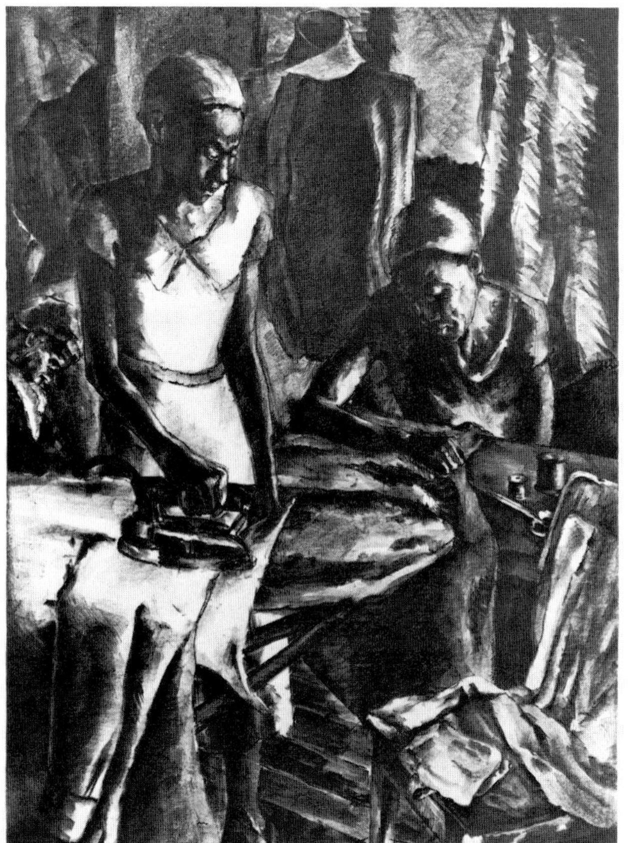

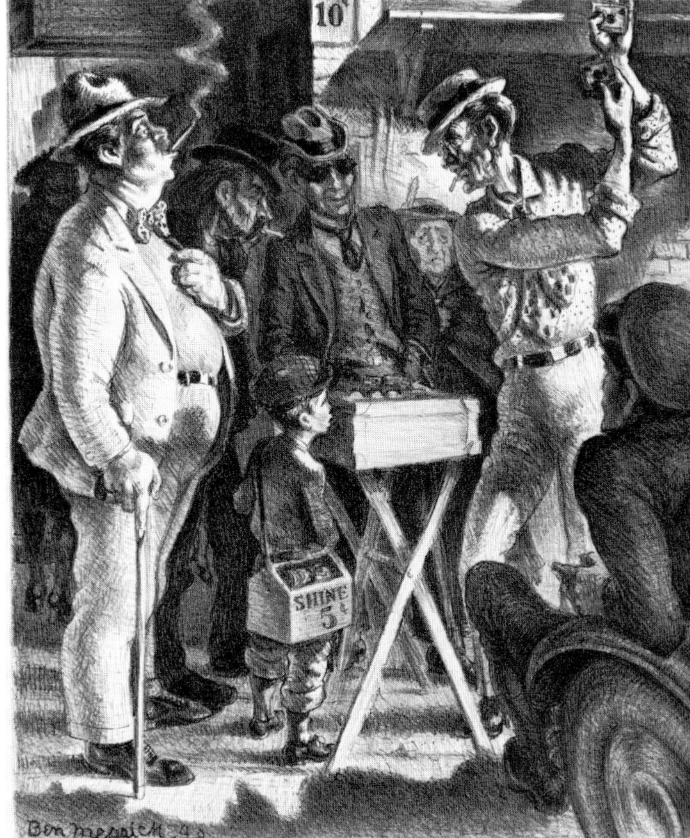

43. Oscar Van Young, *The Laundresses,* 1939

44. Benjamin Newton Messick, *The Pitchman,* 1940

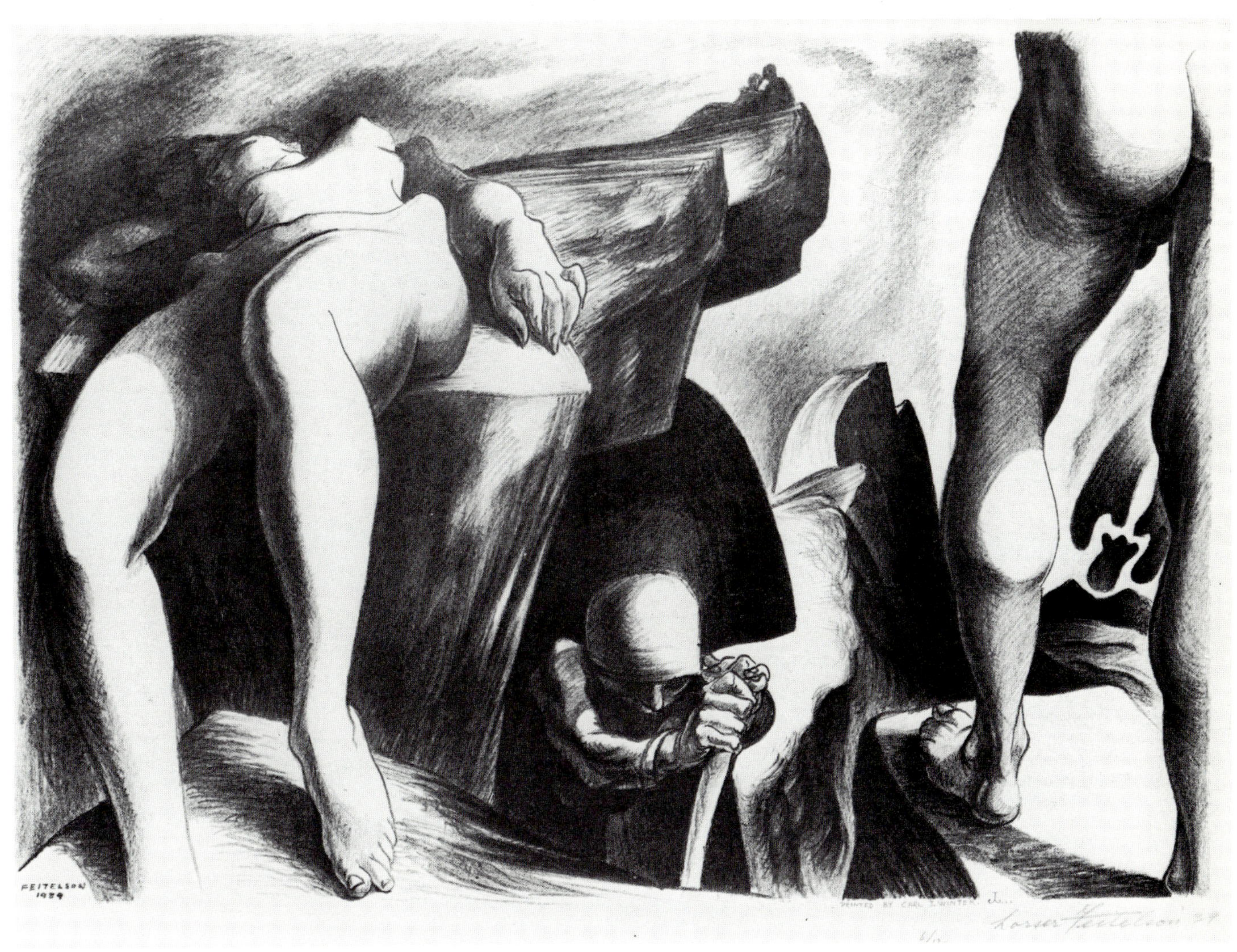

45. Lorser Feitelson, *Post-Surreal Configuration: Biological Symphony,* 1939

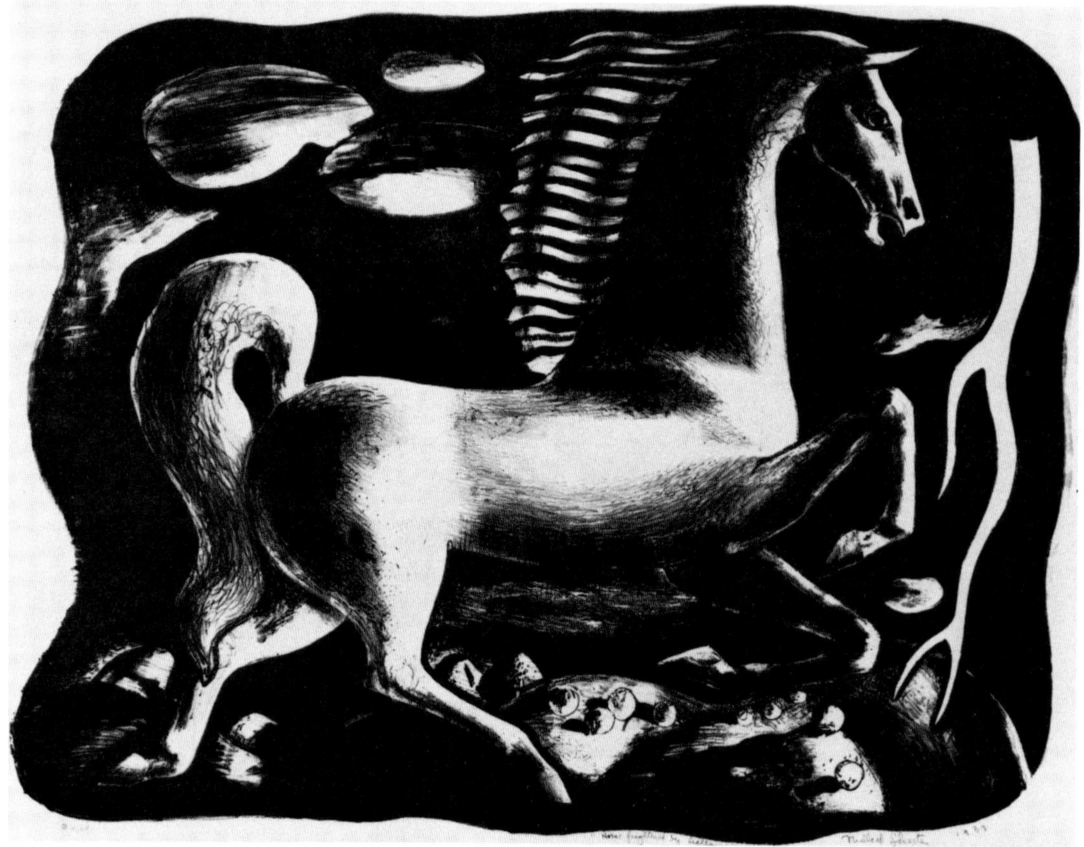

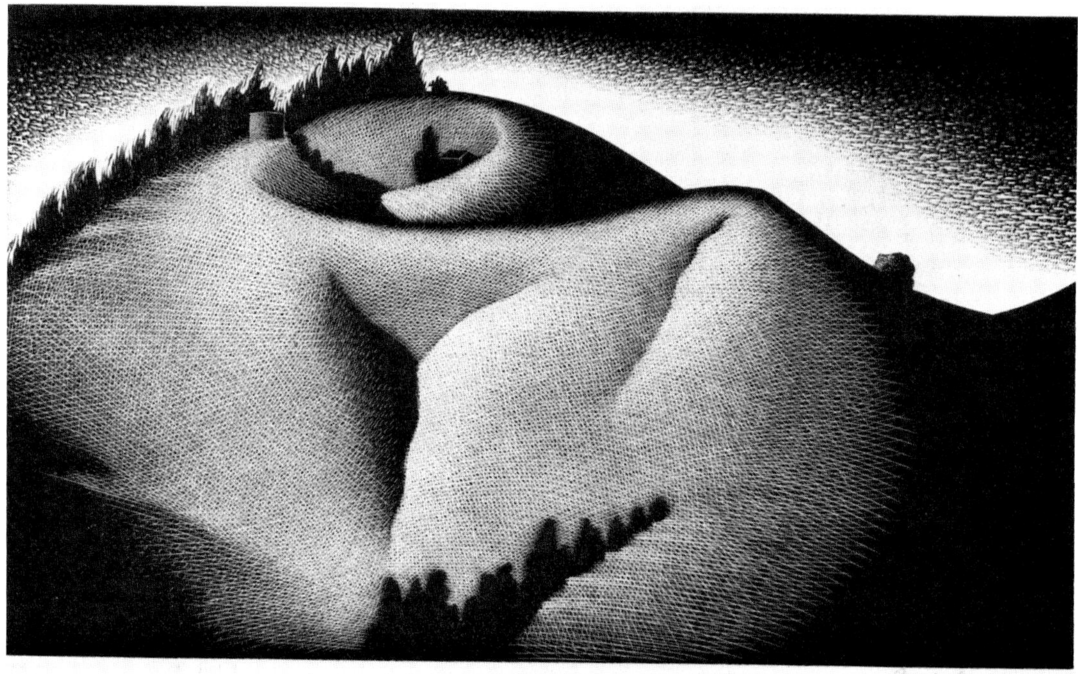

46. Millard Sheets, *Horse Frightened by Lightning,* 1939

48. Paul Landacre, *Hill,* c. 1940

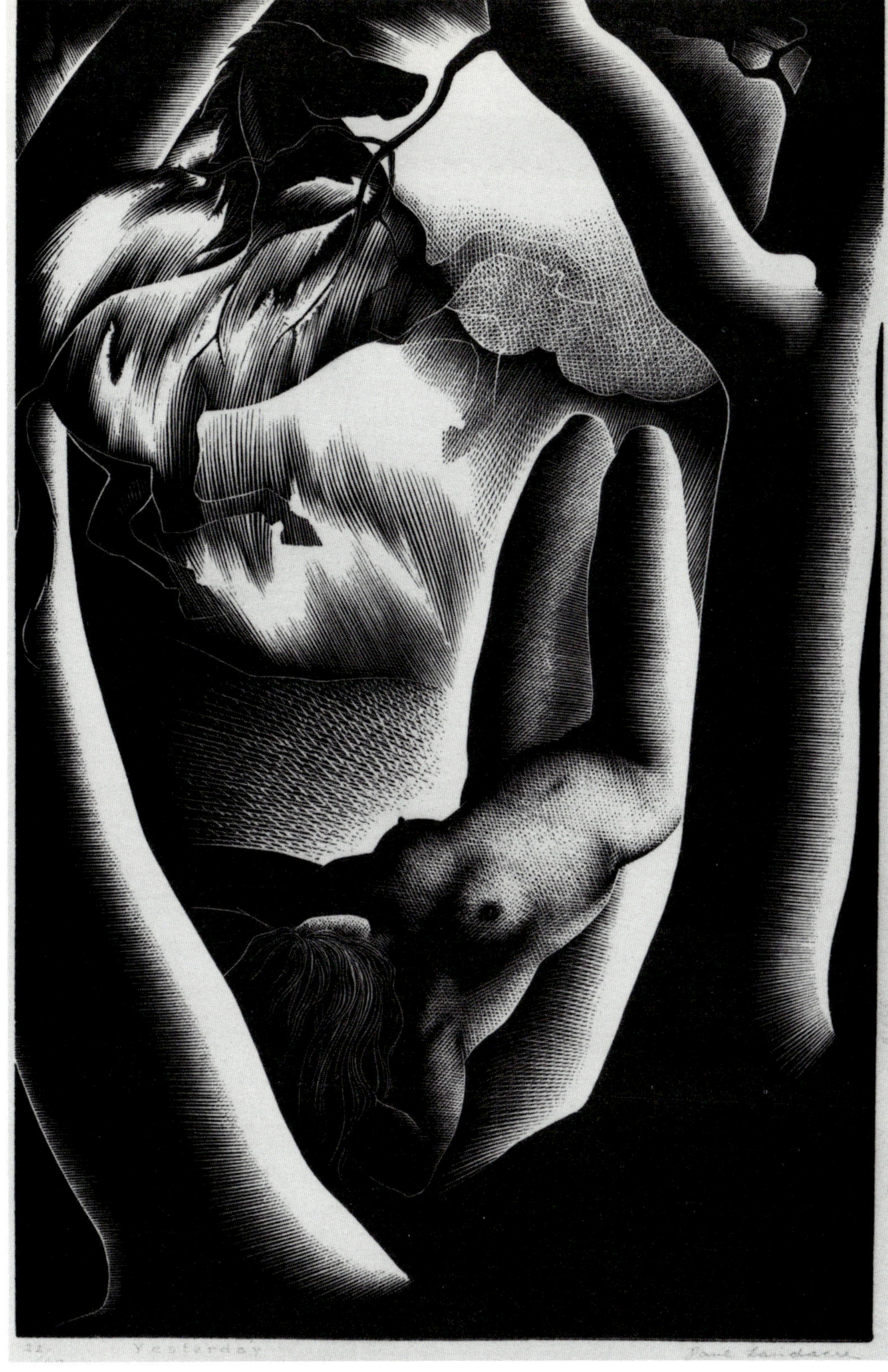

47. Paul Landacre, *Yesterday,* 1941

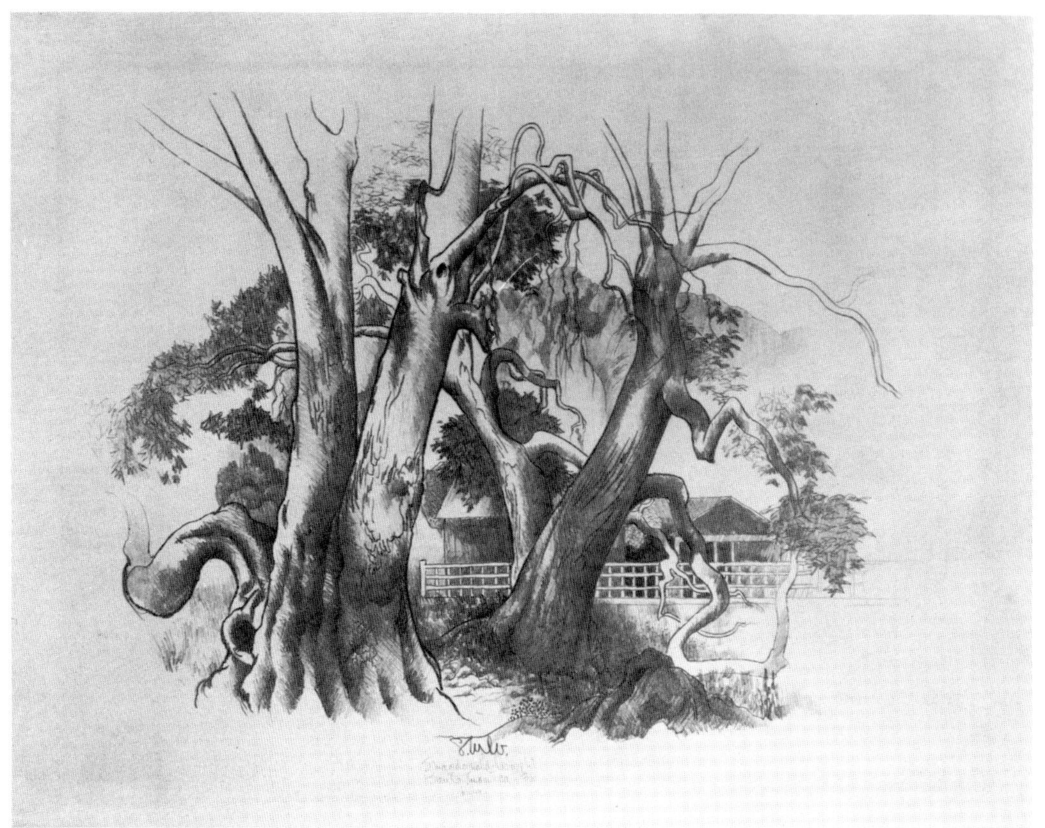

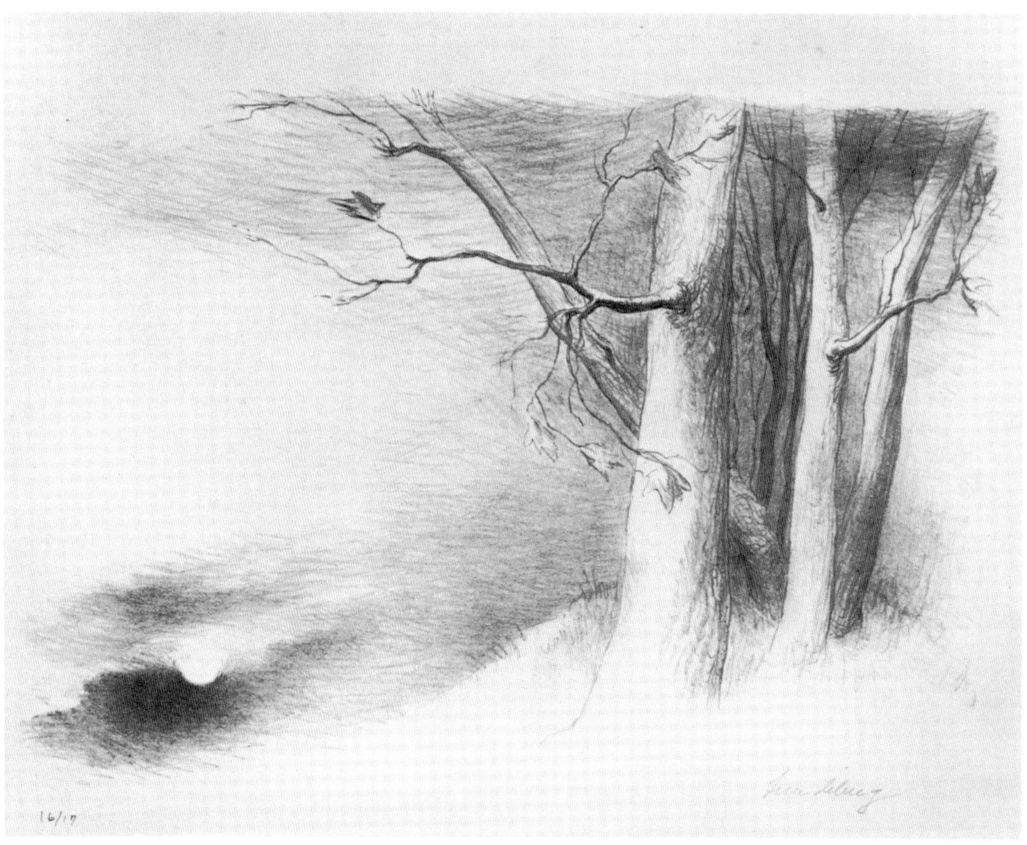

50. Stanton Macdonald-Wright, *Clump of Trees before a House,* 1938

51. Helen Lundeberg, *Moonrise,* 1948

LOS ANGELES PRINTS, 1883–1980

Addenda and errata

Three additional works by Paul Landacre were added to the exhibition too late to be included in the catalog:

Death of a Forest
Wood engraving
8¼ x 11 in. (21 x 27.9 cm.)
Lent by Mr. and Mrs. Joseph Landacre

Smoke Tree Ranch
Wood engraving
6¾ x 10 in. (17.2 x 25.4 cm.)
Lent by Mr. and Mrs. Joseph Landacre

Through the Pass
Wood engraving
10½ x 13½ in. (26.7 x 34.3 cm.)
Lent by Mr. and Mrs. Joseph Landacre

Prints by Helen Lundeberg (cat. nos. 35, 36, and 51) and Boris Deutch (cat. no. 42) were loaned by Helen Lundeberg Feitelson.

Prints by Lorser Feitelson (cat. nos. 45 and 52) were loaned by the Lorser Feitelson and Helen Lundeberg Feitelson Arts Foundation.

Los Angeles County Museum of Art

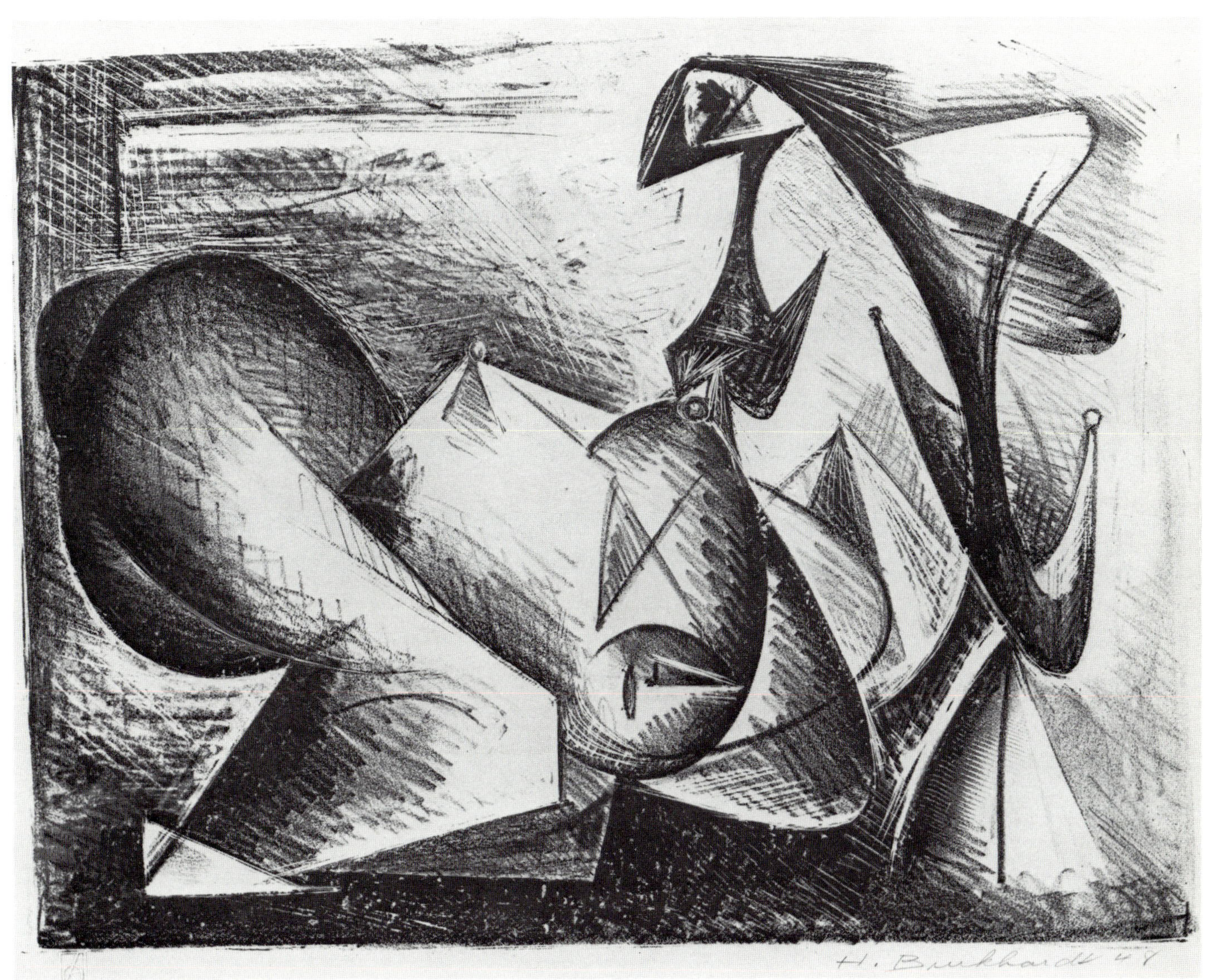

59. Hans Gustav Burkhardt, *Lovers,* 1948

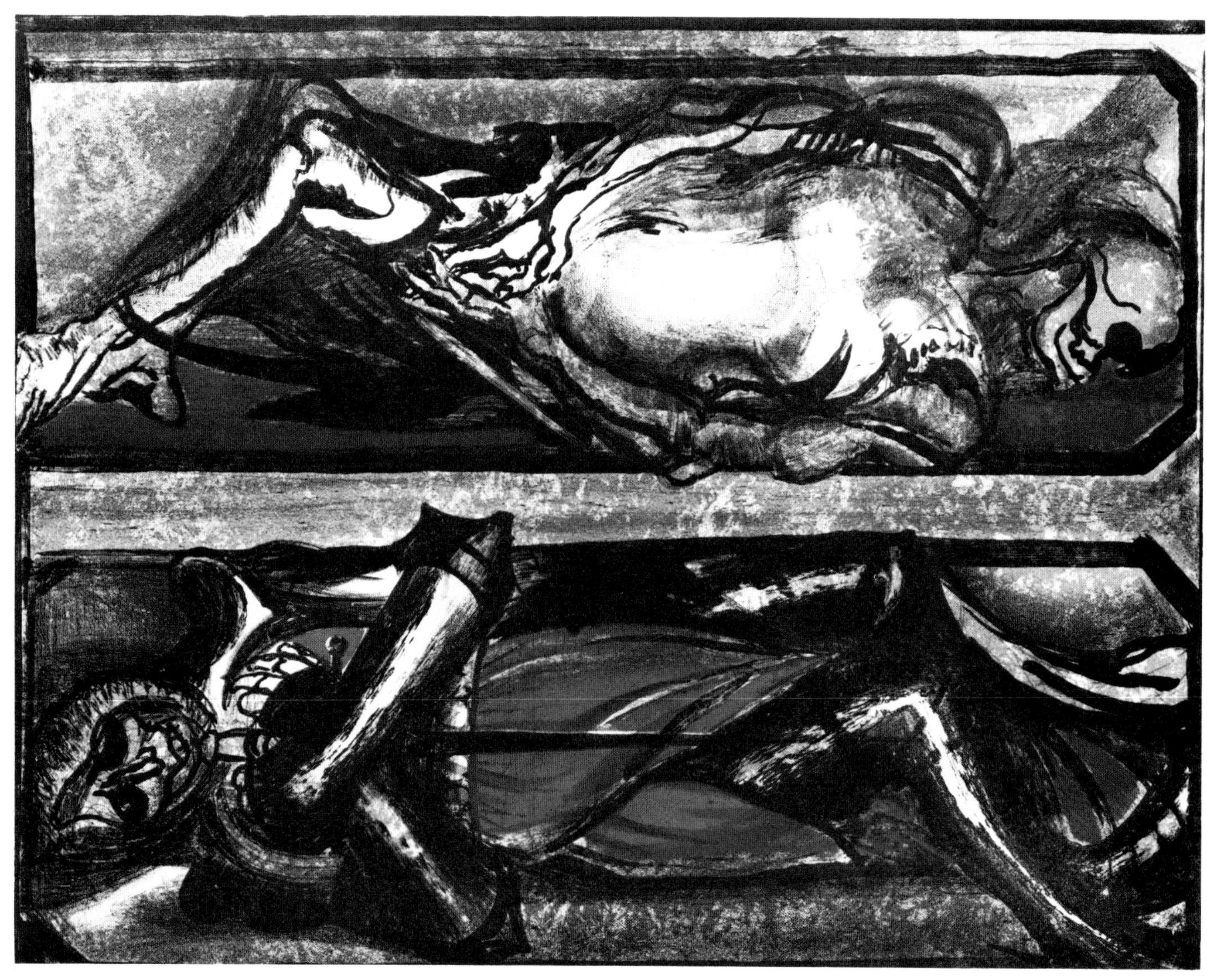

54. Rico Lebrun, *Man and Armor,* 1945

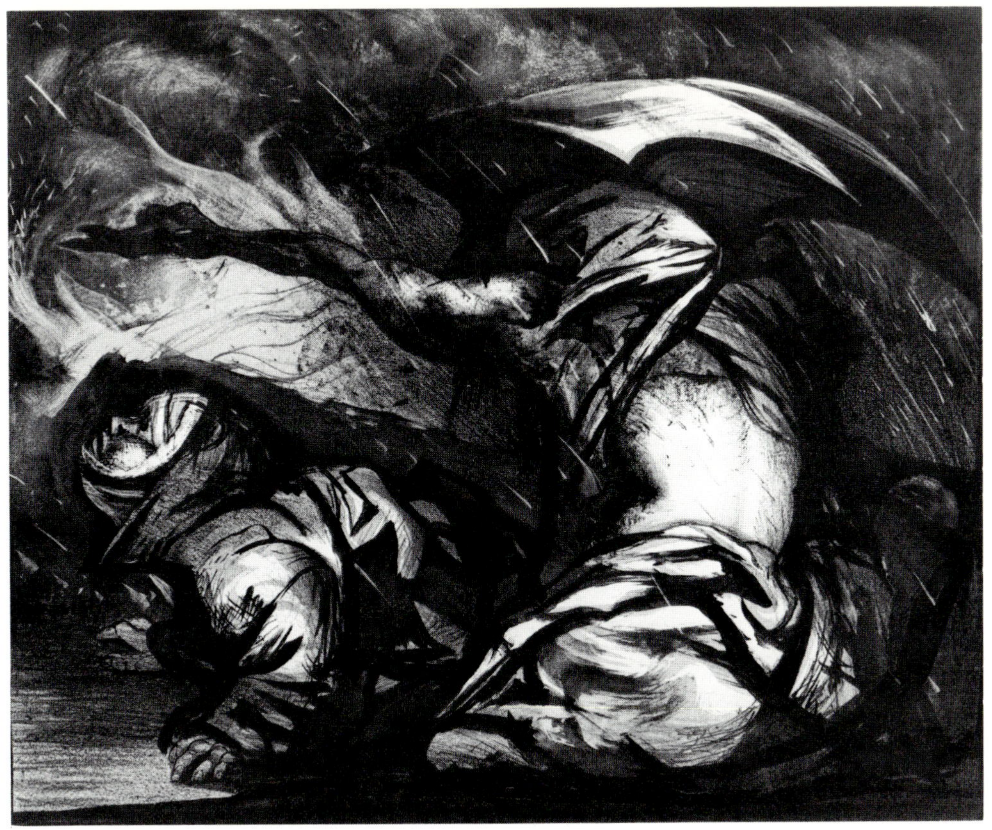

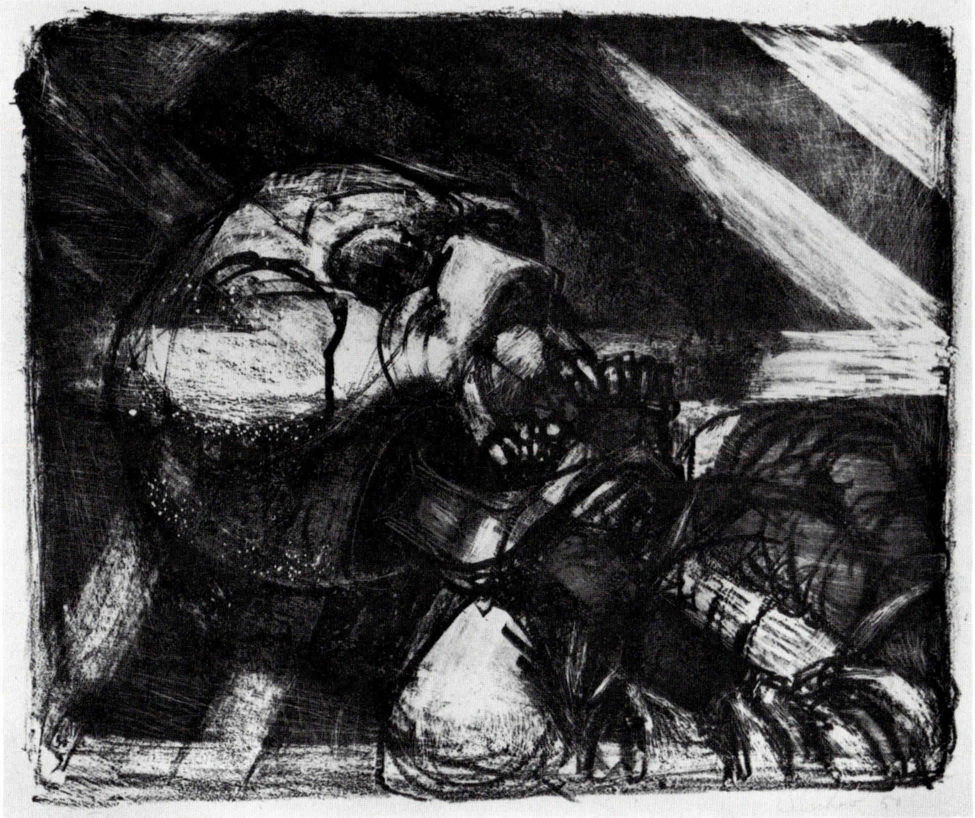

55. Rico Lebrun, *Rain of Ashes,* 1945

56. Howard Warshaw, *Head of Traffic Victim,* c. 1950

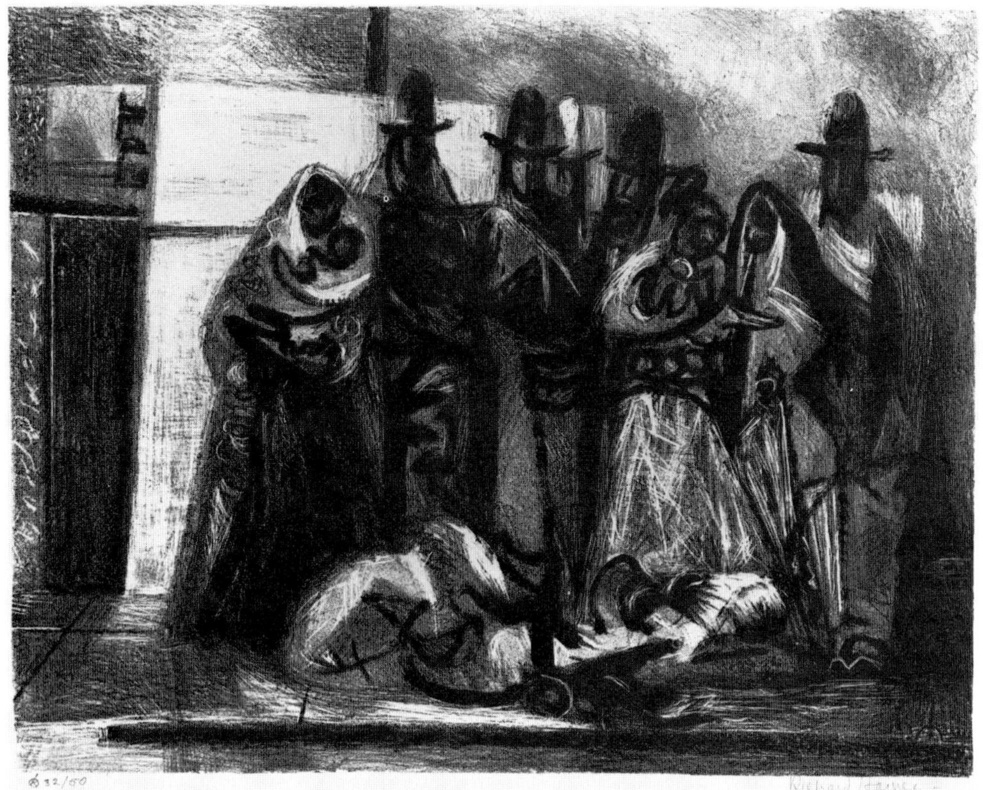

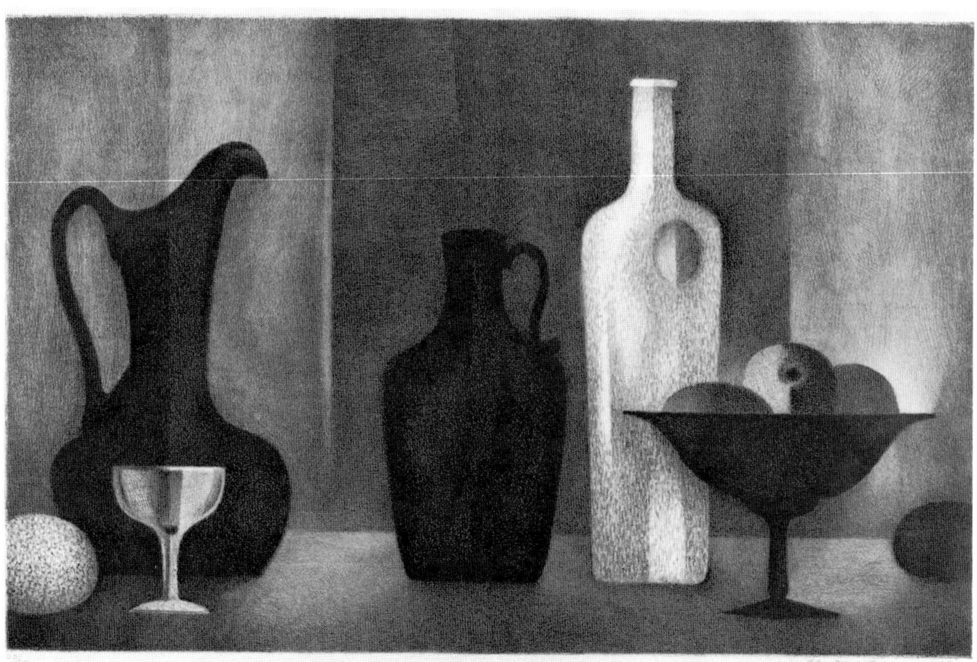

60. Richard Haines, *Bus Stop,* 1948

61. Clinton Adams, *Silver Bottle,* 1950

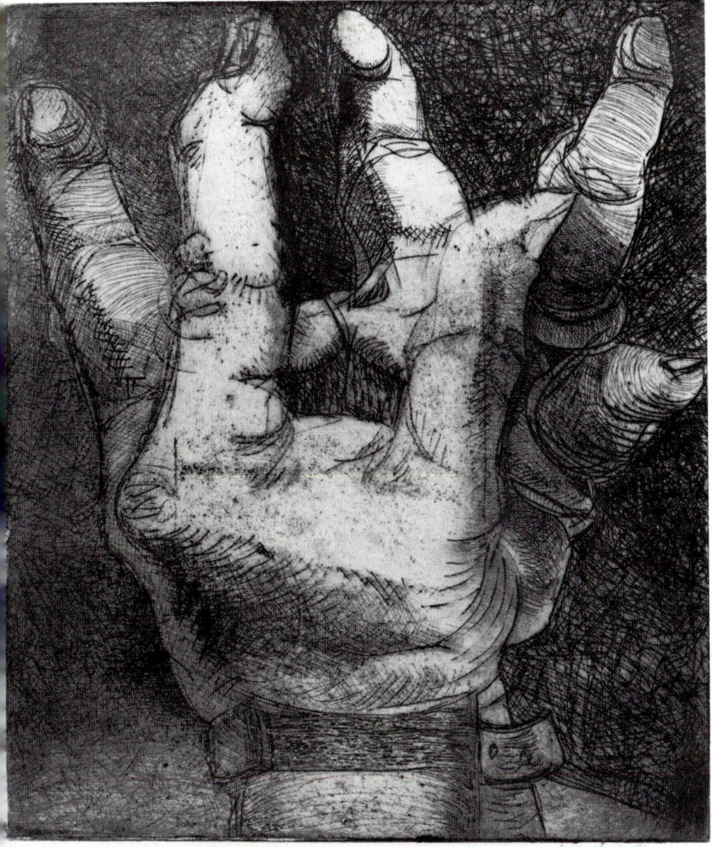

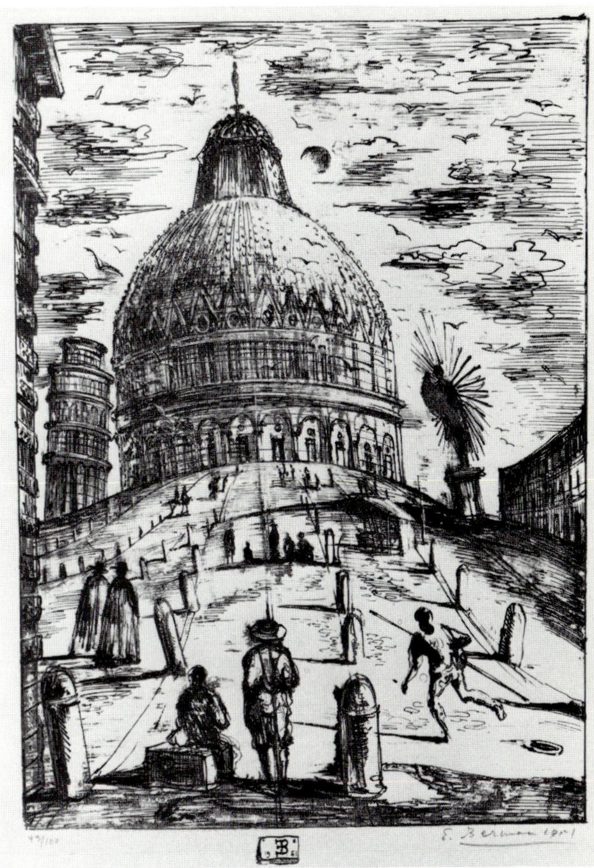

57. Howard Warshaw, *Hands,* 1951

62. Eugene Berman, *Pisan Fantasy,* 1951

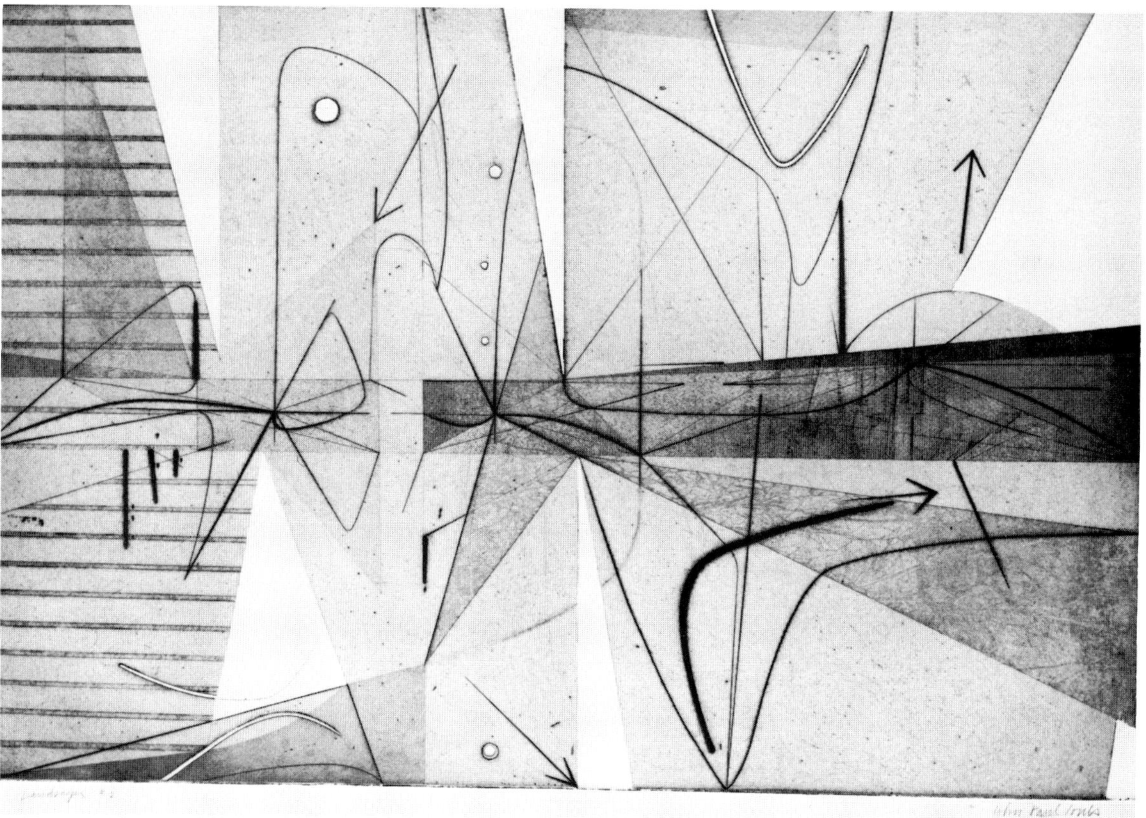

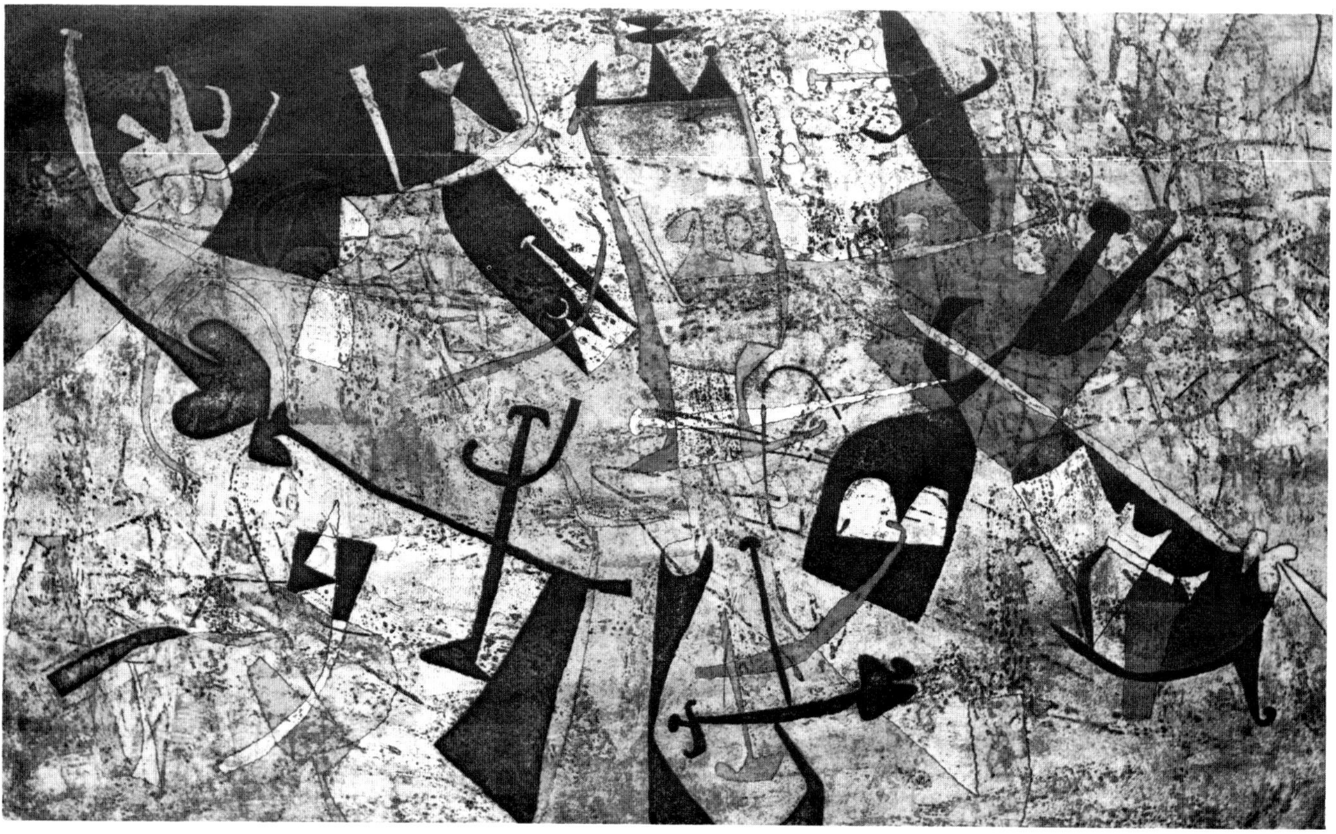

63. John Paul Jones, *Landscape #2,* 1950

66. Leonard Edmondson, *Escarpment,* 1956

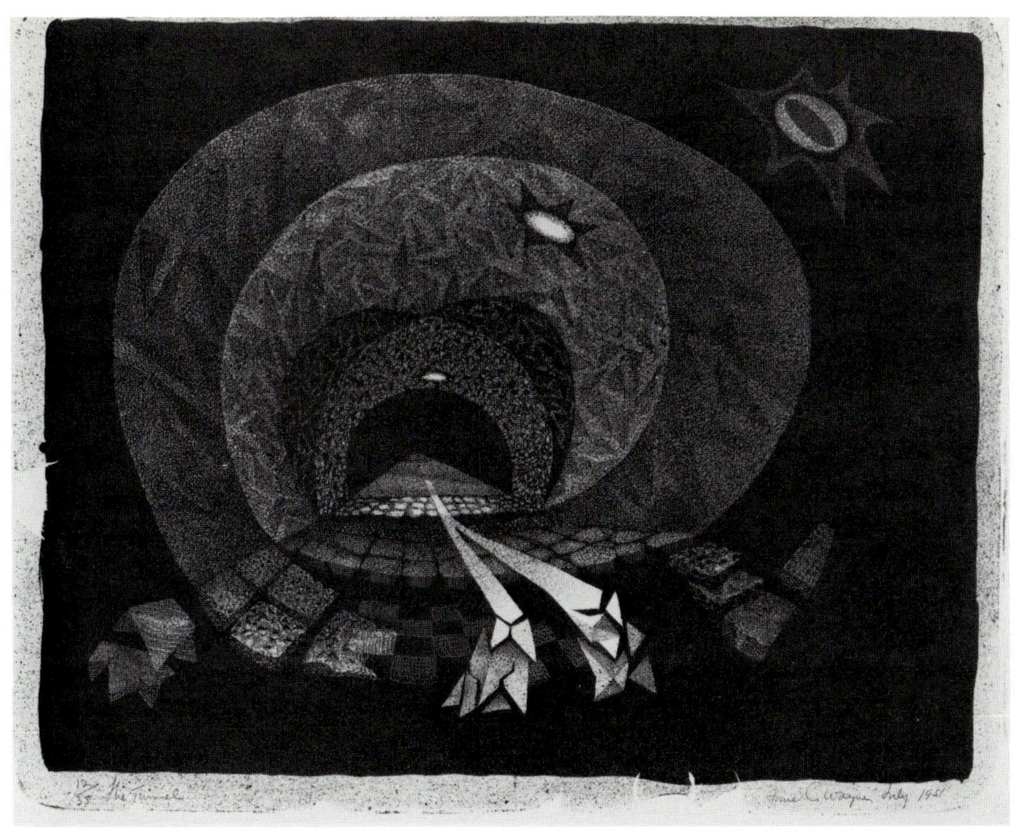

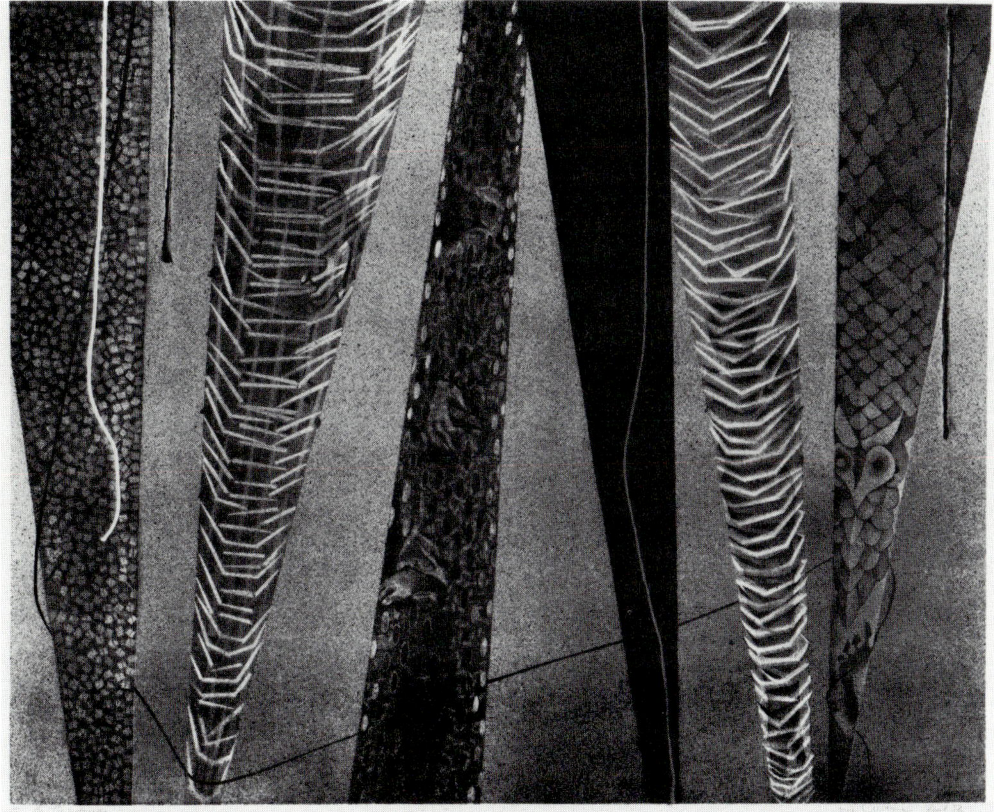

68. June Wayne, *The Tunnel,* 1951

69. June Wayne, *The Witnesses,* 1952

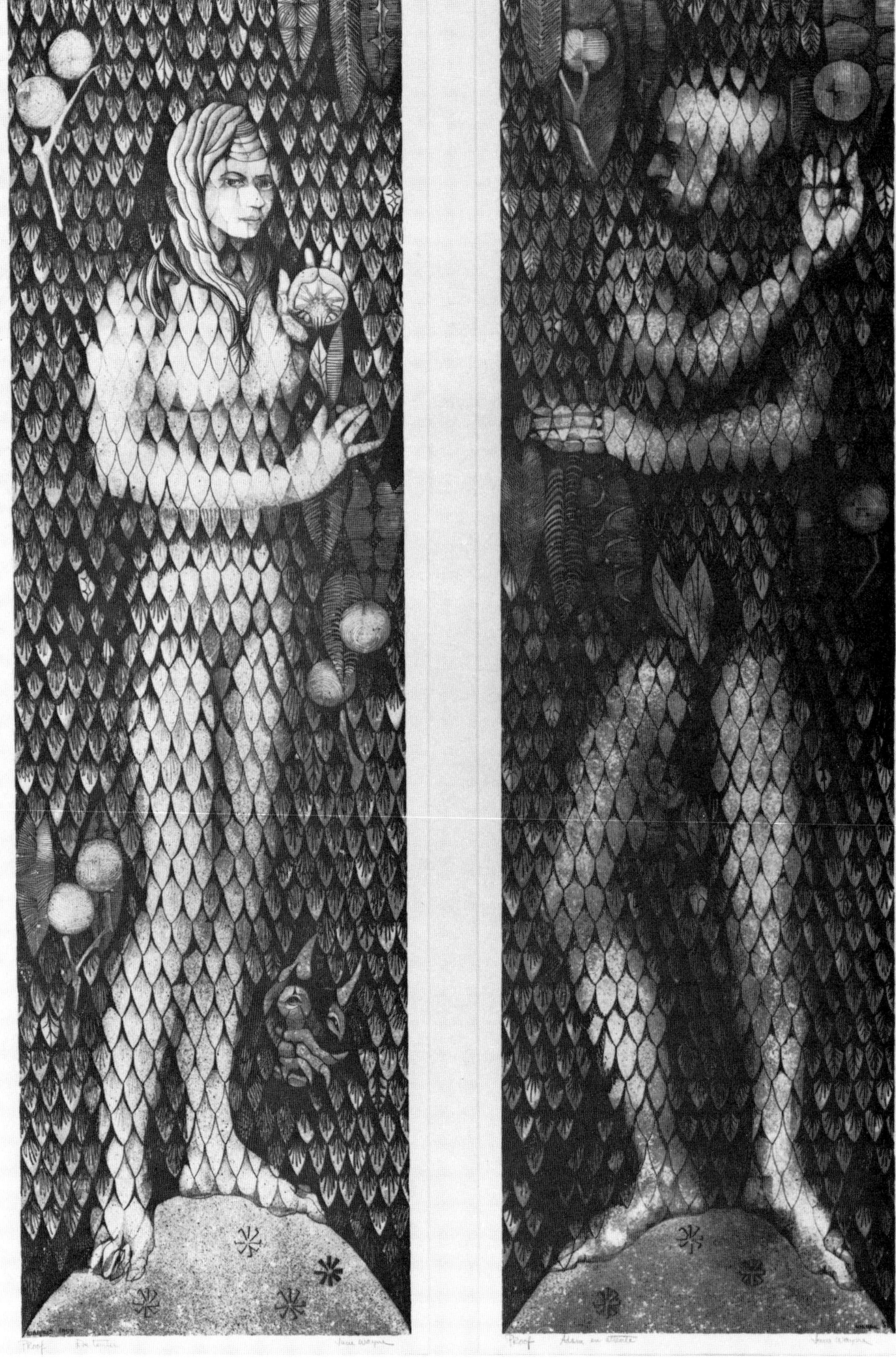

70. June Wayne, *Eve Tentée, Adam en Attente,* 1958

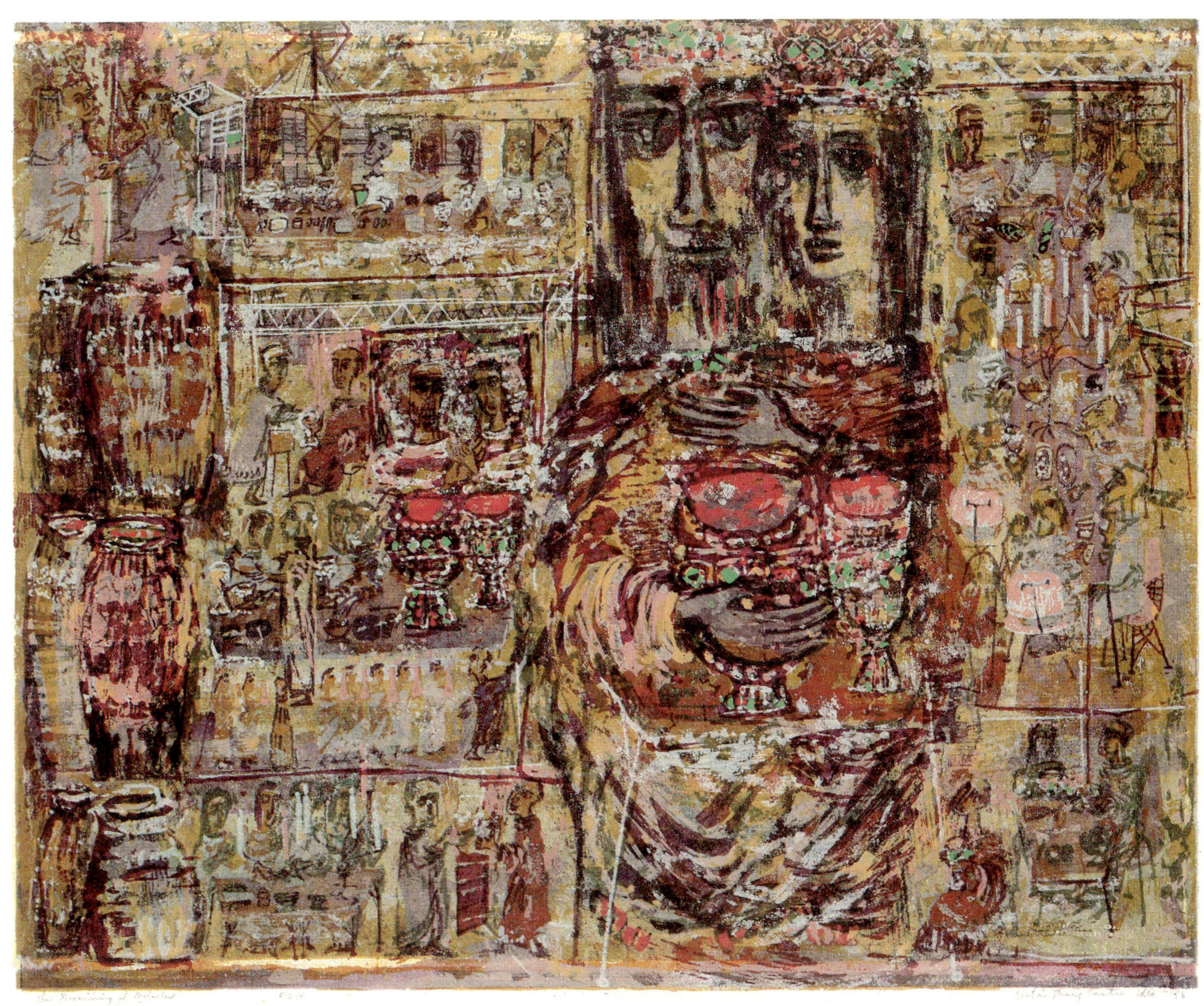

4. Sister Mary Corita, *This Beginning of Miracles,* 1953

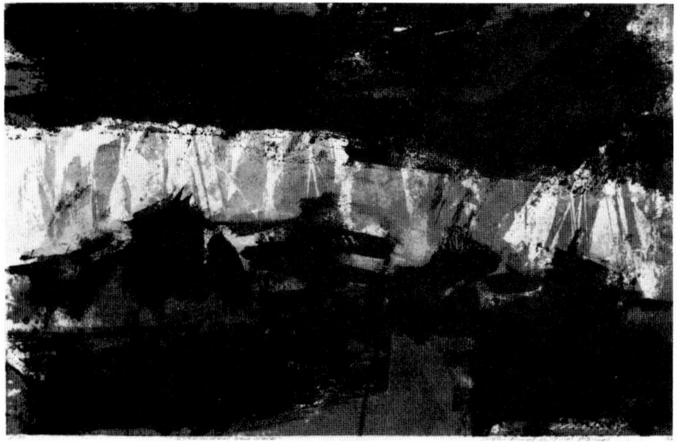

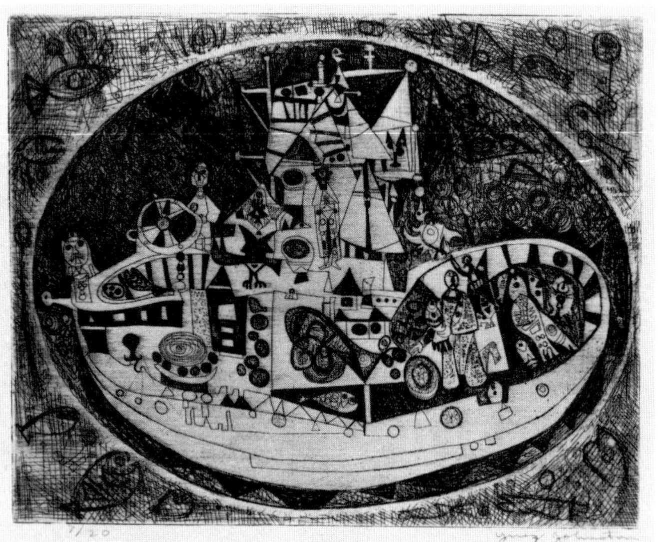

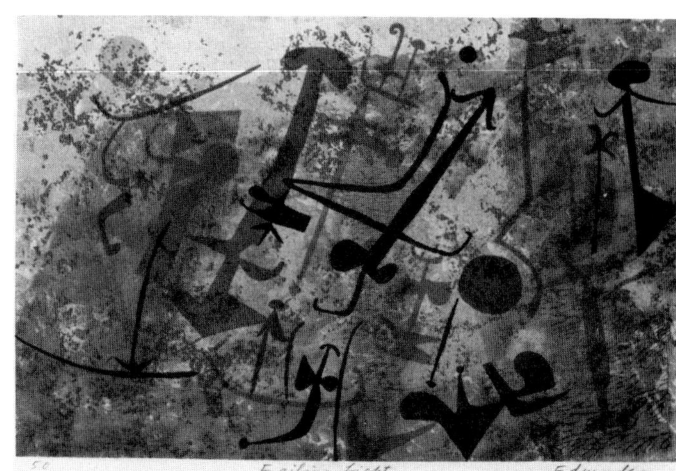

76. Dorothy Bowman, *Sleeping City,* c. 1957–58

75. Howard Bradford, *Suspended Seawave,* 1956

71. Ynez Johnston, *Ship and Storm,* 1949

65. Leonard Edmondson, *Failing Light,* 1950

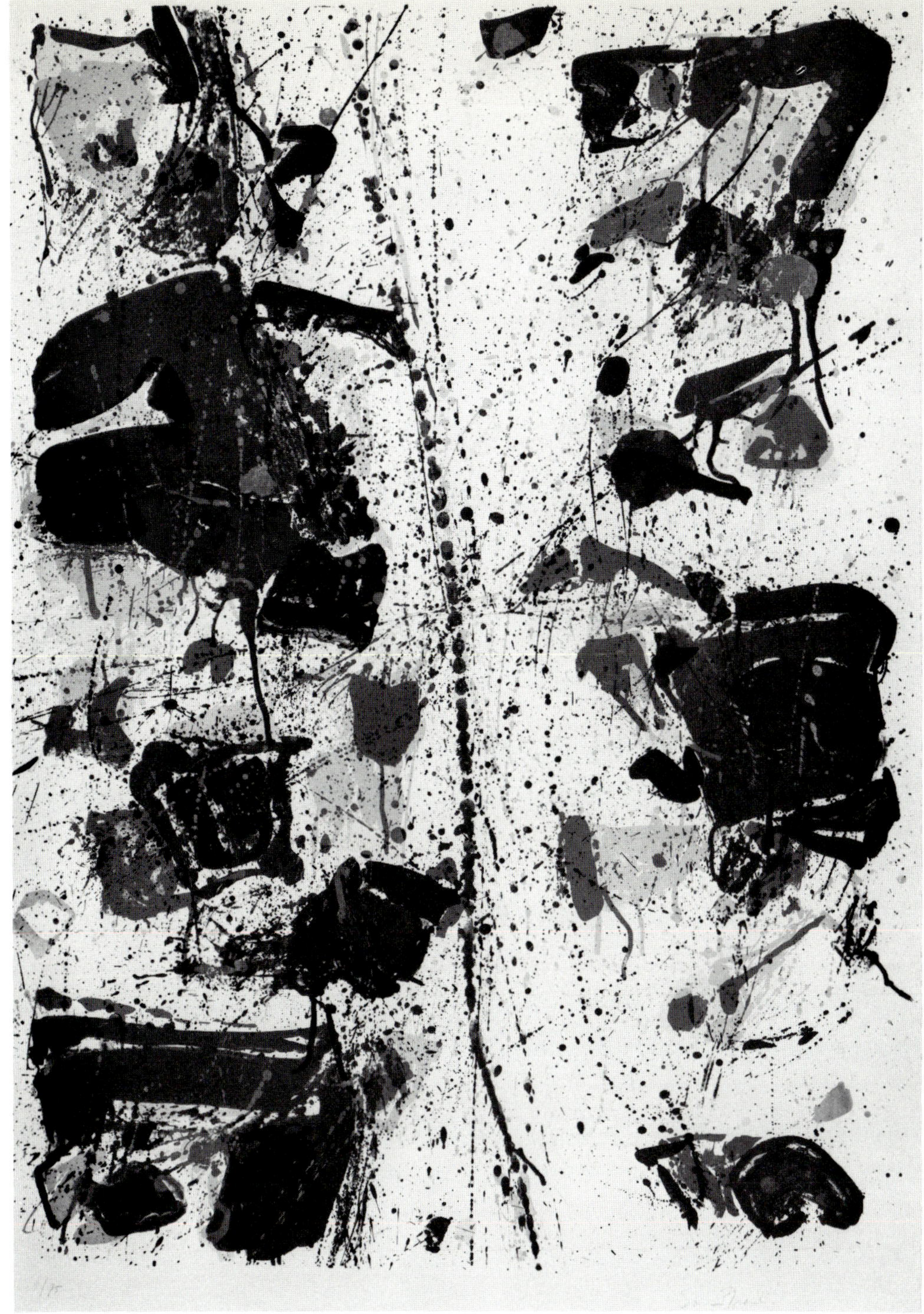

77. Sam Francis, *The White Line,* 1960

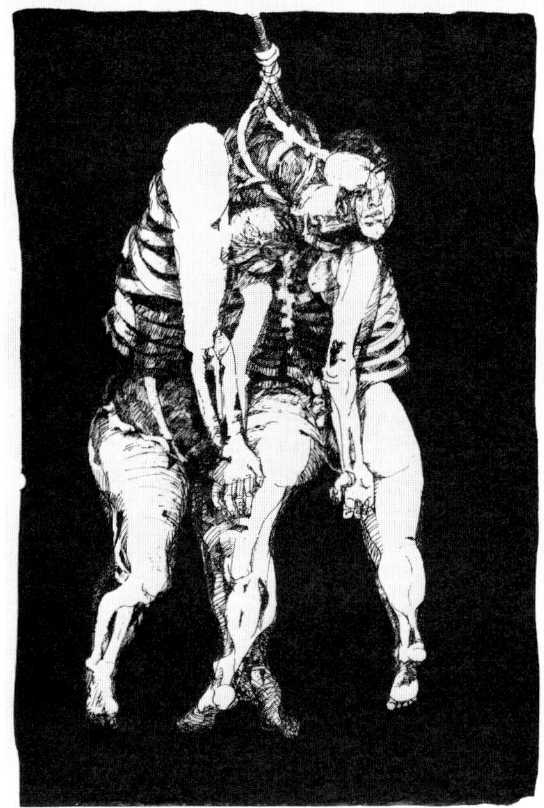

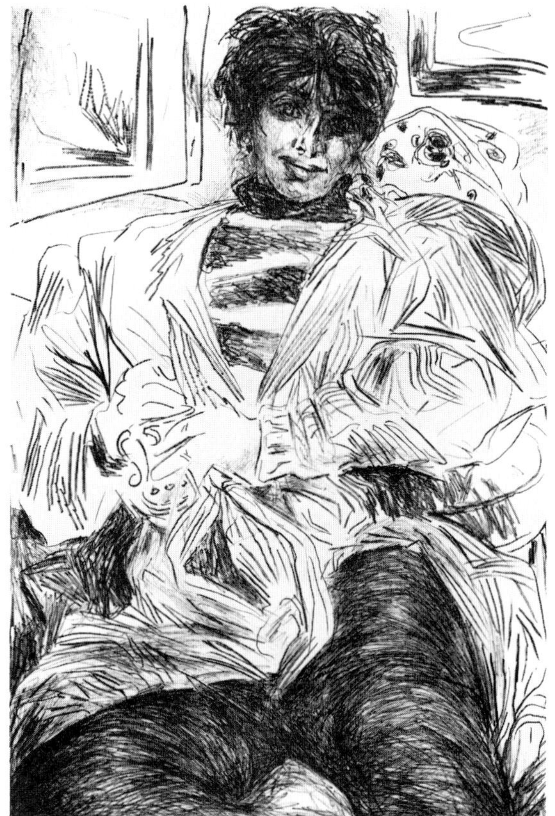

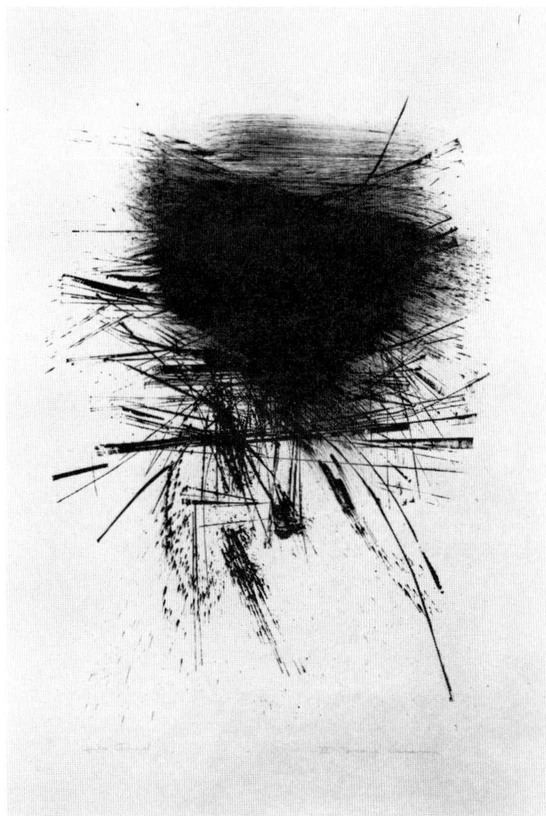

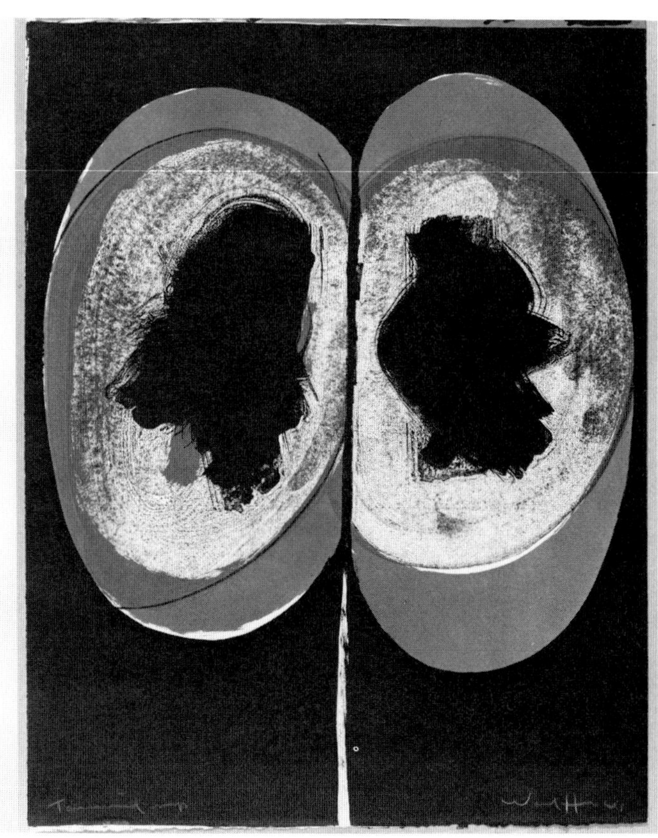

78. Connor Everts, *Execution,* 1960

79. Jules Engel, *Curfew,* 1960

80. William Brice, *Striped Robe,* 1961

81. Emerson Woelffer, *Untitled,* 1961

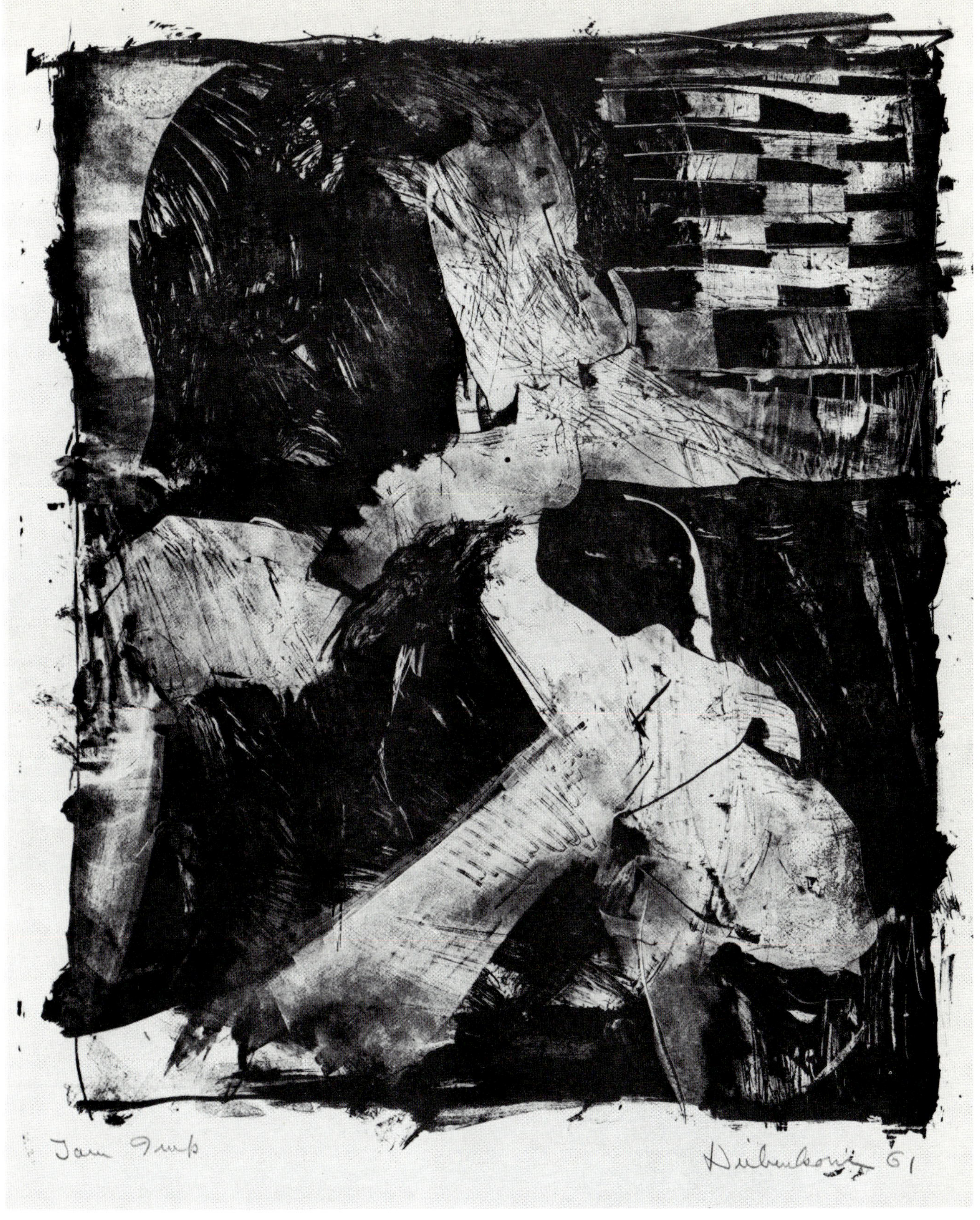

82. Richard Diebenkorn, *Untitled,* 1961

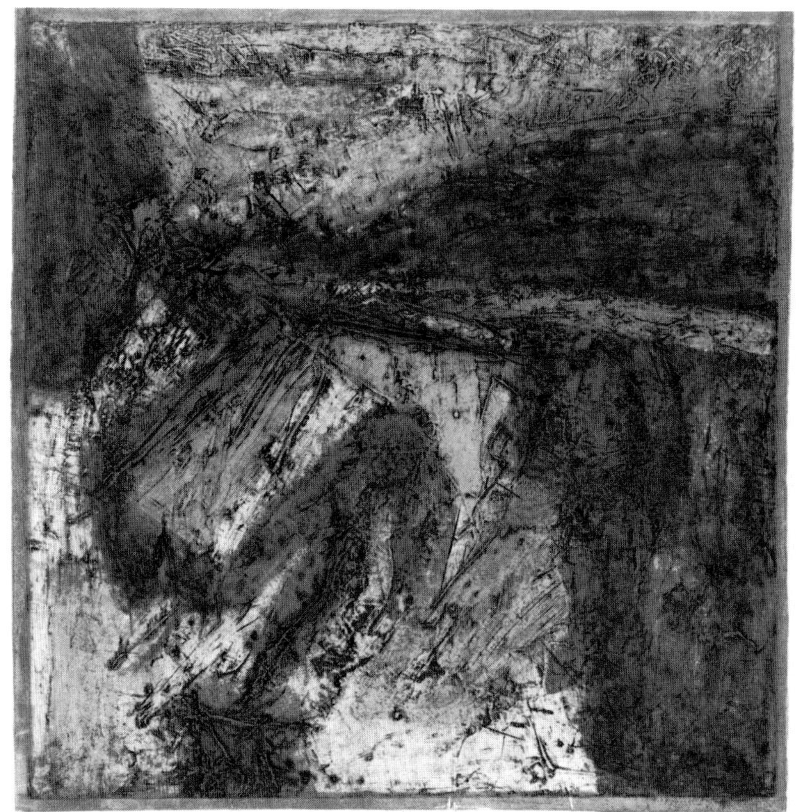

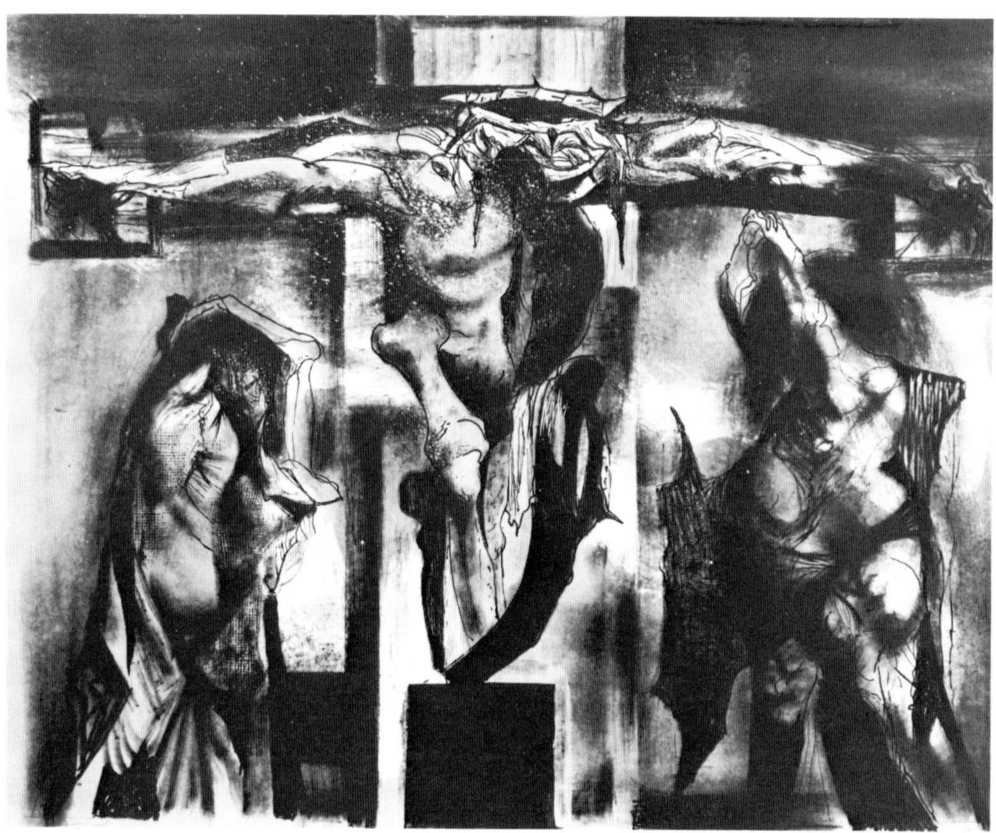

83. Tom Fricano, *Umbria #1*, 1961

84. Rico Lebrun, *Grünewald Study II*, 1961

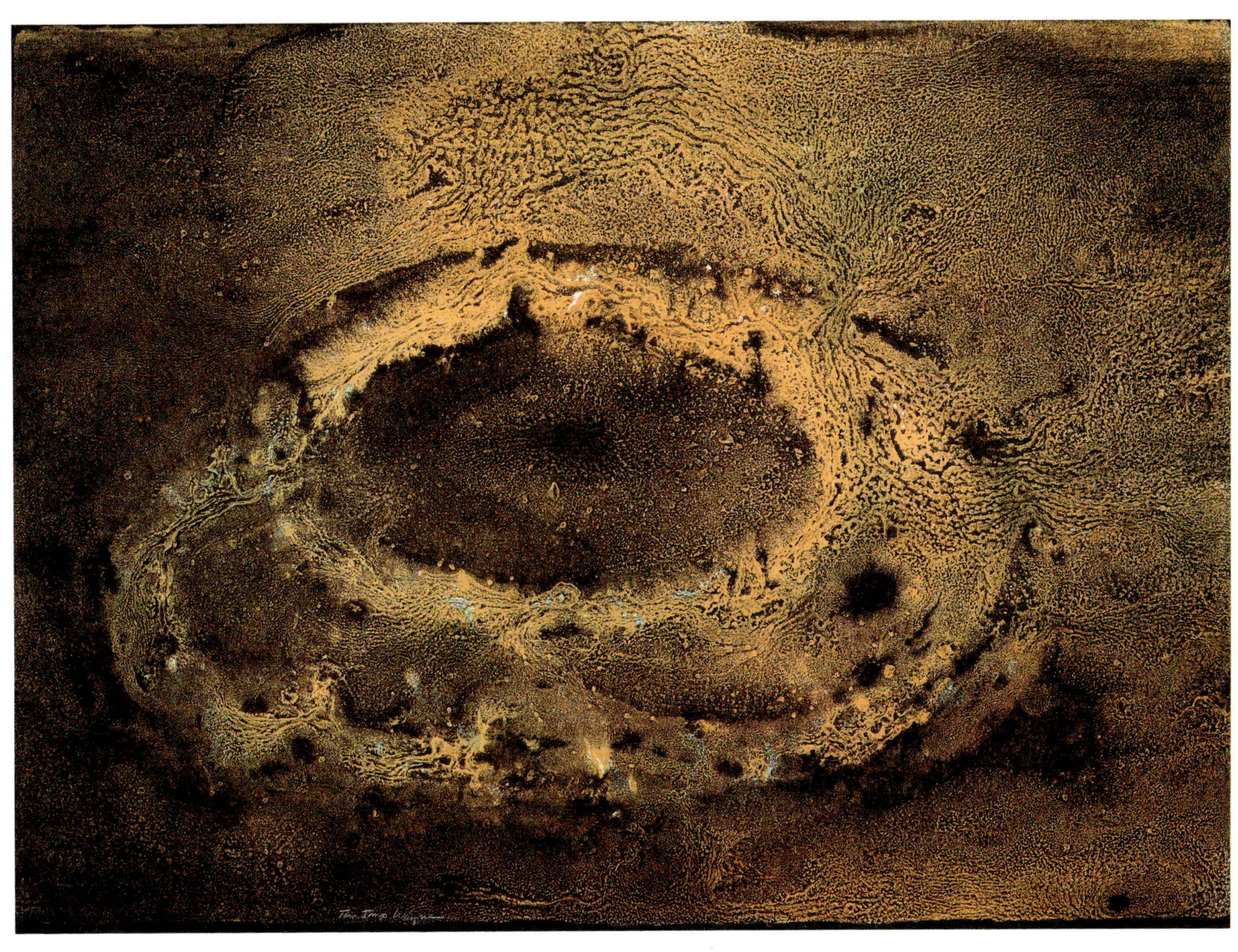

36. June Wayne, *At Last a Thousand II,* 1965

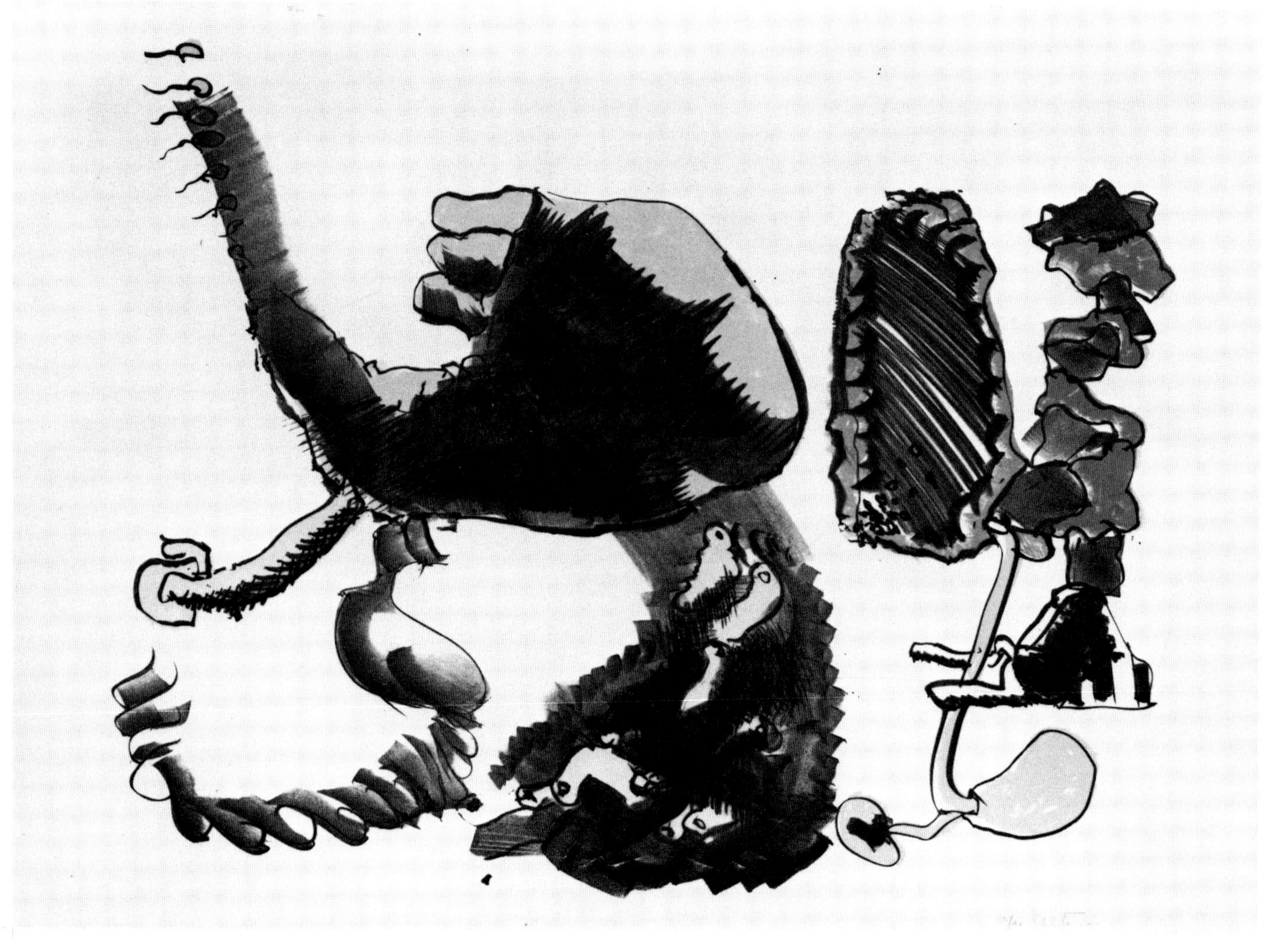

88. John Altoon, *Untitled,* 1966

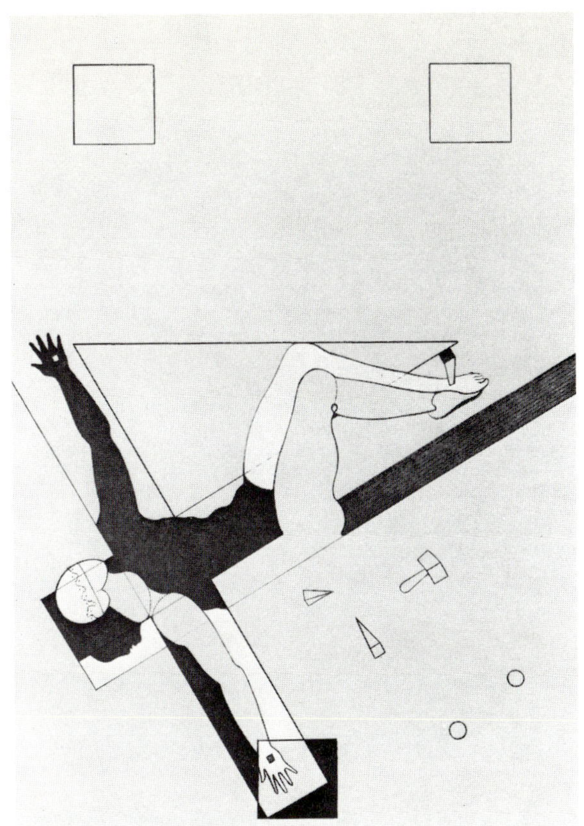

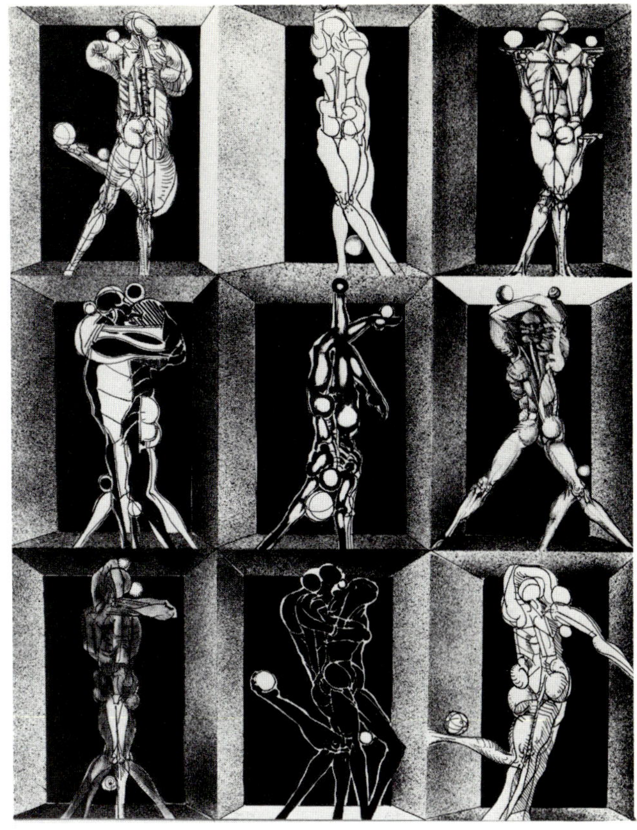

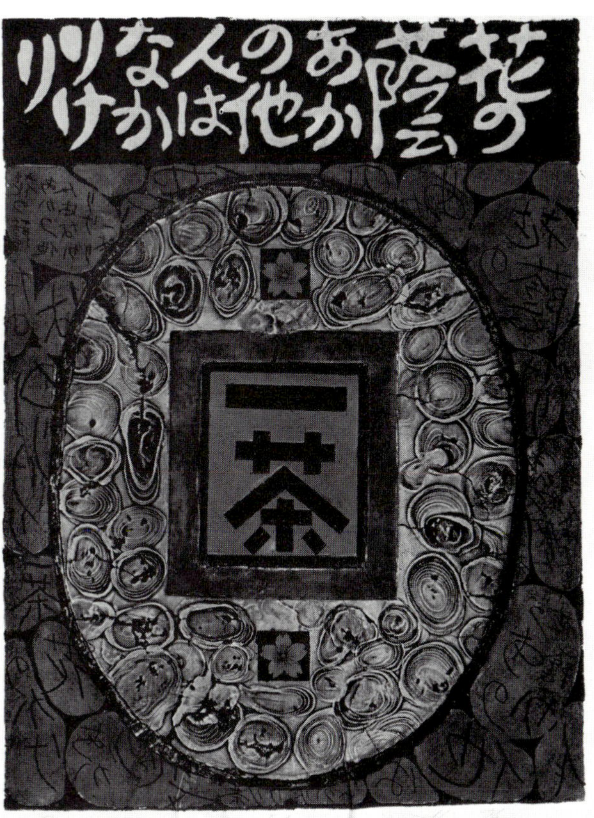

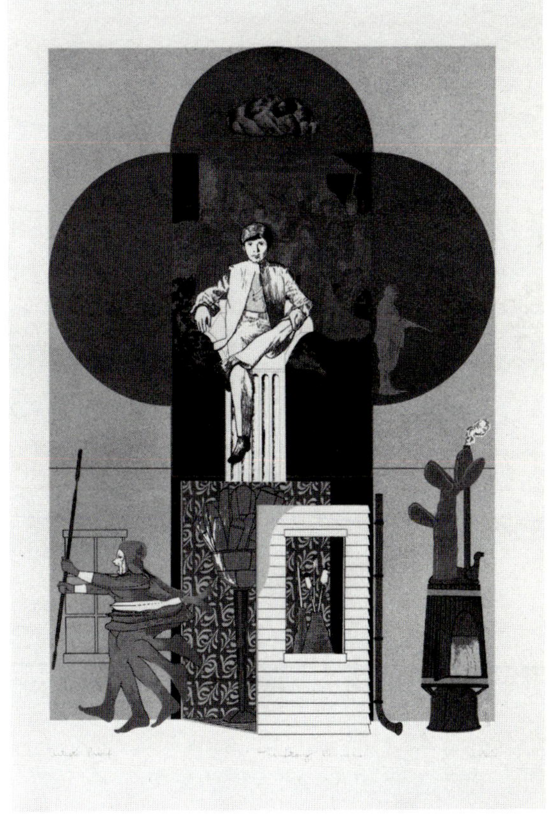

90. Robert Cremean, *The Fourteen Stations of the Cross,* 1966–67

91. Shiro Ikegawa, *Issa,* 1966

102. Jan Stussy, *Family of Acrobatic Jugglers,* 1970

107. Walter Askin, *Transitory Passions,* 1971

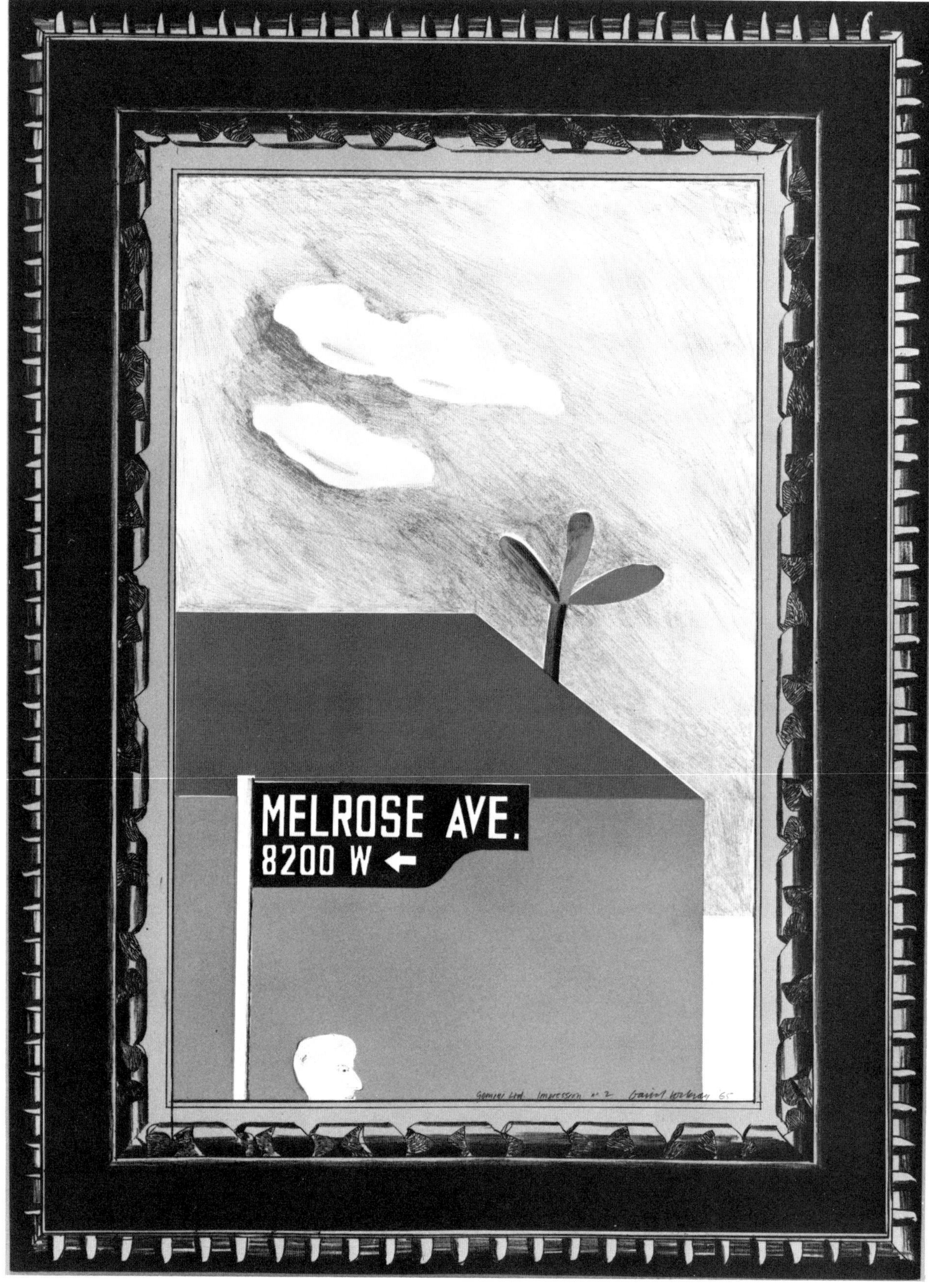

87. David Hockney, *Picture of Melrose Avenue with an Ornate Gold Frame,* 1965

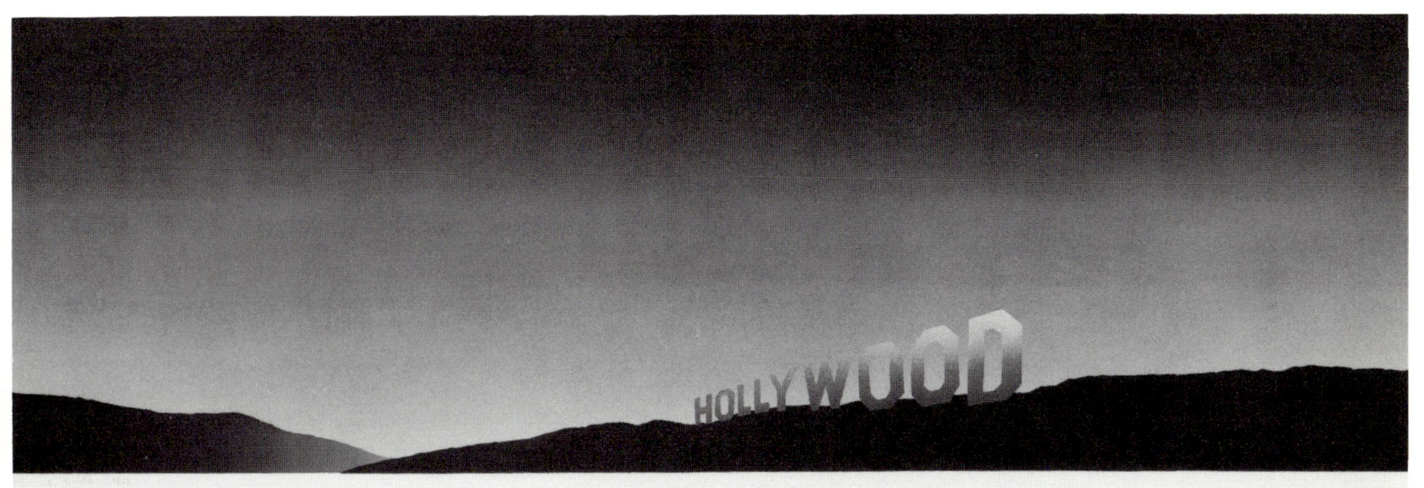

Ed Ruscha, *Hollywood,* 1968

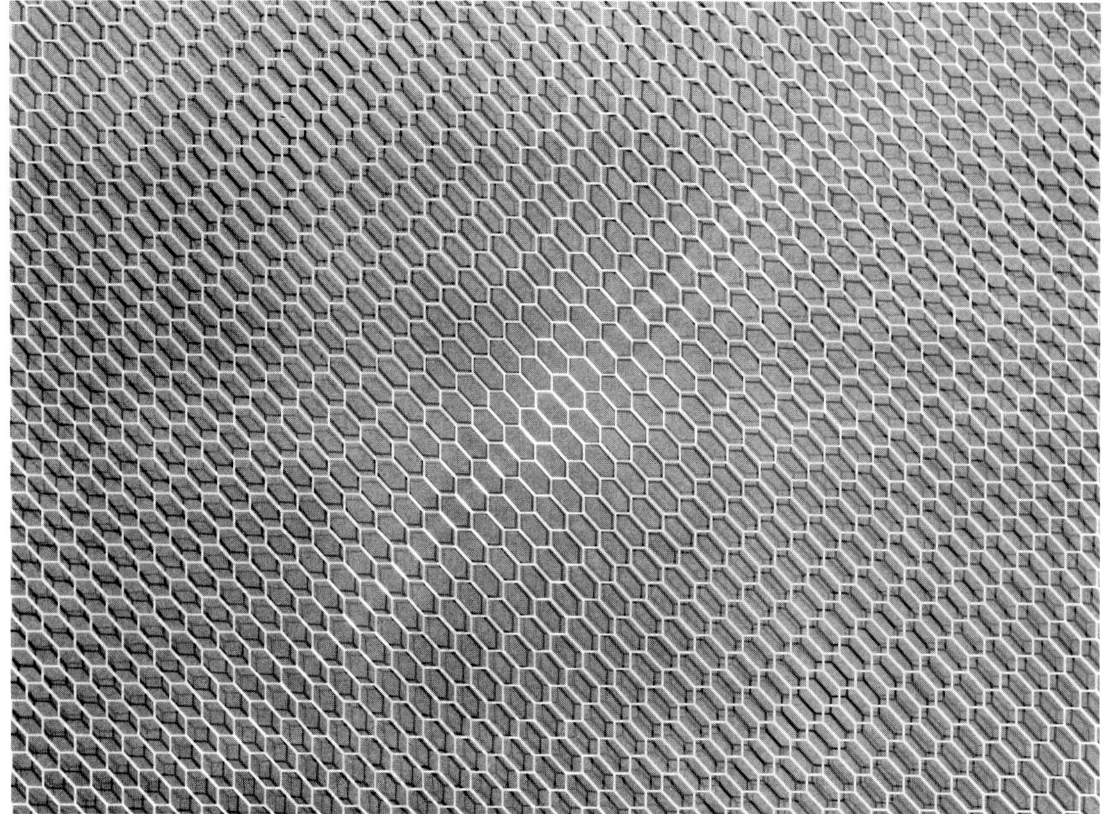

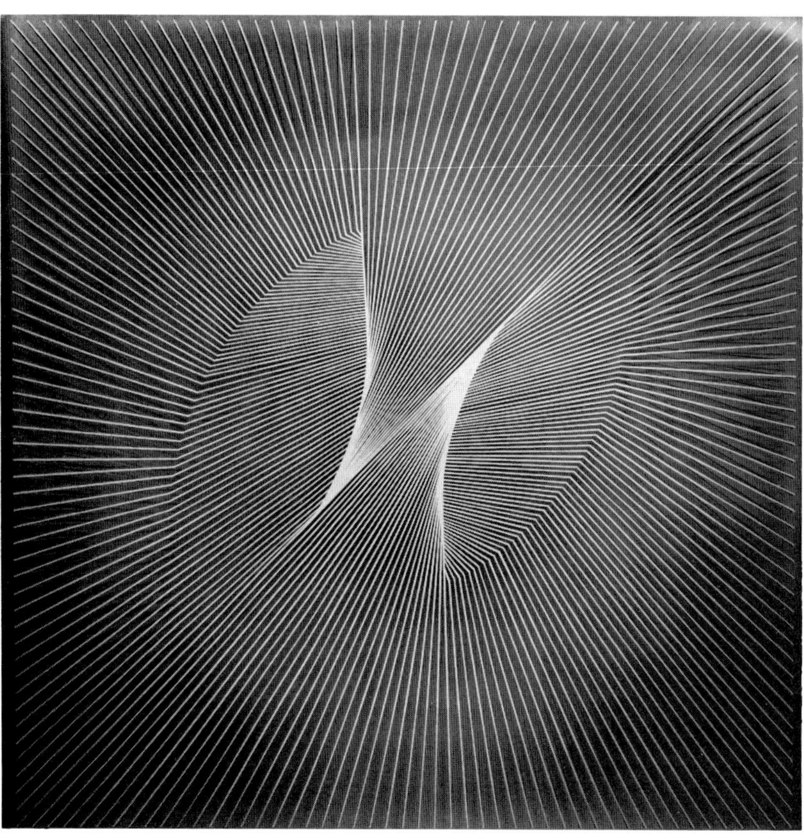

93. Norman Zammitt, *Untitled,* 1967

116. Gene Gill, *Untitled,* 1972

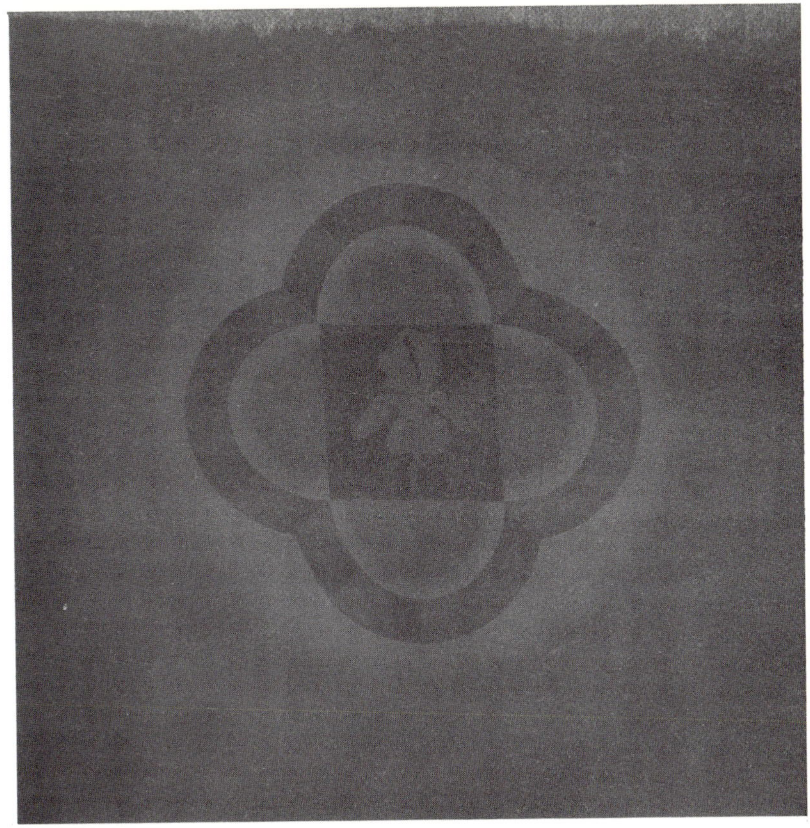

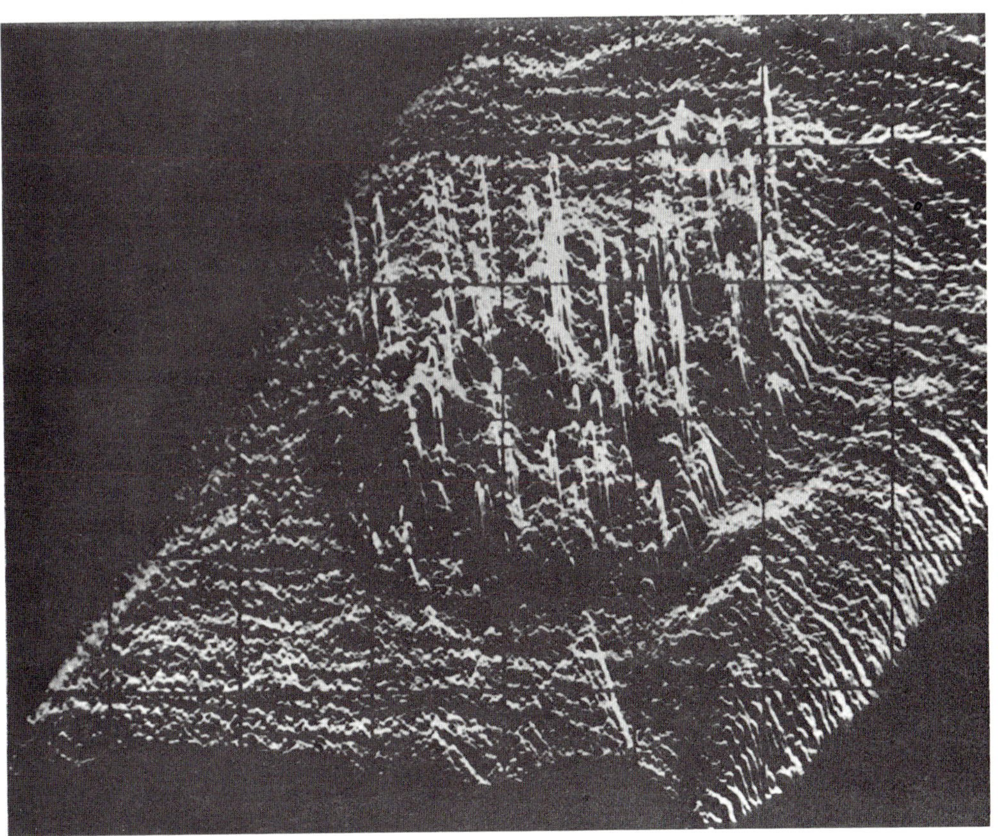

95. Billy Al Bengston, *Mecca Dracula,* 1968

108. Craig Kauffman, *Untitled,* 1971

85. John McLaughlin, *Untitled,* 1962

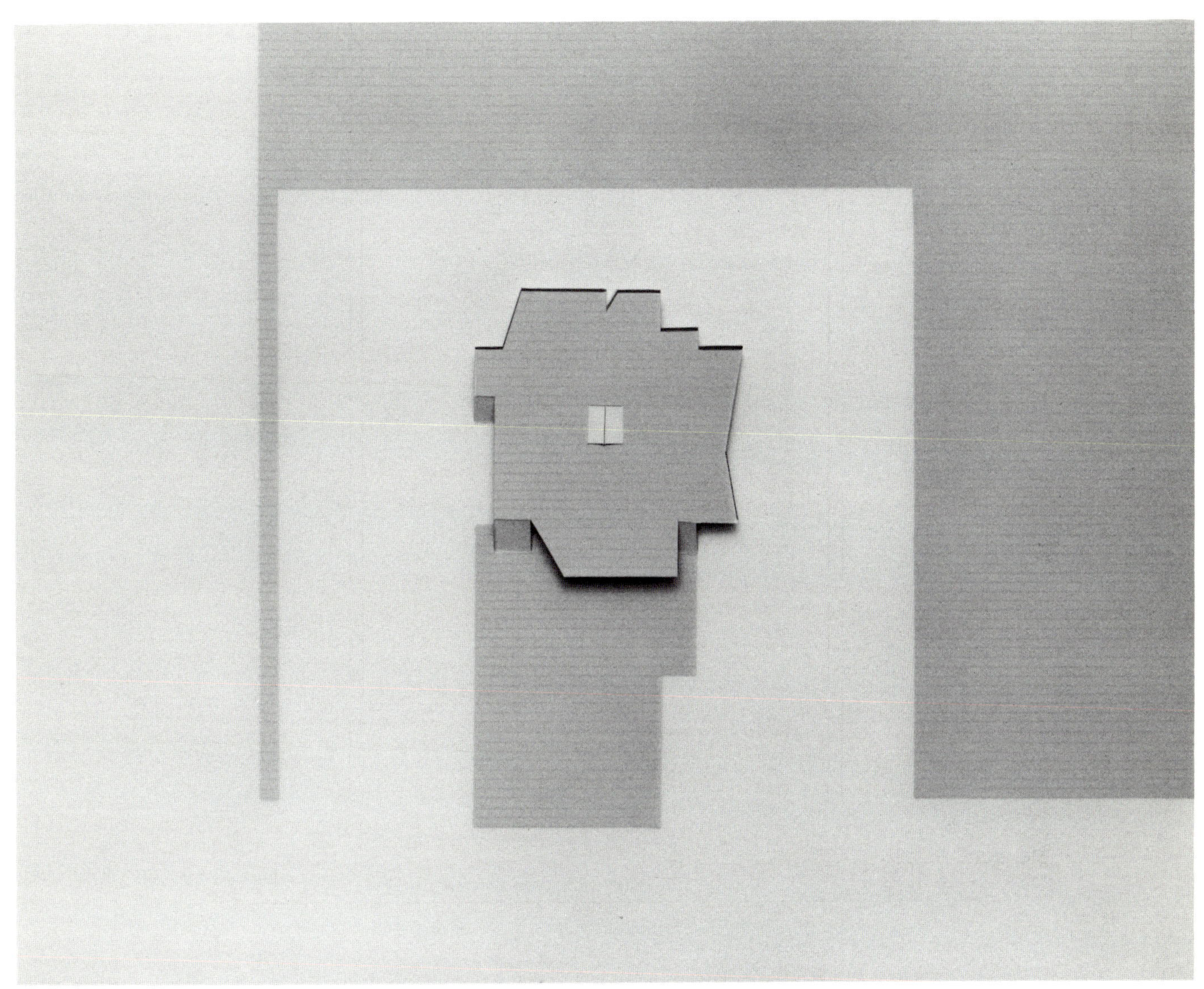

96. Ed Moses, *Untitled,* 1968

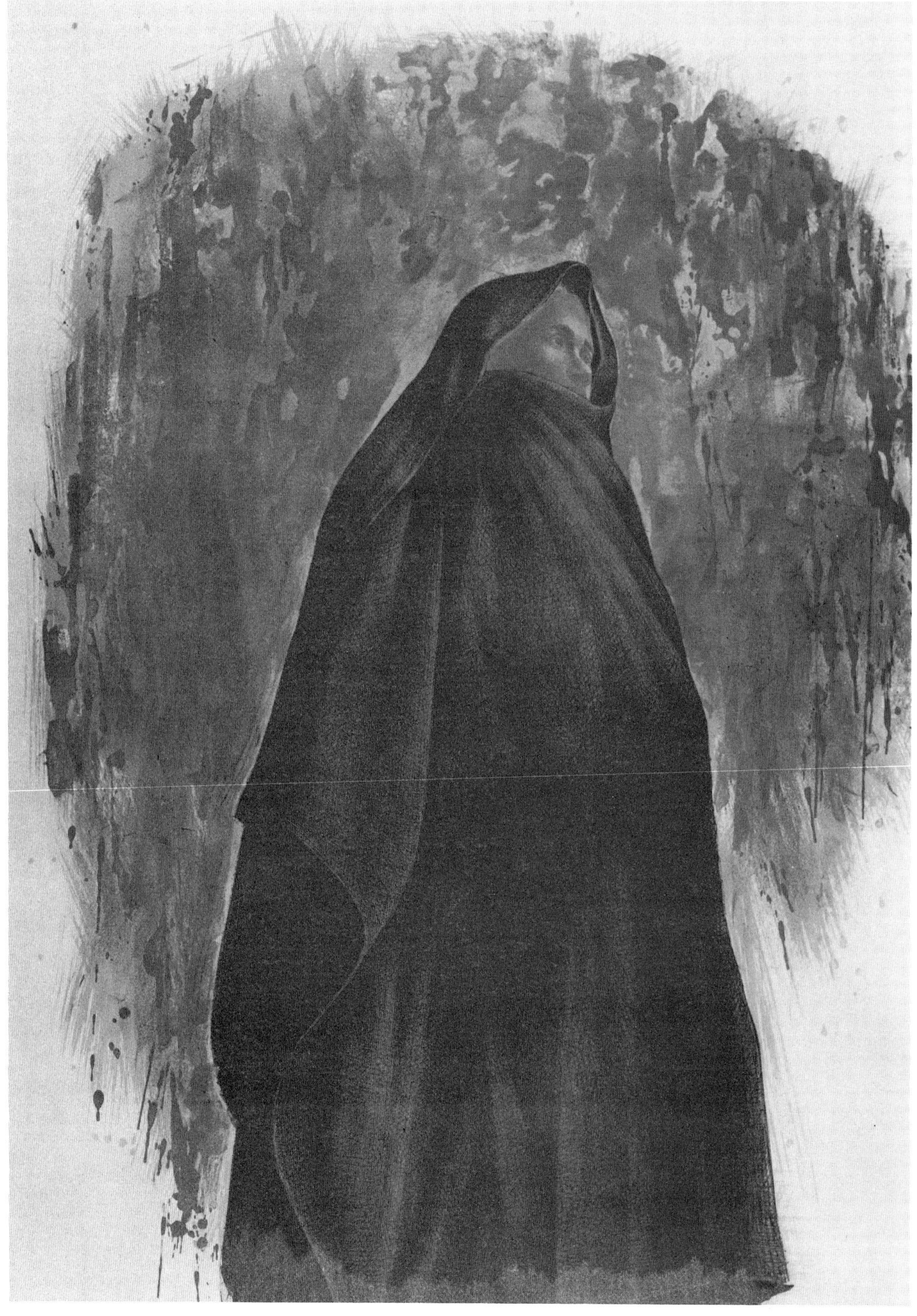

89. Charles White, *Exodus II,* 1966

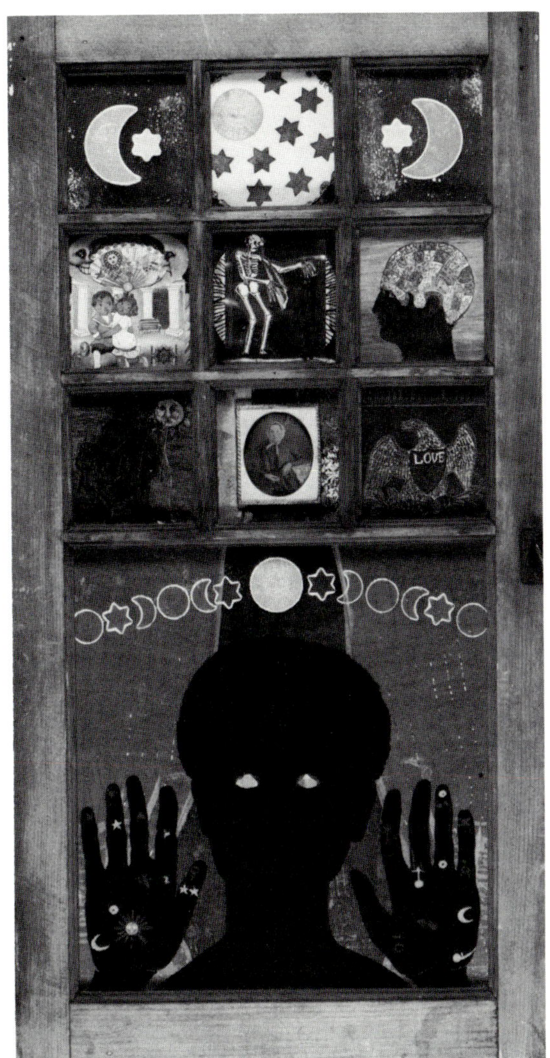

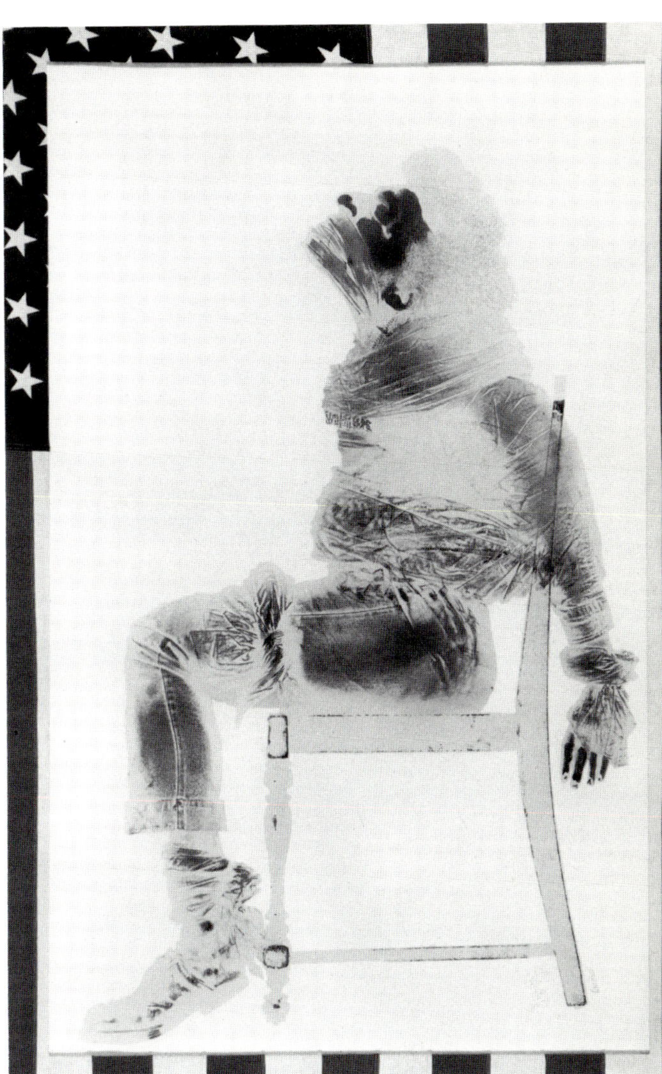

100. Betye Saar, *Black Girl's Window,* 1969

101. David Hammons, *Injustice Case,* 1970

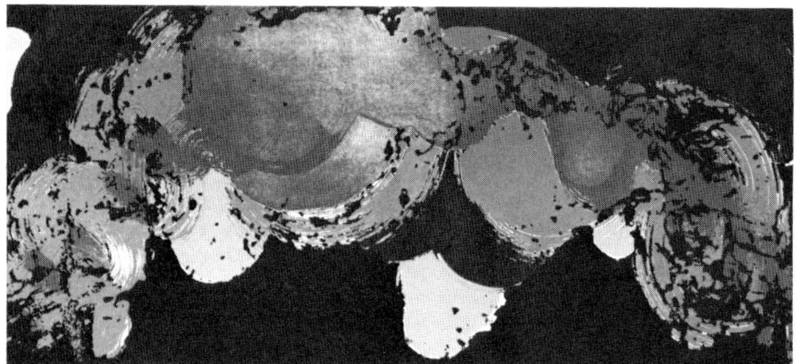

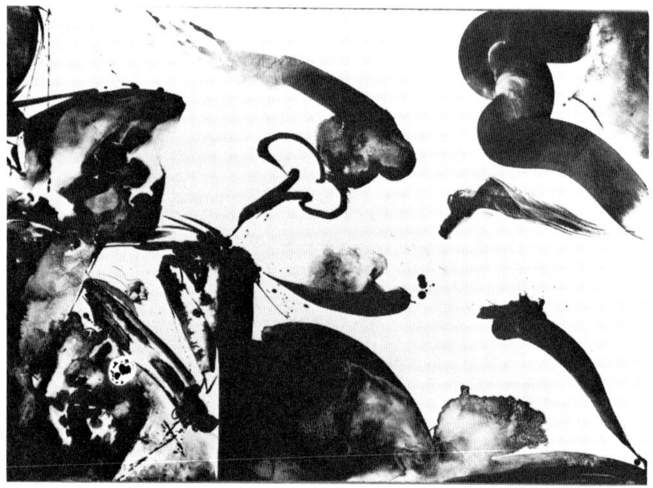

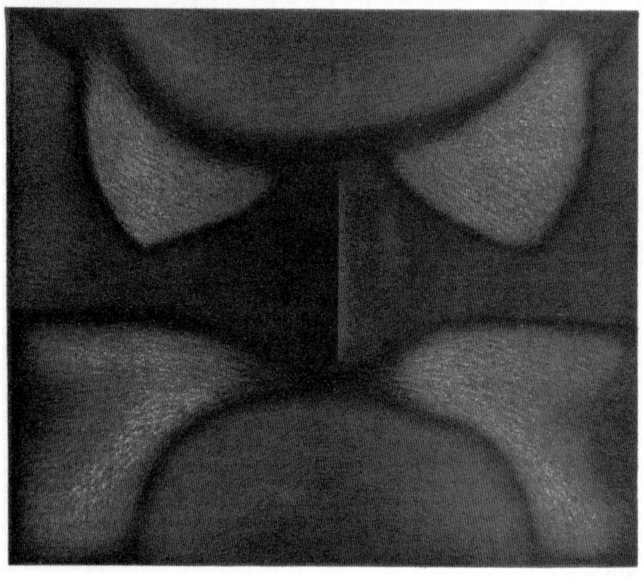

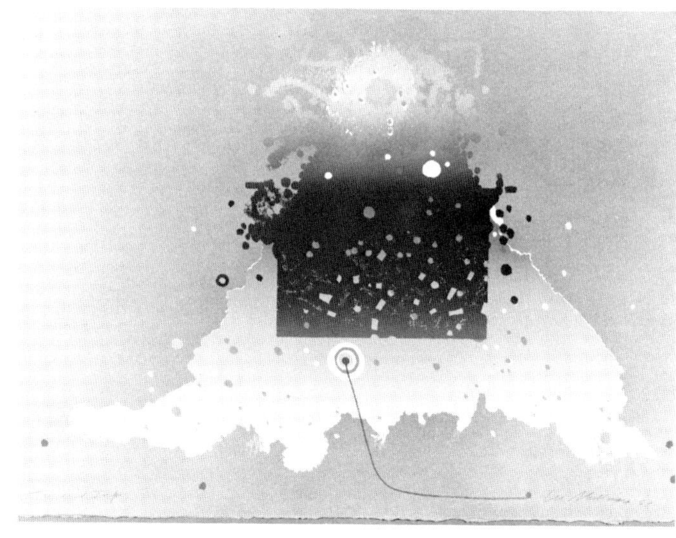

104. William Pettet, *Untitled,* 1970

105. Matsumi Kanemitsu, *Number Six State II,* 1970

92. Clinton Adams, *Venus in Cibola,* 1967–69

99. Lee Mullican, *The Mountain,* 1969

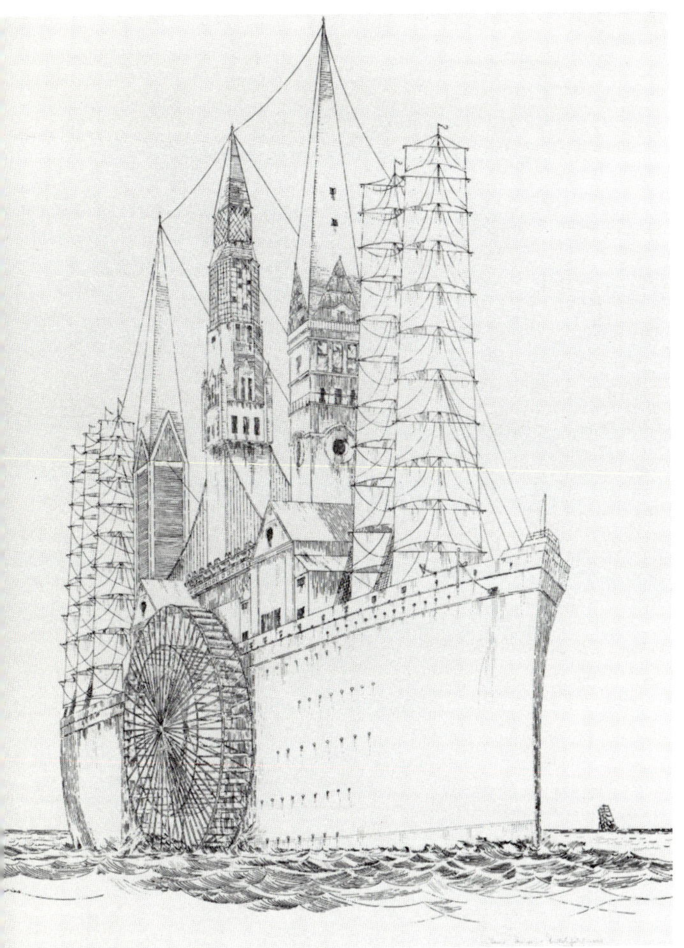

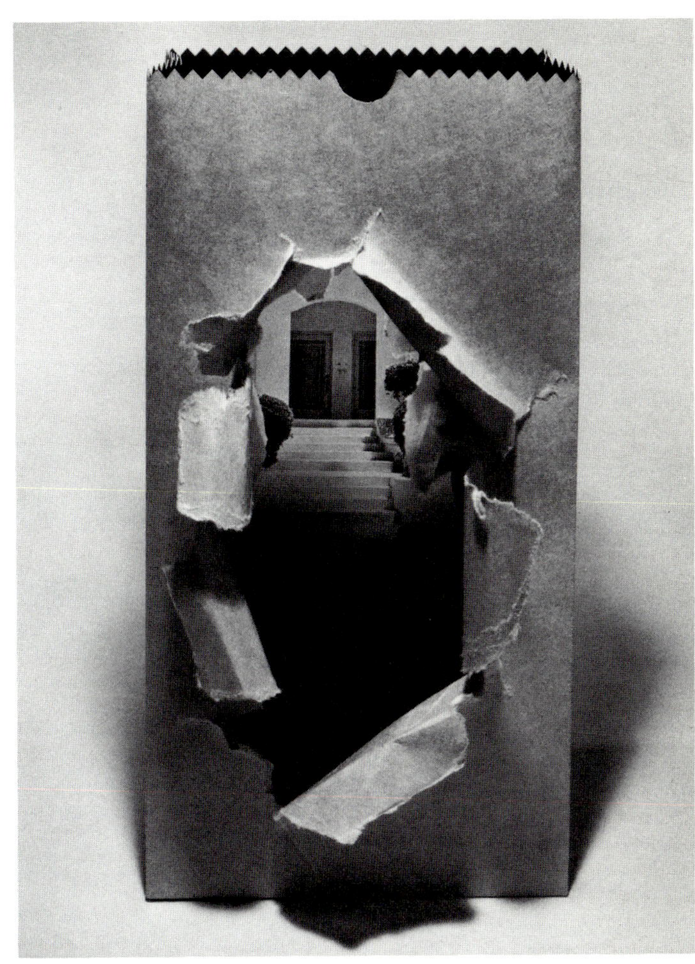

6. William Crutchfield, *Tamarind-Tanic,* 1970

113. Jerry McMillan, *Porch Bag,* 1971

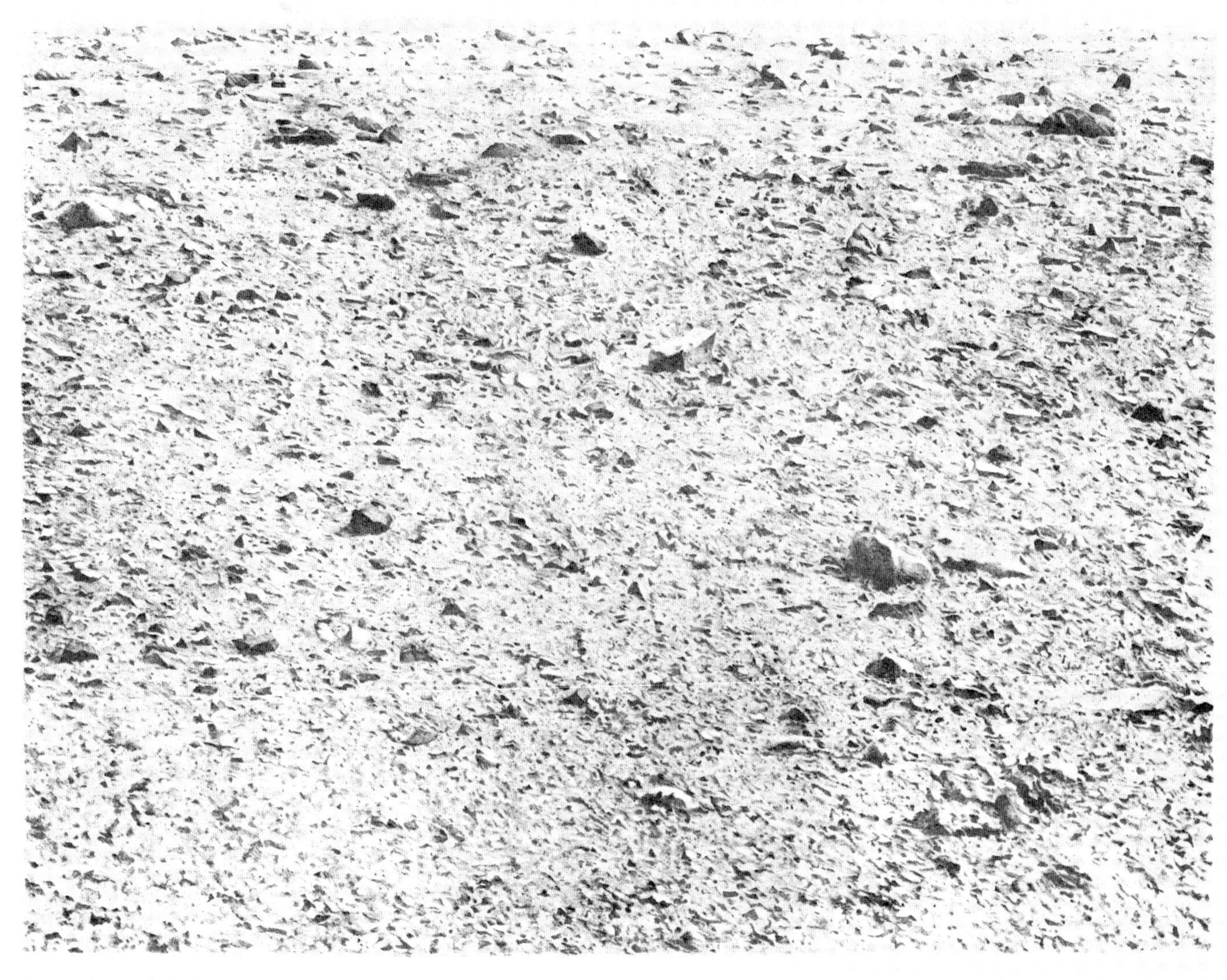

111. Vija Celmins, *Untitled,* 1971

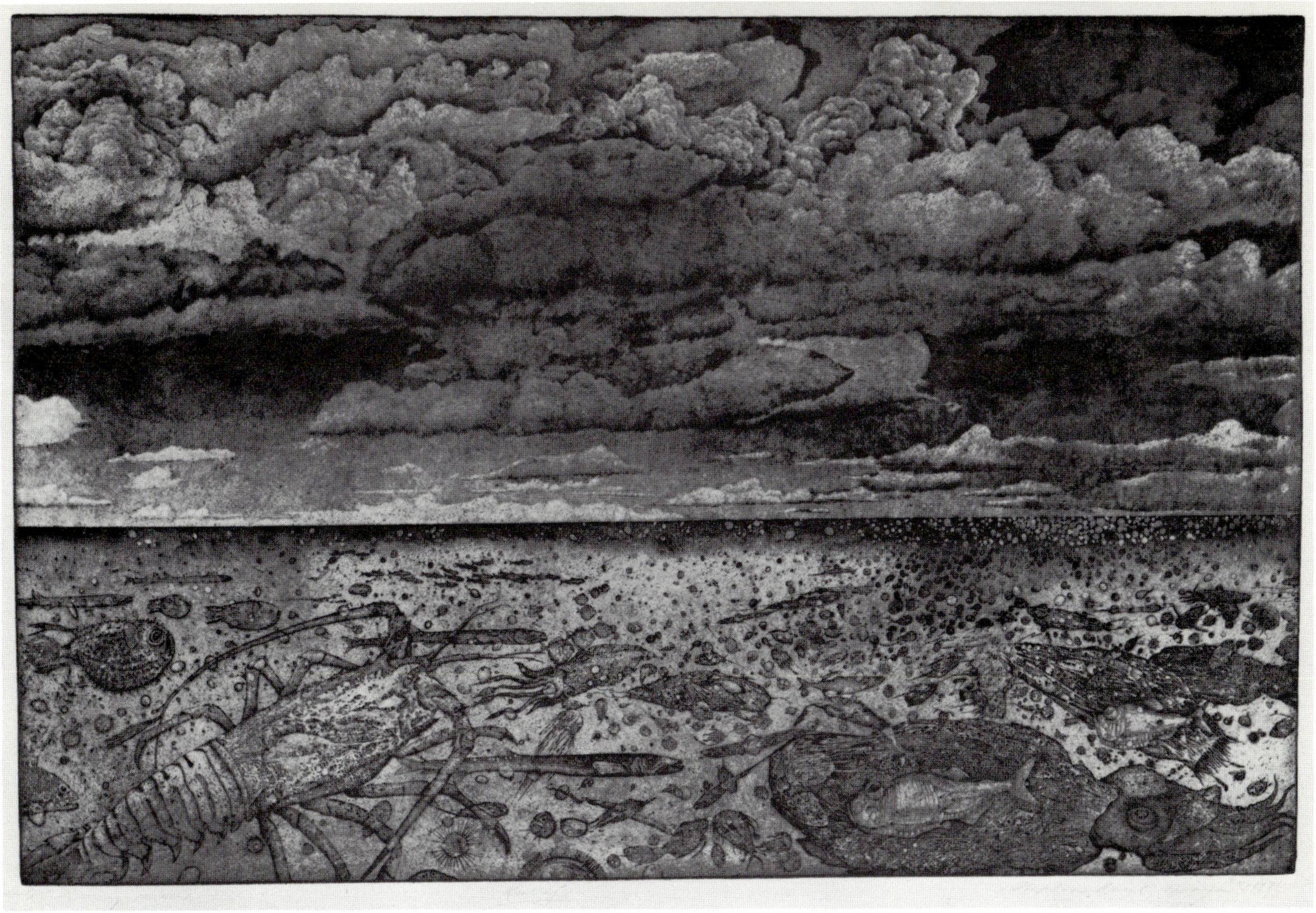

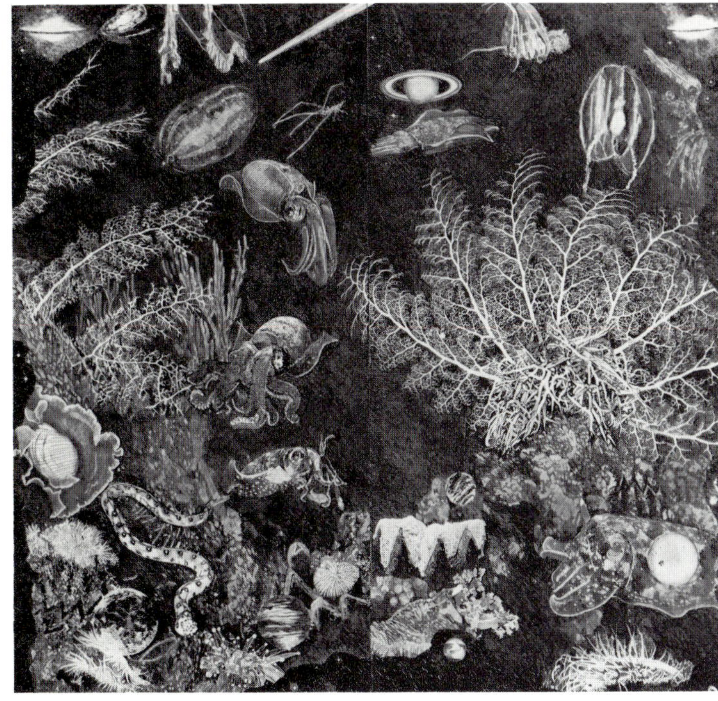

9. Stephen Anaya, *Kuraje,* 1971

1. Ann McCoy, *The Night Sea,* 1978

110. Lorser Feitelson, *Untitled,* 1971

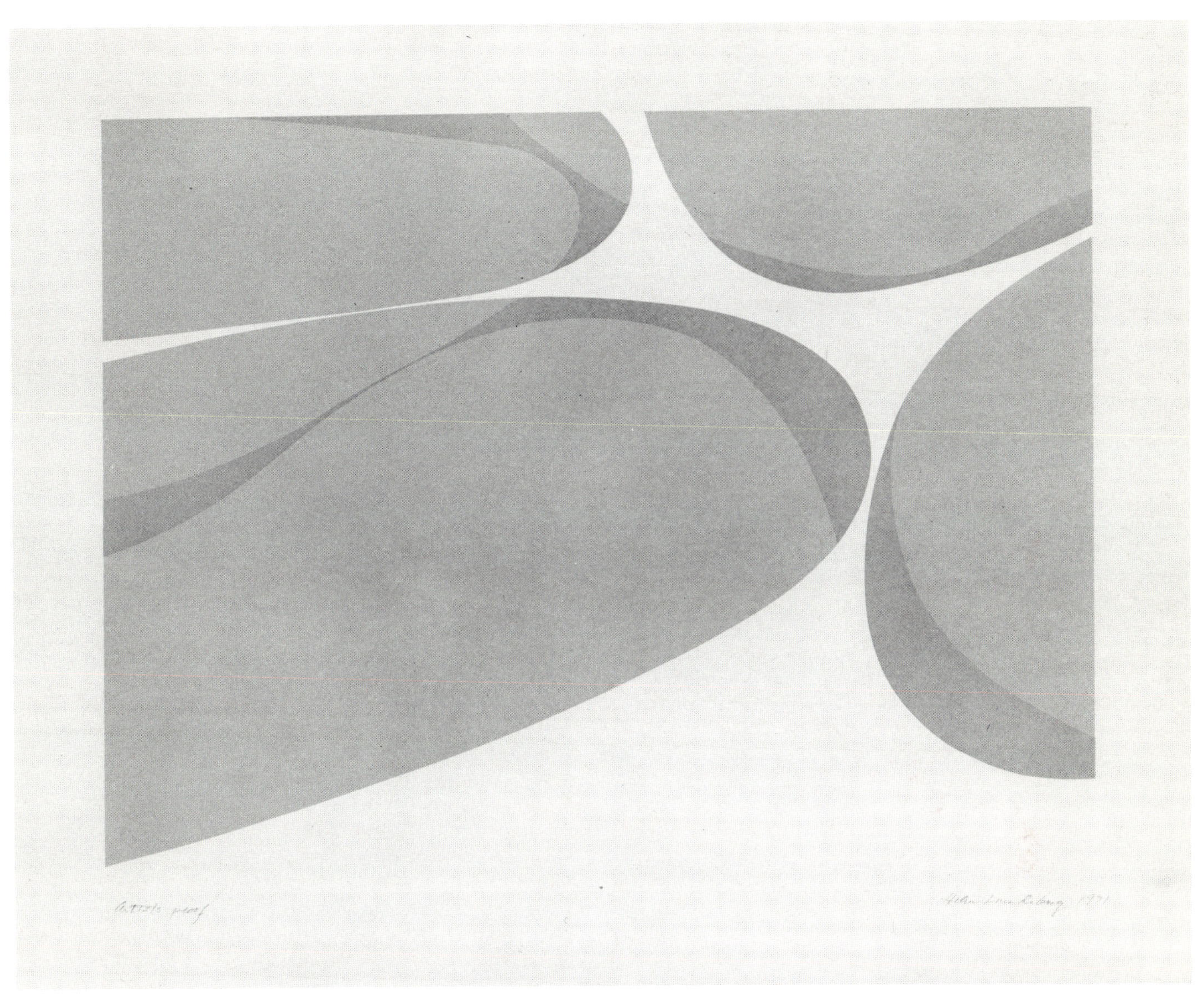

12. Helen Lundeberg, *Untitled,* 1971

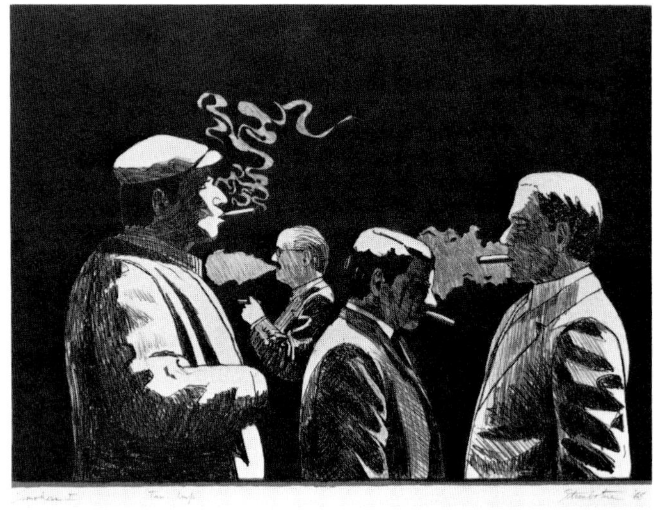

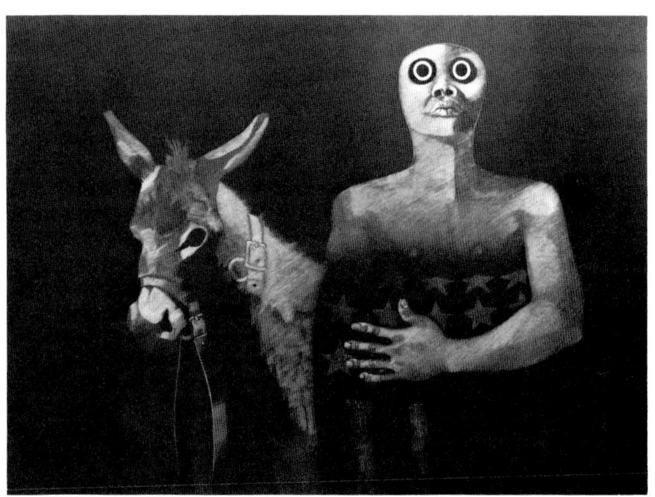

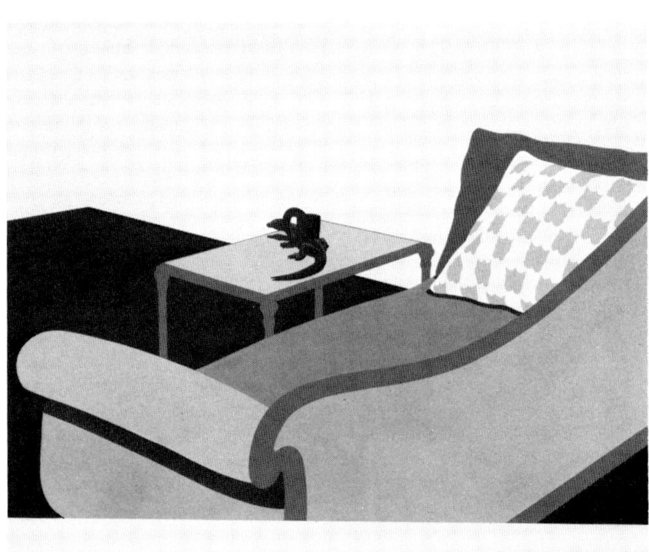

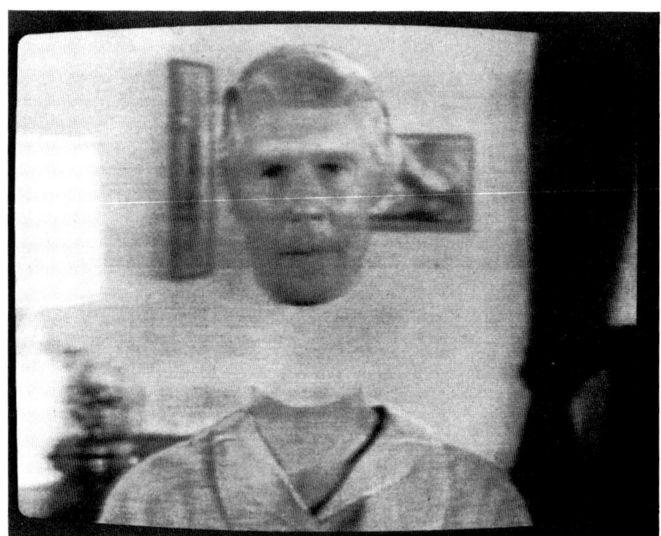

98. James Strombotne, *Smokers,* 1968

103. Timothy Washington, *One Nation Under God,* 1970

114. Ken Price, *Lizard Cup,* 1971 © Gemini G.E.L., Los Angeles, California

118. Peter Alexander, *Anacin II,* 1972

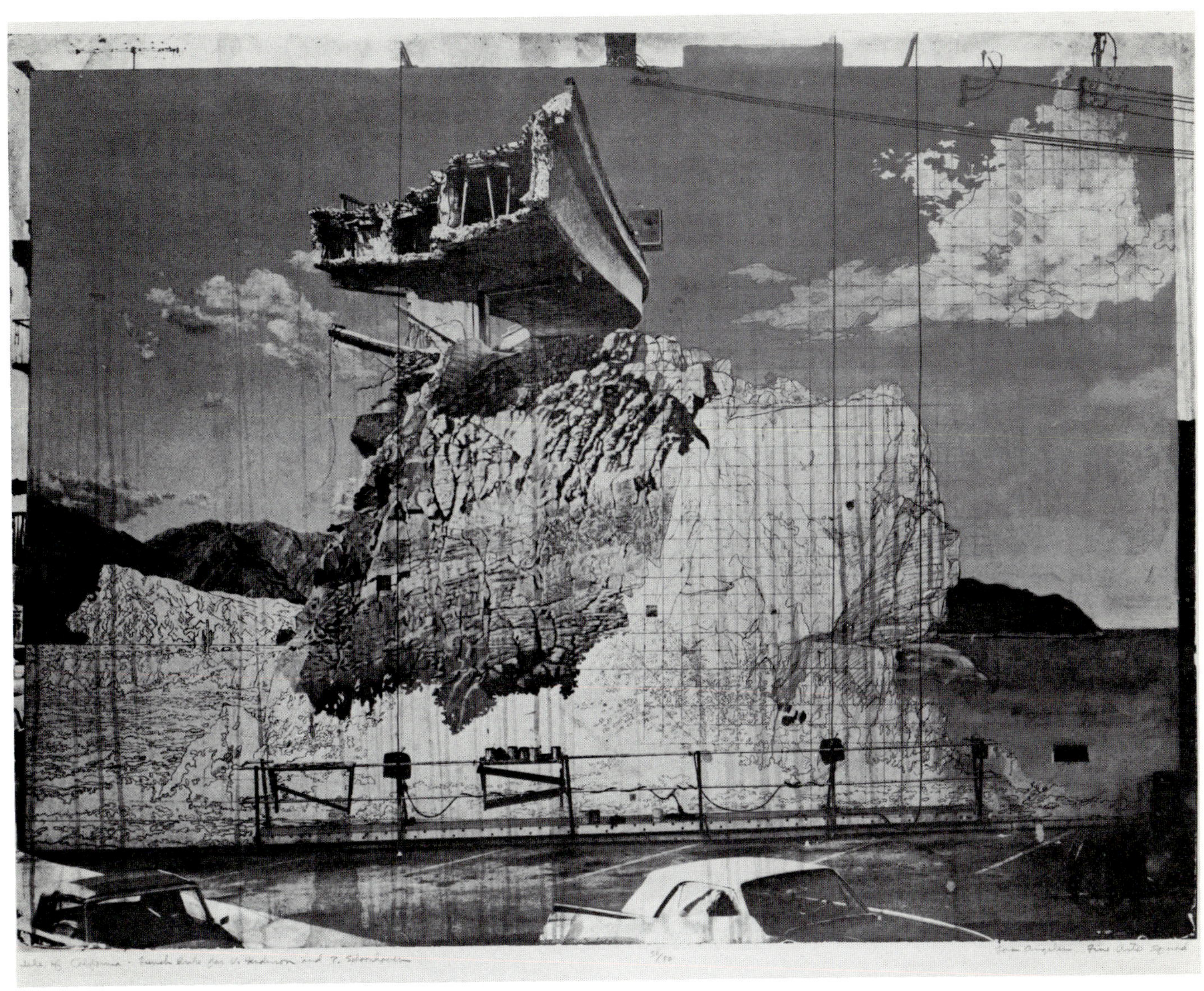

24. Los Angeles Fine Arts Squad (Vic Henderson and Terry Schoonhoven), *Isle of California,* 1973

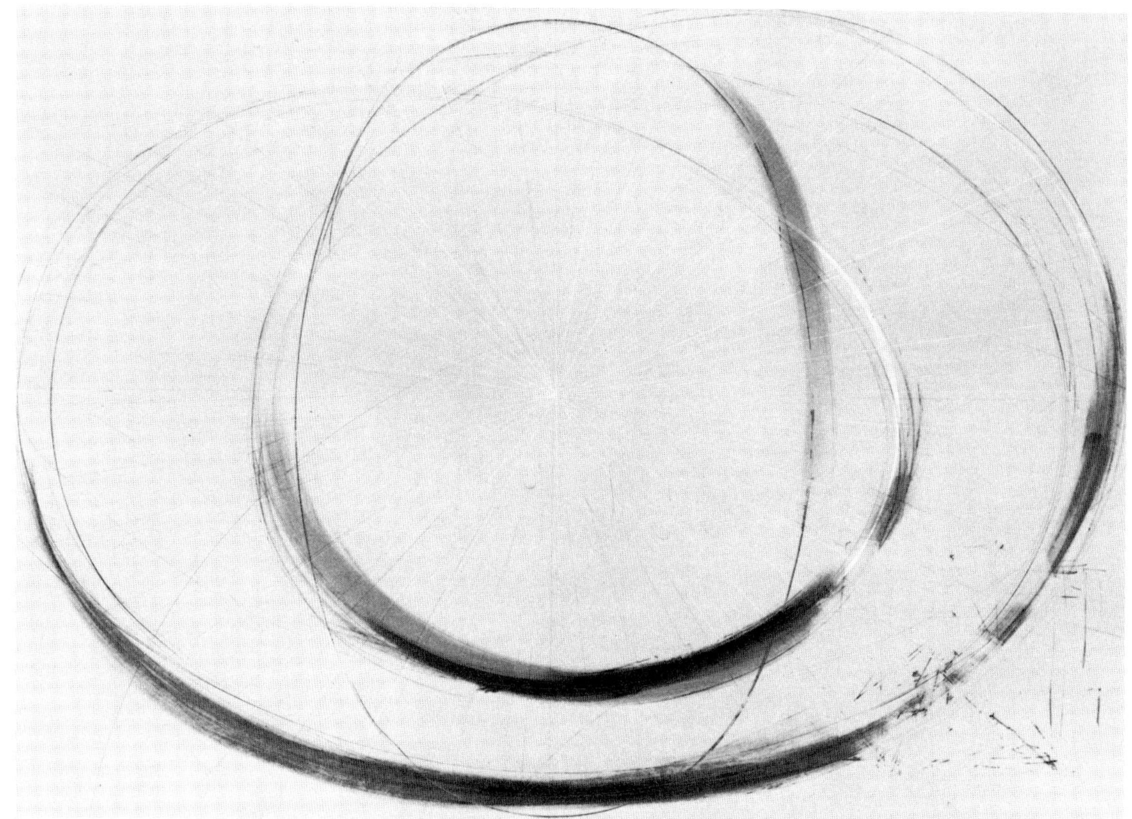

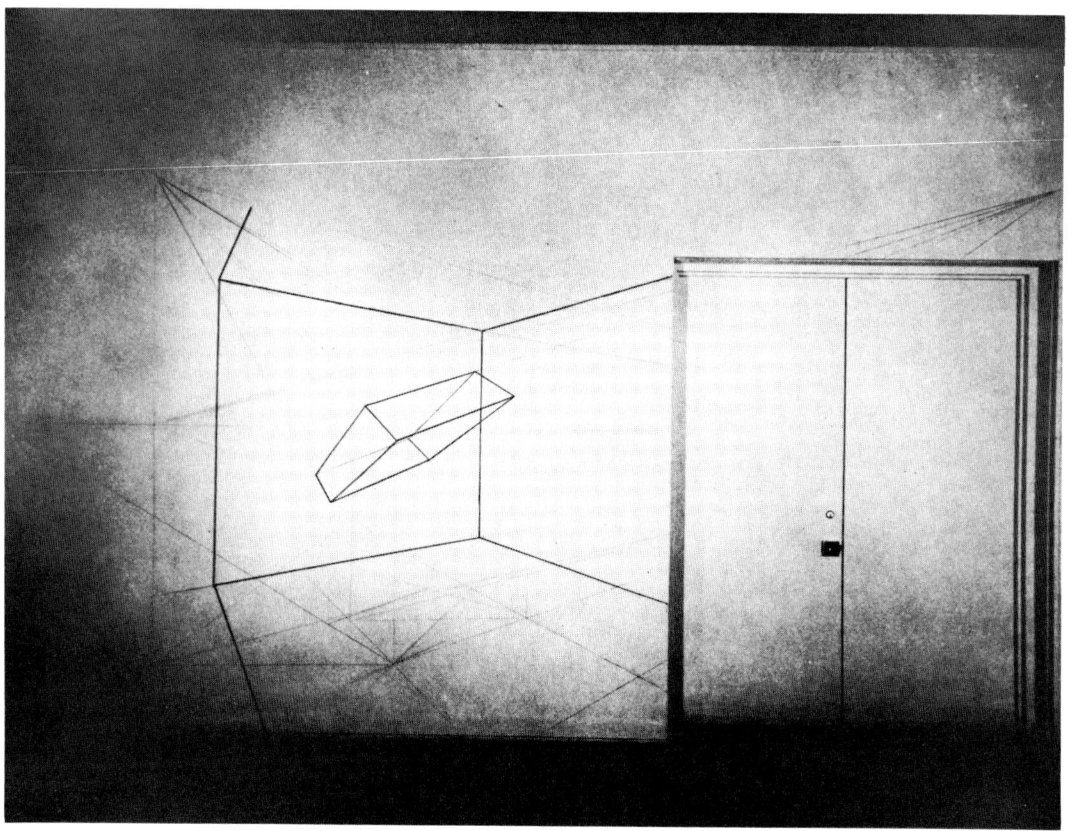

115. Bruce Nauman, *Untitled,* 1971

119. Ron Cooper, *Tri-axial Rotation of a Floating Volume of Light,* 1972

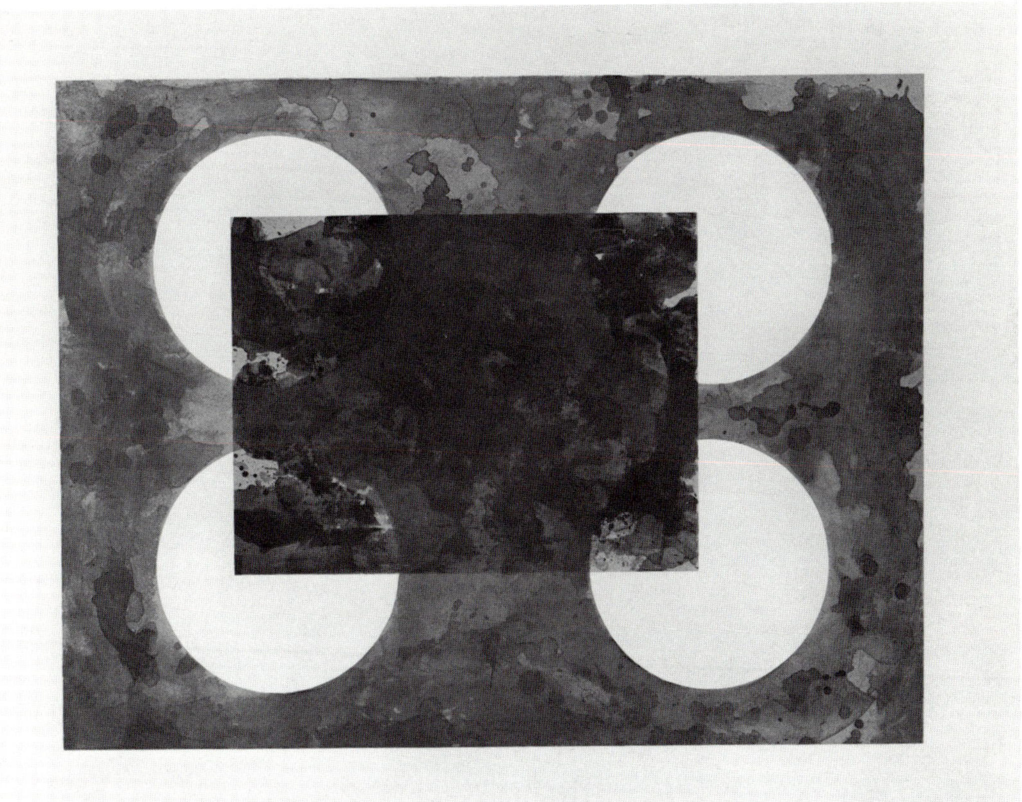

120. Greg Card, *Untitled,* 1972

123. Ron Davis, *Four Circle,* 1972

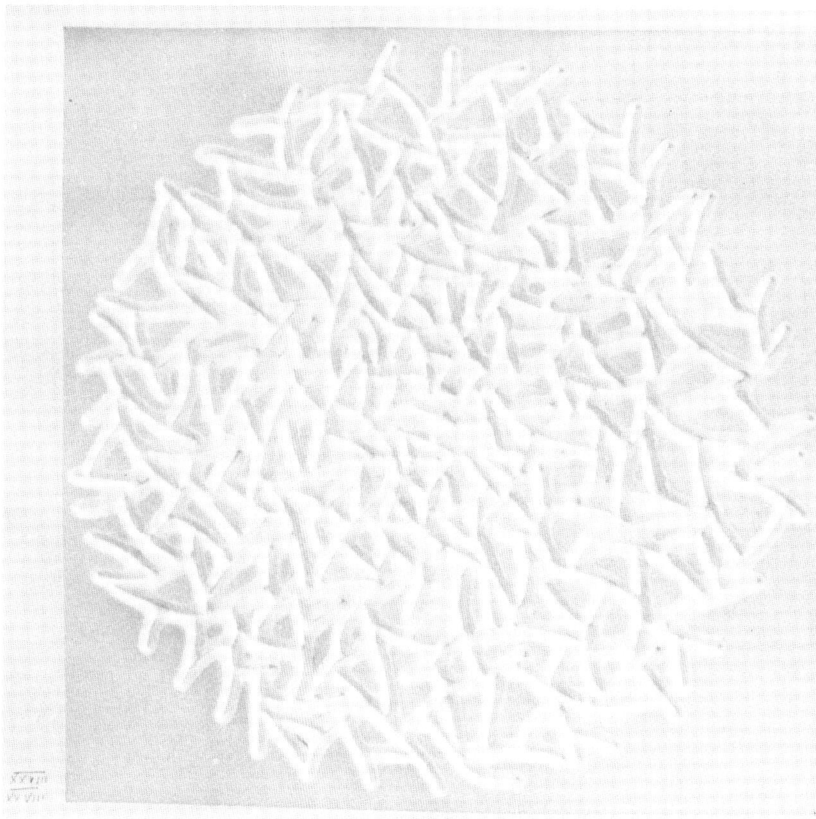

121. Claire Falkenstein, *Struttura Grafica,* 1972

122. Tony DeLap, *Karnak, I,* 1972

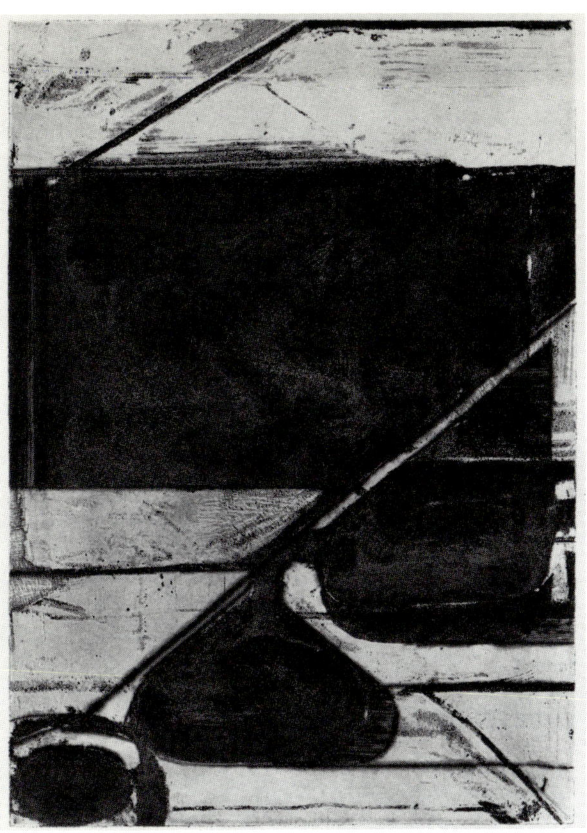

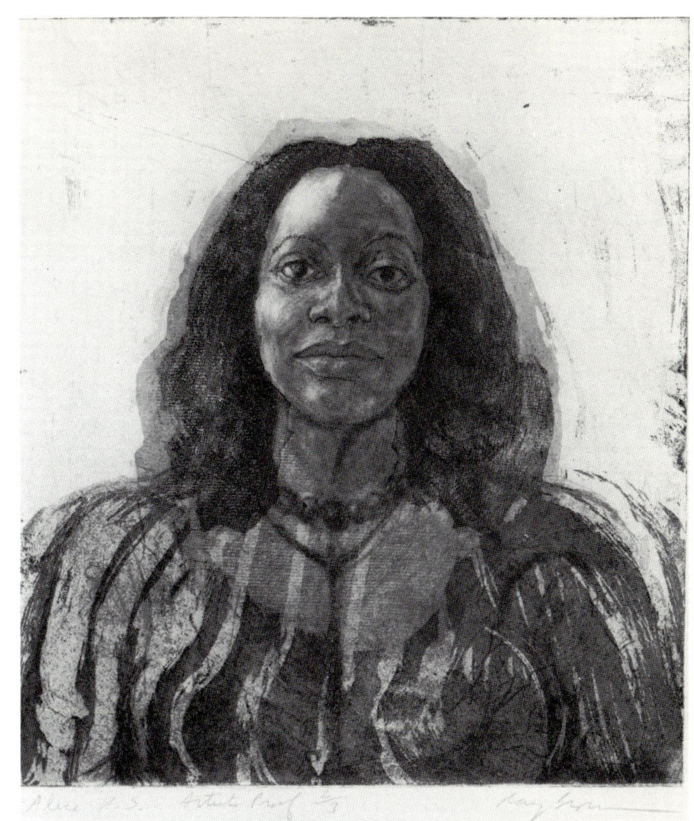

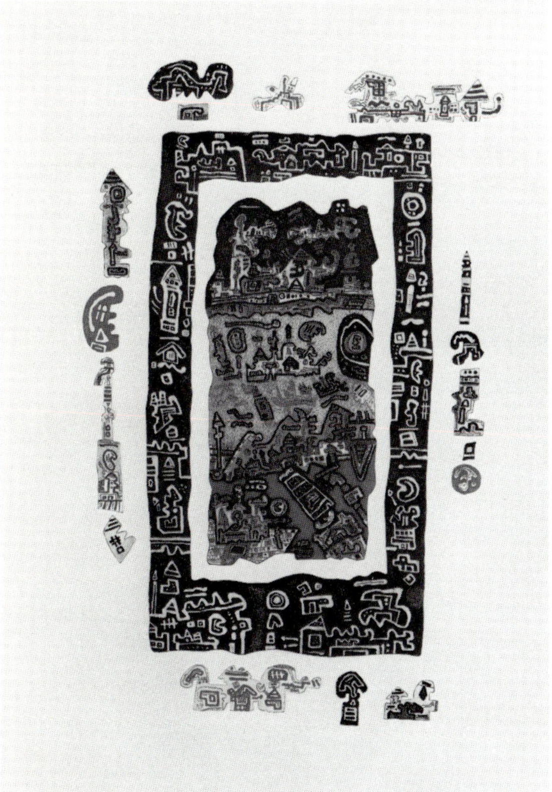

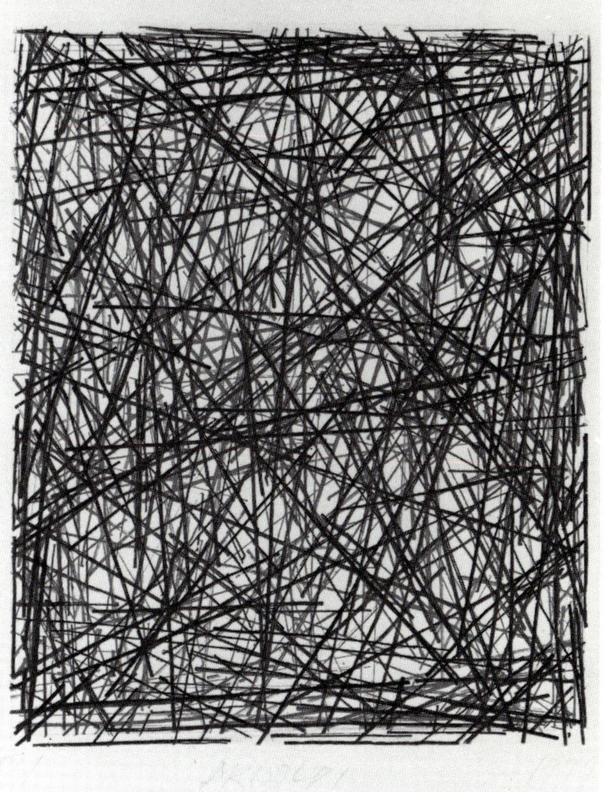

132. Richard Diebenkorn, *Untitled #5*, 1978

126. Ray Brown, *Alice N.S.*, 1975

127. Ynez Johnston, *The Secret Landscape*, 1976

134. Chuck Arnoldi, *Untitled*, 1979

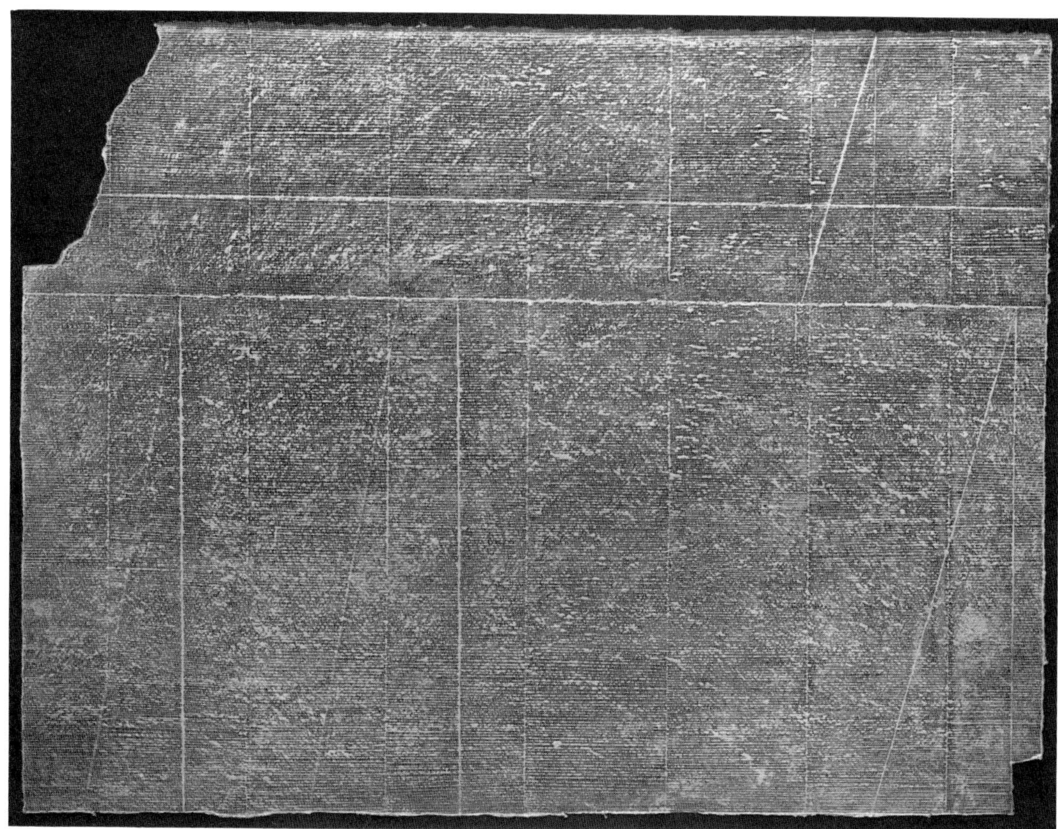

128. Eugene Sturman, *Quadrant #4*, 1977

129. Jay McCafferty, *#1 Alive*, 1977

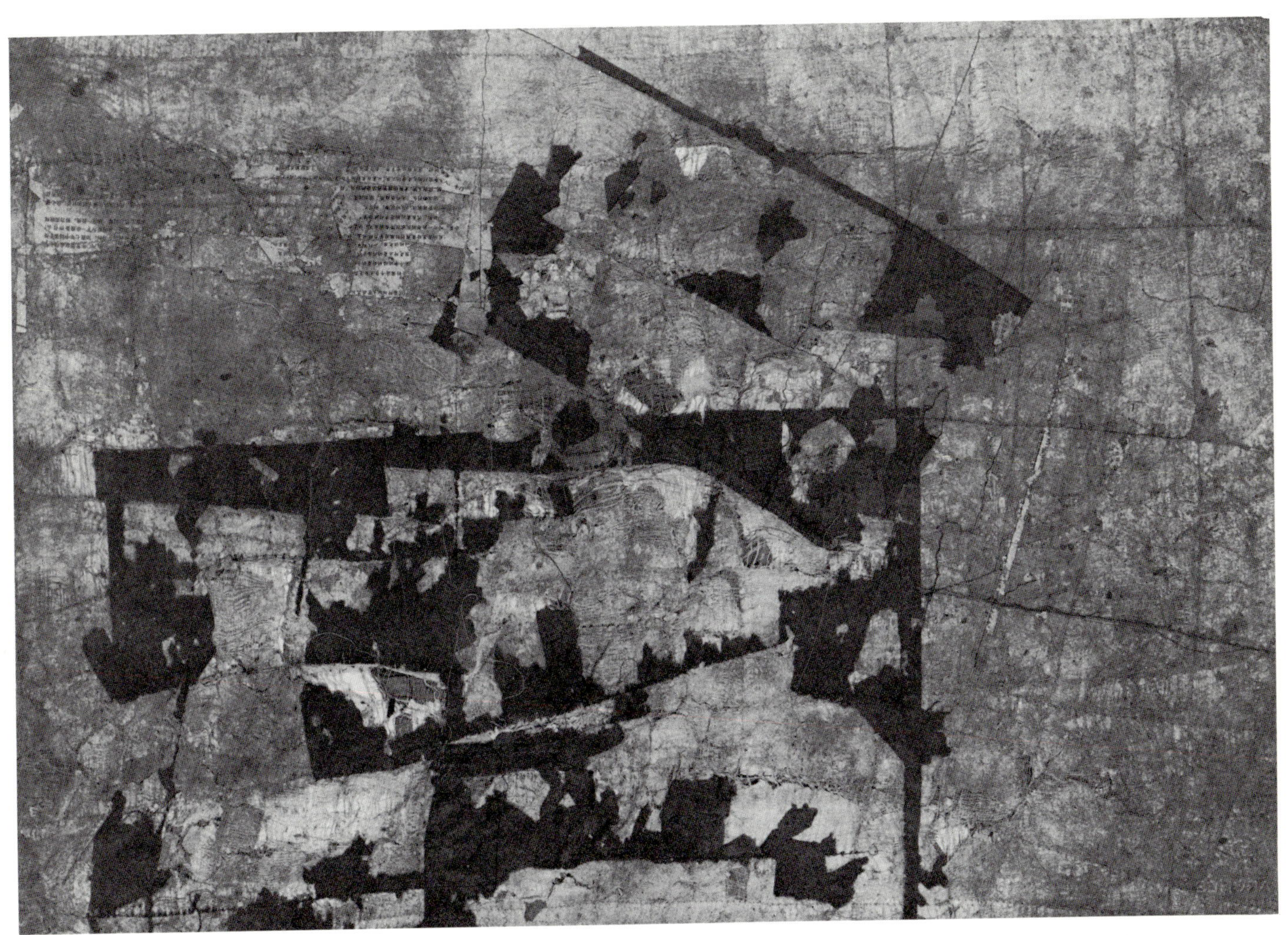

○. Charles Christopher Hill, *Lightning,* 1977

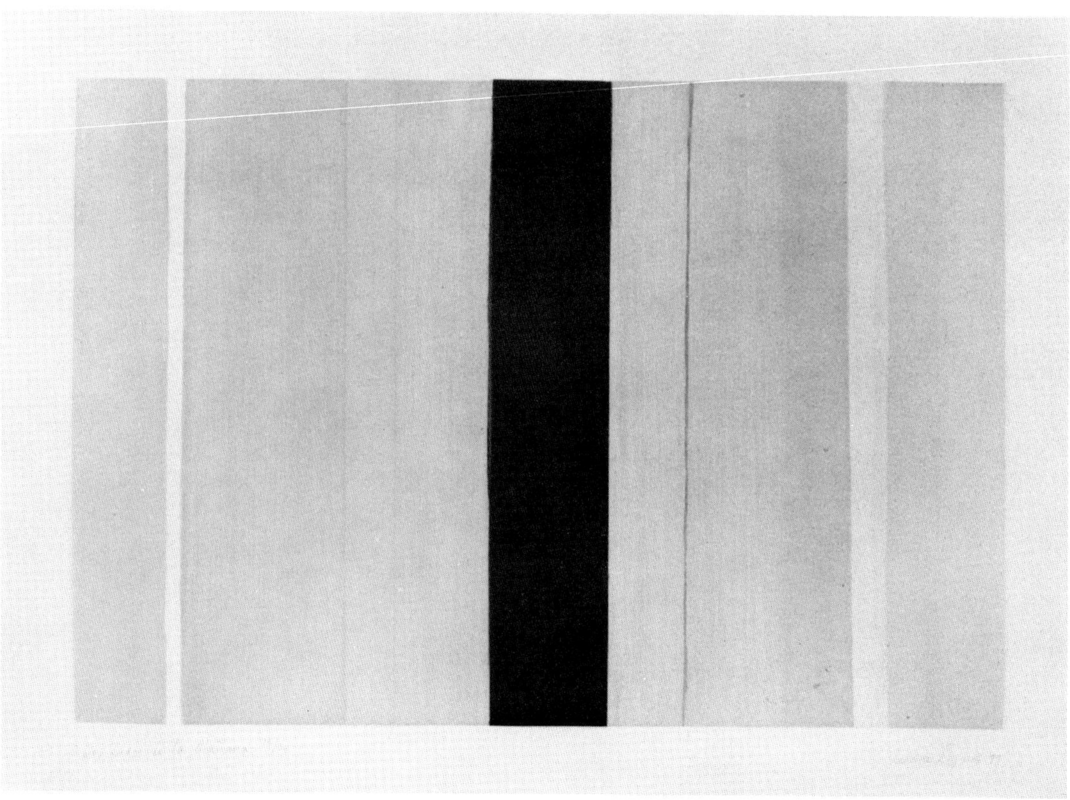

125. Joel Bass, *Horizontals–C,* 1974

135. Eleanore Lazarof, *Dos Lados de la Mañana,* 1979

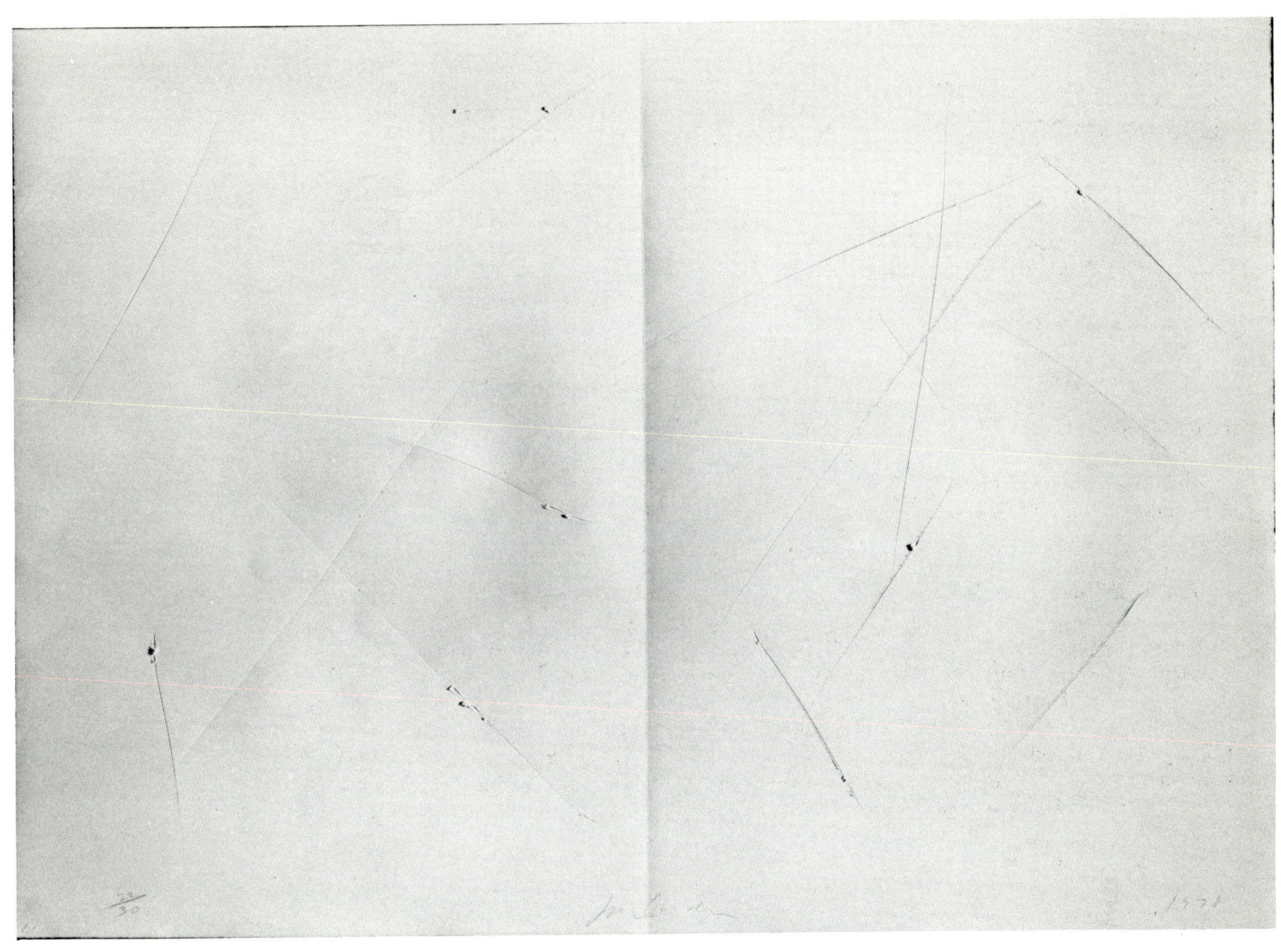

33. Joe Goode, *Untitled,* 1978

Henry Chapman Ford
b. Livonia, New York, 1828
d. Santa Barbara, California, 1894

1a. *Mission San Gabriel*
1b. *Mission Santa Barbara*
1c. *Mission San Juan Capistrano*
1d. *Mission San Fernando*
1e. *Mission San Diego*
Five etchings from the series *Etchings of the Franciscan Missions of California,* published in 1883
6⅞ x 12⅞ in. (17.5 x 32.7 cm.)
Graphic Arts Council Fund
M.79.53.1–.24
1b–1e not illustrated

Frances Gearhart
b. Illinois
d. Pasadena, California, 1958

2. *When Summer Comes,* c. 1925–30
Color woodcut
11 x 9 in. (27.9 x 22.9 cm.)
Lent by Joseph and Nancy Moure

Benjamin Chambers Brown
b. Marion, Arkansas, 1865
d. Pasadena, California, 1942

3. *At the Paint-Wharf,* 1919
Color soft-ground etching
9 x 8 in. (22.9 x 20.3 cm.)
Gift of the Print Makers Society
19.2.2

4. *Grand Canyon,* c. 1915–20
Monotype
4⅛ x 7 in. (10.5 x 17.8 cm.)
Lent by The Fine Arts Museums of San Francisco, Achenbach Foundation for Graphic Arts, California State Library Long Loan

May Gearhart
b. Gladstone, Illinois, 1872
d. Altadena, California, 1951

5. *A Japanese Restaurant,* c. 1918
Color soft-ground etching
7 x 5½ in. (17.8 x 14 cm.)
Gift of Wallace L. Dewolf
19.4.13
Not illustrated

6. *Two Gentlemen of Xochimilco,* c. 1915–20
Color soft-ground etching
3 x 4 in. (7.6 x 10.2 cm.)
Lent by The Fine Arts Museums of San Francisco, Achenbach Foundation for Graphic Arts, California State Library Long Loan

Franz Geritz
b. Budapest, Hungary, 1894
d. Los Angeles, California, 1945

7. *Margrethe Mather,* 1922
Etching
6¼ x 4⅞ in. (15.9 x 12.4 cm.)
Graphic Arts Council Curatorial Discretionary Fund
M.79.246.1

Frank Morley Fletcher
b. Whiston, Lancashire, England, 1866
d. Ojai, California, 1949

8. *The Bookworm,* c. 1920–25
Color woodcut
9¾ x 8¼ in. (24.8 x 21 cm.)
Lent by the San Diego Museum of Art, Gift of the University Women's Club

Henrietta Shore
b. Toronto, Canada

9. *Gypsy Encampment,* c. 1925–30
Lithograph
14½ x 10 in. (36.8 x 25.4 cm.)
Lent by The Oakland Museum

Arthur Millier
b. Somersetshire, England, 1893
d. Hackensack, New Jersey, 1975

10. *Eucalypti,* 1922
Etching
7¾ x 7⅜ in. (19.7 x 18.7 cm.)
Paul Rodman Mabury Bequest
39.12.38.6–b
Not illustrated

11. *Plaza Night,* 1922
Etching
5¾ x 6⅞ in. (14.6 x 17.5 cm.)
Paul Rodman Mabury Bequest
39.12.52

Prescott Chaplin
b. Seattle, Washington, 1897
12. *Market Day, Mexico,* 1926–27
Color woodcut
9⅛ x 11⅝ in. (23.2 x 29.5 cm.)
Lent by the Green Altar Corporation
13. *The Potter,* 1926–27
Woodcut
10¼ x 7¾ in. (26 x 19.7 cm.)
Lent by the Green Altar Corporation
Not illustrated

Loren Roberta Barton
b. Oxford, Massachusetts, 1893
d. Claremont, California, 1975
14. *Manuel,* 1923
Drypoint
14½ x 10½ in. (36.8 x 26.7 cm.)
Gift of Miss Bella Mabury
M.49.4.1

Peter Krasnow
b. Zawill, Ukraine, 1887
d. Los Angeles, California, 1979
15. *Untitled,* 1928
Monotype
18¼ x 12⅛ in. (46.4 x 30.8 cm.)
Lent by Mr. and Mrs. Monroe E. Price
16. *The Slave,* c. 1927–29
Lithograph
14 x 10¼ in. (35.6 x 26 cm.)
Lent anonymously
Not illustrated
17. *Glory,* c. 1927–29
Lithograph
12½ x 17¼ in. (31.8 x 43.8 cm.)
Lent anonymously
18. *The Family,* c. 1927–29
Woodcut
9⅞ x 5⅜ in. (25.1 x 13.7 cm.)
Lent anonymously

Willard Ayer Nash
b. Philadelphia, Pennsylvania, 1898
d. Hollywood, California, 1943
19. *Landscape,* 1927
Etching
5 x 7 in. (12.7 x 17.8 cm.)
Gift of Mr. and Mrs. Lorser Feitelson
56.15.2

Bertha Lum
b. Tipton, Iowa, 1897
d. Genoa, Italy, 1954
20. *Spinning Goddess,* c. 1930–35
Embossed woodcut, hand-colored
22 x 14½ in. (55.9 x 36.8 cm.)
Graphic Arts Council Fund
M.79.246.2

Wilson Silsby
b. New Haven, Connecticut, 1896
d. Los Angeles, California, 1952
21. *Stairway in Meudon, France,* c. 1930
Linocut
8 x 11½ in. (20.3 x 29.2 cm.)
Gift of Mr. and Mrs. Clifford Silsby
M.70.15.336

Charles Keeler
b. Cedar Rapids, Iowa, 1882
d. 1965
22. *In the Street of Life and Death, Segovia,* c. 1929
Aquatint
9¼ x 12 in. (23.5 x 30.5 cm.)
Gift of Associated Members of the Print Makers Society
29.20.3

Nicholas Brigante
b. Naples, Italy, 1895
23. *Spanish Canyon,* 1930
Etching
11⅛ x 8½ in. (28.3 x 21.6 cm.)
Gift of Dr. Robert E. Barela
M.72.122.43

Orpha Klinker
b. Fairfield, Idaho, 1891
d. Los Angeles, California, 1964
24. *Road to Dreams,* c. 1930–35
Aquatint
11¾ x 8⅞ in. (29.8 x 22.5 cm.)
Lent by Dr. and Mrs. Pratapaditya Pal

Douglas Parshall
b. New York, New York, 1899
25. *Bathers,* 1930
Color lithograph
11½ x 15⅞ in. (29.2 x 40.3 cm.)
Lent by Mr. and Mrs. Monroe E. Price

Lawton Parker
b. Nebraska, 1868
d. 1954

26. *Reclining Nude,* c. 1930
Etching
7¼ x 9¼ in. (18.4 x 23.5 cm.)
Lent by Mildred Bryant Brooks

Jean Charlot
b. Paris, France, 1898
d. Honolulu, Hawaii, 1979

27. *Woman Standing, Child on Back,* 1934
Color lithograph
26½ x 19½ in. (67.3 x 49.5 cm.)
Gift of Merle Armitage
40.2.1

Fletcher Martin
b. Palisade, Colorado, 1904
d. New York, New York, 1979

28. *Trouble in Frisco,* c. 1935
Lithograph
11¼ x 11⅛ in. (28.6 x 28.3 cm.)
Lent by Abe Tankenson in memory of Mary Donovan Tankenson

Palmer Schoppe
Active, 1930s and 1940s

29. *Head of a Negro,* 1935
Lithograph
18¾ x 15⅛ in. (47.6 x 38.4 cm.)
Lent by Mr. and Mrs. Monroe E. Price

Stephen de Hospodar
b. Nagy Mihaly, Hungary, 1902
d. Los Angeles, California, 1959

30. *Bather,* c. 1930
Woodcut
7½ x 5⅜ in. (19.1 x 13.7 cm.)
Gift of the artist
32.15.1

Richard Day
b. Canada, 1896
d. Los Angeles, California, 1972

31. *Boats in the Ways,* c. 1931
Lithograph
9⅞ x 7⅞ in. (25 x 20 cm.)
Gift of Merle Armitage
46.60.1

Carl Oscar Borg
b. Grinstad, Sweden, 1879
d. Santa Barbara, California, 1947

32. *Navajo Chief,* c. 1930–35
Woodcut
11 x 9¼ in. (27.9 x 23.5 cm.)
Gift of Miss Bella Mabury
M.48.3

Conrad Buff
b. Speicher, Switzerland, 1886
d. Laguna Hills, California, 1975

33. *American Pioneers,* c. 1935
Lithograph
13 x 20 in. (33 x 50.8 cm.)
General Acquisitions Funds
M.79.119

Harold Doolittle
b. Pasadena, California, 1883
d. Temple City, California, 1974

34. *Rugged Cliffs,* c. 1935
Aquatint
8⅞ x 12 in. (22.5 x 30.5 cm.)
Museum Associates General Acquisitions Funds
M.79.107

Helen Lundeberg
b. Chicago, Illinois, 1908

35. *The Mirror,* 1937
Lithograph
11⅞ x 9 in. (30.1 x 22.9 cm.)
Lent by the artist

36. *Red Planet,* 1937
Lithograph
11⅞ x 9 in. (30.2 x 22.9 cm.)
Lent by the artist
Not illustrated

Fletcher Martin
b. Palisade, Colorado, 1904
d. New York, New York, 1979

37. *Shower,* c. 1930–32
Wood engraving
10 x 6 in. (25.4 x 15.2 cm.)
Lent by Takako and Irwin Weinberg

Edward Biberman
b. Philadelphia, Pennsylvania, 1904

38. *Self-Portrait,* c. 1936–40
Lithograph
22⅜ x 17 in. (56.8 x 43.2 cm.)
Lent by Mr. and Mrs. Monroe E. Price
Not illustrated

39. *Pietà,* c. 1936–40
Lithograph
16 x 11½ in. (40.6 x 29.2 cm.)
Lent by the artist

Mildred Bryant Brooks
b. Maryville, Missouri, 1901

40. *Companions,* 1937
Etching
8¾ x 8¾ in. (22.2 x 22.2 cm.)
Gift of Associated Members of the Print Makers Society
37.22

Marion Hebert
b. Spencer, Iowa, 1899
d. Santa Barbara, California, 1960

41. *Rose Arrangement,* 1938
Aquatint
9¾ x 7¾ in. (24.8 x 19.7 cm.)
Lent by Dr. and Mrs. Pratapaditya Pal

Boris Deutsch
b. Krasnagorka, Lithuania, 1892
d. Los Angeles, California, 1978

42. *Mother and Child,* 1938
Lithograph
20 x 15 in. (50.8 x 38.1 cm.)
Lent by the Lorser Feitelson Revocable Trust

Oscar Van Young
b. Vienna, Austria, 1906

43. *The Laundresses,* 1939
Lithograph
19¾ x 14 in. (50.2 x 35.6 cm.)
Gift of Mr. and Mrs. Oscar Van Young
M.80.37

Benjamin Newton Messick
b. Strafford, Missouri, 1901

44. *The Pitchman,* 1940
Lithograph
16¼ x 13⅜ in. (41.3 x 34 cm.)
Gift of the Friends of the Museum
44.5

Lorser Feitelson
b. Savannah, Georgia, 1898
d. Los Angeles, California, 1978

45. *Post-Surreal Configuration: Biological Symphony,* 1939
Lithograph
13¼ x 18 in. (33.7 x 45.7 cm.)
Lent by the Lorser Feitelson Revocable Trust

Millard Sheets
b. Claremont, California, 1907

46. *Horse Frightened by Lightning,* 1939
Lithograph
17¾ x 22½ in. (45.1 x 57.2 cm.)
Gift of Gordon Holmes
58.3

Paul Landacre
b. Columbus, Ohio, 1893
d. Los Angeles, California, 1963

47. *Yesterday,* 1941
Wood engraving
9¼ x 6⅛ in. (23.5 x 15.6 cm.)
Museum Purchase
41.3.24

48. *Hill,* c. 1940
Wood engraving
5¼ x 9 in. (13.3 x 22.9 cm.)
Gift of Jake Zeitlin
41.3.25

49. *Storm,* c. 1940
Wood engraving
7⅞ x 10⅛ in. (20 x 25.7 cm.)
Graphic Arts Council Fund
M.73.40.2
Not illustrated

Stanton Macdonald-Wright
b. Charlottesville, Virginia, 1890
d. Los Angeles, California, 1973

50. *Clump of Trees before a House,* 1938
Lithograph
15 x 20 in. (38.1 x 50.8 cm.)
Gift of Mr. and Mrs. Lorser Feitelson
56.15.1

Helen Lundeberg
b. Chicago, Illinois, 1908

51. *Moonrise,* 1948
Lithograph
12¼ x 16⅞ in. (31.1 x 42.9 cm.)
Lent by the artist

Lorser Feitelson
b. Savannah, Georgia, 1898
d. Los Angeles, California, 1978

52. *Girl Reading,* 1948
Lithograph
11½ x 16 in. (29.2 x 40.6 cm.)
Lent by the Lorser Feitelson Revocable Trust
Not illustrated

Rico Lebrun
b. Naples, Italy, 1900
d. Malibu, California, 1964

53. *François Villon: From the Living,* 1945
Color lithograph
17½ x 13½ in. (44.5 x 34.3 cm.)
Gift of Dr. Kurt Wagner
M.75.12.1
Not illustrated

54. *Man and Armor,* 1945
Color lithograph
11½ x 18 in. (29.2 x 45.7 cm.)
Gift of Dr. Kurt Wagner
M.75.12.3

55. *Rain of Ashes,* 1945
Color lithograph
13¼ x 17 in. (33.7 x 43.2 cm.)
Gift of Dr. Kurt Wagner
M.75.12.4

Howard Warshaw
b. New York, New York, 1920
d. Carpinteria, California, 1977

56. *Head of Traffic Victim,* c. 1950
Lithograph
9¾ x 12 in. (24.8 x 30.5 cm.)
Gift of Frank Perls
50.34.1

57. *Hands,* 1951
Color etching
14 x 11¾ in. (35.6 x 29.8 cm.)
Gift of Frank Perls
53.28

Hans Gustav Burkhardt
b. Basel, Switzerland, 1904

58. *Untitled,* 1948
Lithograph
17 x 12½ in. (43.2 x 31.8 cm.)
Lent by Dr. and Mrs. Pratapaditya Pal
Not illustrated

59. *Lovers,* 1948
Lithograph
12½ x 16⅞ in. (31.8 x 42.9 cm.)
Lent by Dr. and Mrs. Pratapaditya Pal

Richard Haines
b. Marion, Iowa, 1906

60. *Bus Stop,* 1948
Lithograph
9¾ x 12¾ in. (24.8 x 32.4 cm.)
Lent anonymously

Clinton Adams
b. Glendale, California, 1918

61. *Silver Bottle,* 1950
Lithograph
10 x 15¼ in. (25.4 x 38.7 cm.)
Gift of Mrs. Harry Ormiston
M.61.34.1

Eugene Berman
b. St. Petersburg, Russia, 1899
d. Rome, Italy, 1972

62. *Pisan Fantasy,* 1951
Lithograph
17¼ x 12½ in. (43.8 x 31.8 cm.)
Lent by Lynton R. Kistler

John Paul Jones
b. Indianola, Iowa, 1924

63. *Landscape #2,* 1950
Etching
16 x 24 in. (40.6 x 61 cm.)
Lent by the Grunwald Center for the Graphic Arts, University of California, Los Angeles

64. *Double Portrait,* 1957
Intaglio
23½ x 32 in. (59.7 x 81.3 cm.)
Museum Associates, Junior Art Council Purchase Award
M.58.20
Not illustrated

Leonard Edmondson
b. Sacramento, California, 1916

65. *Failing Light,* 1950
Serigraph
11 x 16¾ in. (27.9 x 42.5 cm.)
Gift of Mr. and Mrs. Oscar Salzer
57.45.19

66. *Escarpment,* 1956
Color etching
13¼ x 21¾ in. (33.7 x 55.2 cm.)
Lent by the Grunwald Center for the Graphic Arts, University of California, Los Angeles

June Wayne
b. Chicago, Illinois, 1918

67. *Quiet One,* 1950
Lithograph
21¼ x 12⅜ in. (54 x 31.4 cm.)
Gift of the artist
55.20.1
Not illustrated

68. *The Tunnel,* 1951
Lithograph
15⅜ x 19⅜ in. (39.1 x 49.2 cm.)
Gift of the artist
55.20.2

69. *The Witnesses,* 1952
Lithograph
23¾ x 29¾ in. (60.3 x 75.6 cm.)
Gift of the artist
55.20.7

70a. *Adam en Attente,* 1958
Lithograph
35 x 11¼ in. (88.9 x 28.6 cm.)
Gift of Mr. and Mrs. Dalzell Hatfield
59.18.1

70b. *Eve Tentée,* 1958
Lithograph
35 x 11½ in. (88.9 x 29.2 cm.)
Gift of Mr. and Mrs. Dalzell Hatfield
59.18.2

Ynez Johnston
b. Berkeley, California, 1920

71. *Ship and Storm,* 1949
Etching
6¾ x 8¾ in. (17.1 x 22.2 cm.)
Gift of California Centennials of Art
49.40.12

72. *Square with Monuments,* 1952
Color etching
18 x 22 in. (45.7 x 55.9 cm.)
Lent by the Mekler Gallery
Not illustrated

Sister Mary Corita
b. Fort Dodge, Iowa, 1918

73. *The Lord Is with Thee,* 1951
Serigraph
22½ x 15⅜ in. (57.2 x 39.1 cm.)
Gift to Museum Associates from June Wayne
M.62.60.9
Not illustrated

74. *This Beginning of Miracles,* 1953
Serigraph
16 x 20 in. (40.6 x 50.8 cm.)
Gift of Mr. and Mrs. Fred Grunwald
53.9.1

Howard Bradford
b. Toronto, Ontario, 1919

75. *Suspended Seawave,* 1956
Serigraph
16⅝ x 25½ in. (42.2 x 64.8 cm.)
Gift of Mr. and Mrs. Oscar Salzer
57.45.21

Dorothy Bowman
b. Hollywood, California, 1927

76. *Sleeping City,* c. 1957–58
Serigraph
29¾ x 11 in. (75.6 x 27.9 cm.)
Gift of Mr. and Mrs. Oscar Salzer
57.45.35

Sam Francis
b. San Mateo, California, 1923

77. *The White Line,* 1960
Color lithograph
35½ x 24¼ in. (90.2 x 61.6 cm.)
Lent by Margo Leavin

Connor Everts
b. Bellingham, Washington, 1928
78. *Execution,* 1960
Lithograph
41 x 29 in. (104.1 x 73.7 cm.)
Gift of Dorothy and Michael Blankfort through the Modern and Contemporary Art Council
M.61.40.94

Jules Engel
b. Budapest, Hungary, 1915
79. *Curfew,* 1960
Lithograph
42 x 30 in. (106.7 x 76.2 cm.)
Gift of Dorothy and Michael Blankfort through the Modern and Contemporary Art Council
M.62.44.12

William Brice
b. New York, New York, 1921
80. *Striped Robe,* 1961
Lithograph
41½ x 29 in. (105.4 x 73.7 cm.)
Gift of Dorothy and Michael Blankfort through the Modern and Contemporary Art Council
M.63.53.8

Emerson Woelffer
b. Chicago, Illinois, 1914
81. *Untitled,* 1961
Color lithograph
22 x 17 in. (55.9 x 43.2 cm.)
Gift of Dorothy and Michael Blankfort through the Modern and Contemporary Art Council
M.66.53.25

Richard Diebenkorn
b. Portland, Oregon, 1922
82. *Untitled,* 1961
Lithograph
29 x 21 in. (73.7 x 53.3 cm.)
Lent by Dorothy and Michael Blankfort

Tom Fricano
b. Chicago, Illinois, 1930
83. *Umbria #1,* 1961
Cardboard cut
27¾ x 27½ in. (70.5 x 69.9 cm.)
Gift of Otis Art Associates
62.11.9

Rico Lebrun
b. Naples, Italy, 1900
d. Malibu, California, 1964
84. *Grünewald Study II,* 1961
Lithograph
25¼ x 35¼ in. (64.1 x 89.5 cm.)
Gift of Dorothy and Michael Blankfort through the Modern and Contemporary Art Council
M.79.224.6

John McLaughlin
b. Sharon, Massachusetts, 1898
d. Laguna Beach, California, 1976
85. *Untitled,* 1962
Lithograph
22¼ x 30 in. (56.5 x 76.2 cm.)
Gift of Dorothy and Benjamin B. Smith through the Modern and Contemporary Art Council
M.75.126.61

June Wayne
b. Chicago, Illinois, 1918
86. *At Last a Thousand II,* 1965
Color lithograph
24 x 34 in. (61 x 86.4 cm.)
Lent anonymously

David Hockney
b. Bradford, Yorkshire, England, 1937
87. *Picture of Melrose Avenue with an Ornate Gold Frame,* 1965
Color lithograph
30 x 22 in. (76.2 x 55.9 cm.)
Gift of Mr. and Mrs. David Gensburg
M.68.72.18

John Altoon
b. Los Angeles, California, 1925
d. Los Angeles, California, 1969
88. *Untitled,* 1966
Color lithograph
30 x 42½ in. (76.2 x 108 cm.)
Gift of Mr. and Mrs. David Gensburg
M.68.72.28

Charles White
b. Chicago, Illinois, 1918
d. Los Angeles, California, 1979

89. *Exodus II,* 1966
Color lithograph
40 x 32 in. (101.6 x 81.3 cm.)
Gift of Mr. and Mrs. David Gensburg
M.68.72.31

Robert Cremean
b. Toledo, Ohio, 1932

90. *The Fourteen Stations of the Cross,* 1966–67
Three from suite of fourteen color lithographs
22 x 15 in. (55.9 x 38.1 cm.)
Museum Purchase
67.7.8–.21

Shiro Ikegawa
b. Tokyo, Japan, 1933

91. *Issa,* 1966
Color intaglio
29¾ x 22 in. (75.6 x 55.9 cm.)
Gift of the Container Corporation of America
M.66.38

Clinton Adams
b. Glendale, California, 1918

92. *Venus in Cibola,* 1967–69
Four from suite of ten color lithographs
12½ x 10 in. (31.8 x 25.4 cm.)
Museum Purchase with Museum Associates Acquisitions Fund
M.70.81.172–.181

Norman Zammitt
b. Toronto, Ontario, 1931

93. *Untitled,* 1967
Color lithograph
29½ x 42½ in. (74.9 x 108 cm.)
Museum Purchase
67.8.149

Ed Ruscha
b. Omaha, Nebraska, 1937

94. *Hollywood,* 1968
Silkscreen
17½ x 44½ in. (44.5 x 113 cm.)
Lent by Douglas S. Cramer

Billy Al Bengston
b. Dodge City, Kansas, 1934

95. *Mecca Dracula,* 1968
Color lithograph
21½ x 21½ in. (54.6 x 54.6 cm.)
Museum Purchase
M.68.4.76

Ed Moses
b. Long Beach, California, 1926

96. *Untitled,* 1968
Color lithograph
13¼ x 16¾ in. (33.7 x 42.5 cm.)
Museum Purchase
M.70.81.12

97. *Untitled,* 1968
Color lithograph
13¼ x 16¾ in. (33.7 x 42.5 cm.)
Museum Purchase
M.70.81.15
Not illustrated

James Strombotne
b. Watertown, South Dakota, 1934

98. *Smokers,* 1968
Color lithograph
20 x 66 in. (50.8 x 167.6 cm.)
Museum Purchase
68.4.190

Lee Mullican
b. Chickasha, Oklahoma, 1919

99. *The Mountain,* 1969
Color lithograph
22 x 30 in. (55.9 x 76.2 cm.)
Museum Purchase
M.70.81.468

Betye Saar
b. Los Angeles, California, 1926

100. *Black Girl's Window,* 1969
Mixed media
35¾ x 18 x 1½ in. (90.8 x 45.7 x 3.8 cm.)
Lent by the artist

David Hammons
b. Springfield, Illinois, 1943
101. *Injustice Case,* 1970
Body print, mixed media
63 x 40½ in. (160 x 102.9 cm.)
Museum Acquisitions Fund
M.71.7

Jan Stussy
b. Benton County, Missouri, 1921
102. *Family of Acrobatic Jugglers,* 1970
Lithograph
30 x 24 in. (76.2 x 61 cm.)
Museum Purchase
70.4.132

Timothy Washington
b. Los Angeles, California, 1946
103. *One Nation Under God,* 1970
Engraving on aluminum with added color
35 x 48 in. (88.9 x 121.9 cm.)
Museum Purchase with Museum Associates Funds
M.71.8

William Pettet
b. Los Angeles, California, 1942
104. *Untitled,* 1970
Color lithograph
13 x 29 in. (33 x 73.7 cm.)
Museum Purchase
70.4.105

Matsumi Kanemitsu
b. Ogden, Utah, 1922
105. *Number Six State II,* 1970
Lithograph
25 x 36 in. (63.5 x 91.4 cm.)
Museum Purchase
70.4.101

William Crutchfield
b. Indianapolis, Indiana, 1932
106. *Tamarind-Tanic,* 1970
Color lithograph
30 x 22 in. (76.2 x 55.9 cm.)
Museum Purchase
70.4.86

Walter Askin
b. Pasadena, California, 1929
107. *Transitory Passions,* 1971
Silkscreen
40 x 27½ in. (101.6 x 69.9 cm.)
Anonymous Gift
M.72.121

Craig Kauffman
b. Los Angeles, California, 1932
108. *Untitled,* 1971
Set of four color lithographs
21½ x 26¾ in. (54.6 x 67.9 cm.)
Gift of Iris and Allen Mink
M.79.248.5–.8

Stephen Anaya
b. Los Angeles, California, 1946
109. *Kuraje,* 1971
Stipple etching
24 x 36 in. (61 x 91.4 cm.)
Lent by the artist

Lorser Feitelson
b. Savannah, Georgia, 1898
d. Los Angeles, California, 1978
110. *Untitled,* 1971
Silkscreen
30 x 22 in. (76.2 x 55.8 cm.)
Gift of Dr. Robert E. Barela
M.71.91.3

Vija Celmins
b. Latvia, U.S.S.R., 1938
111. *Untitled,* 1971
Lithograph
22¼ x 29 in. (56.5 x 73.7 cm.)
Gift of Iris and Allen Mink
M.79.248.20

Helen Lundeberg
b. Chicago, Illinois, 1908
112. *Untitled,* 1971
Silkscreen
18 x 23⅞ in. (45.7 x 60.6 cm.)
Gift of Dr. Robert E. Barela
M.71.91.6

Jerry McMillan
b. Oklahoma City, Oklahoma, 1936
113. *Porch Bag,* 1971
Mixed media with offset lithograph
11 x 5¾ x 3½ in. (27.9 x 14.6 x 8.9 cm.)
Graphic Arts Council Fund
M.80.28

Ken Price
b. Los Angeles, California, 1935
114. *Lizard Cup,* 1971
Silkscreen
30 x 40 in. (76.2 x 101.6 cm.)
Lent by Gemini G.E.L.

Bruce Nauman
b. Fort Wayne, Indiana, 1941
115. *Untitled,* 1971
Color lithograph
30 x 42 in. (76.2 x 106.7 cm.)
Gift of Iris and Allen Mink
M.79.248.15

Gene Gill
b. Memphis, Tennessee, 1933
116. *Untitled,* 1972
Silkscreen on plastic with aluminum
37 x 37 in. (94 x 94 cm.)
Lent by the artist

Peter Alexander
b. Los Angeles, California, 1939
117. *Anacin I,* 1972
Offset lithograph
11⅛ x 13⅛ in. (28.3 x 33.3 cm.)
Gift of Iris and Allen Mink
M.79.248.1
Not illustrated
118. *Anacin II,* 1972
Offset lithograph
11⅛ x 13⅛ in. (28.3 x 33.3 cm.)
Gift of Iris and Allen Mink
M.79.248.2

Ron Cooper
b. Ojai, California, 1943
119. *Tri-axial Rotation of a Floating Volume of Light,* 1972
Color lithograph
22½ x 29¾ in. (57.2 x 75.6 cm.)
Lent by Cirrus Editions Ltd.

Greg Card
b. Los Angeles, California, 1945
120. *Untitled,* 1972
Silkscreen on Plexiglas
26 x 26 in. (66 x 66 cm.)
Lent by Cirrus Editions Ltd.

Claire Falkenstein
b. Coos Bay, Oregon, 1908
121. *Struttura Grafica,* 1972
Embossed print
20 x 27½ in. (50.8 x 69.9 cm.)
Gift of the Graphic Arts Council
M.73.98

Tony DeLap
b. Oakland, California, 1927
122. *Karnak, I, II, III, IV,* 1972
Set of four color lithographs/embossments
19 x 19 in. (48.3 x 48.3 cm.)
Gift of Iris and Allen Mink
M.79.248.16–.19

Ron Davis
b. Santa Monica, California, 1937
123. *Four Circle,* 1972
Color lithograph/silkscreen
30 x 39¼ in. (76.2 x 99.7 cm.)
Lent by Carl Parsons

Los Angeles Fine Arts Squad
(Vic Henderson and Terry Schoonhoven)
124. *Isle of California,* 1973
Color lithograph
27⅞ x 35½ in. (70.8 x 90.2 cm.)
Gift of Mr. and Mrs. Stuart Buchalter
M.78.42

Joel Bass
b. Los Angeles, California, 1942
125. *Horizontals—C,* 1974
Etching with lead collage
20 x 30 in. (50.8 x 76.2 cm.)
Lent by the Janus Gallery

Ray Brown
b. San Antonio, Texas, 1933

126. *Alice N.S.*, 1975
Color etching
12¾ x 11¼ in. (32.4 x 28.6 cm.)
Gift of the Graphic Arts Council
M.75.38

Ynez Johnston
b. Berkeley, California, 1920

127. *The Secret Landscape*, 1976
Color etching
27¾ x 19 in. (70.5 x 48.3 cm.)
Lent by the Mekler Gallery

Eugene Sturman
b. New York, New York, 1945

128. *Quadrant #4*, 1977
Silkscreen, waxed and gilded
22½ x 30 in. (57.2 x 76.2 cm.)
Lent by Cirrus Editions Ltd.

Jay McCafferty
b. San Pedro, California, 1948

129. *#1 Alive*, 1977
Silkscreen and woodblock
22 x 22 in. (55.9 x 55.9 cm.)
Lent by Cirrus Editions Ltd.

Charles Christopher Hill
b. Greensburg, Pennsylvania, 1948

130. *Lightning*, 1977
Hand-colored lithograph
27½ x 39½ in. (69.9 x 100.3 cm.)
Lent by Cirrus Editions Ltd.

Ann McCoy
b. Boulder, Colorado, 1946

131. *The Night Sea*, 1978
Lithograph, hand-colored, two panels
65¼ x 34¼ in. (165.7 x 87 cm.) each
Lent by the Margo Leavin Gallery and Brooke Alexander, Inc.

Richard Diebenkorn
b. Portland, Oregon, 1922

132. *Untitled #5*, 1978
Aquatint with drypoint
19 x 13 in. (48.3 x 33 cm.)
Lent by the artist

Joe Goode
b. Oklahoma City, Oklahoma, 1937

133. *Untitled*, 1978
Color lithograph
28 x 40 in. (71.1 x 101.6 cm.)
Lent by Cirrus Editions Ltd.

Chuck Arnoldi
b. Dayton, Ohio, 1946

134. *Untitled*, 1979
Color etching
18 x 15 in. (45.7 x 38.1 cm.)
Lent anonymously

Eleanore Lazarof
b. New York, New York, 1928

135. *Dos Lados de la Mañana*, 1979
Color intaglio
29½ x 41½ in. (74.9 x 105.4 cm.)
Gift of the artist
M.80.35

Sam Francis
b. San Mateo, California, 1923

136. *Untitled*, 1980
Monotype
30 x 24½ in. (76.2 x 62.2 cm.)
Gift of the artist
M.80.64
Not illustrated

SELECTED BIBLIOGRAPHY

Ann McCoy: The Red Sea and The Night Sea, The Arts Club of Chicago, 1979.

Adams, C., "Lynton R. Kistler and the Development of Lithography in Los Angeles," *Tamarind Technical Papers,* no. 8, winter 1977–78, pp. 100–109.

Adams, C., "Lithography in Los Angeles: 1933–69," unpublished manuscript accepted by the *American Art Review.*

Antreasian, G. Z., and C. Adams, *The Tamarind Book of Lithography: Art and Techniques,* New York, 1971.

Armitage, M., *The Lithographs of Richard Day,* New York, 1932.

Armitage, M., *Henrietta Shore,* New York, 1933.

Baskett, M. W., *The Art of June Wayne,* New York, 1969.

Bell, M., *Black Dolphin Prints,* Art Galleries, California State University, Long Beach, 1978.

Bloch, E. M., *Tamarind: A Renaissance of Lithography,* International Exhibitions Foundation, Baltimore, 1971–72.

Bloch, E. M., ed., *Made in California: An Exhibition of Five Workshops,* University of California, Los Angeles, 1971.

Bogle, A., *Graphic Works by Edward Ruscha,* Auckland City Art Gallery, 1978.

Bourdon, D., "A Heap of Words About Ed Ruscha," *Art International,* vol. 15, no. 9, 1971, pp. 25–28, 38.

Castleman, R., *Technics and Creativity: Gemini G.E.L.,* New York, Museum of Modern Art, 1971.

Catalogue Raisonné, Gemini G.E.L., Los Angeles, 1966–1977.

David Hammons, Selected Works 1968–1974, California State University, Los Angeles, 1974.

Edelstein, J. M., ed., *A Garland for Jake Zeitlin,* Los Angeles, 1967.

Foster, E. A., *Edward Ruscha: Prints, Drawings and Books 1963–1971,* Minneapolis Institute of Arts, 1972.

Glazebrook, M., *David Hockney: Paintings, Prints and Drawings 1960–1970,* Whitechapel Art Gallery, London, 1970.

Grafton, S., "Tamarind: Where Artist and Craftsman Meet," *Lithopinion,* vol. 5, no. 1, 1967, pp. 18–25.

Higgins, W. H., *Art Collecting in the Los Angeles Area: 1910–1960,* University of California, Los Angeles, Ph.D. dissertation, 1964, University Microfilms, Ann Arbor, Michigan.

Hopps, W., and E. Solomon, *John Altoon: Drawings and Prints,* Whitney Museum of American Art, New York, 1971.

Hoyer, A., *Sam Francis: Exhibition of Drawings and Lithographs,* San Francisco Museum of Art, 1967.

Johnson, U. E., *John Paul Jones: Prints and Drawings 1948–1963,* Brooklyn Museum, New York, 1963.

June Wayne Bibliography, 1950–January 1978, published by the artist, Los Angeles, 1978.

Käthe Kollwitz, Jake Zeitlin Bookshop and Gallery: 1937, The Art Museum and Galleries, California State University, Long Beach, 1979.

Landacre, P., *California Hills and Other Wood Engravings,* foreword by Arthur Millier, Los Angeles, 1931.

Landacre, P., "Wood engraving technique," *The Relief Print,* ed. E. W. Watson and N. Kent, New York, 1945.

Larsen, S., "A Conversation with Vija Celmins," *Los Angeles Institute of Contemporary Art Journal,* no. 20, Oct.–Nov. 1978, pp. 36–39.

Larsen, S., *Vija Celmins, A Survey Exhibition,* Newport Harbor Art Museum, Newport Beach, California, 1979.

Lemos, P. J., "California and its Etchers, What They Mean to Each Other"; Harshe, R. B., "The California Society of Etchers"; Tolerton, Hill, "Etching and Etchers"; *Art in California,* San Francisco, 1916, pp. 113–26.

Leonard Edmondson: Color Etchings, 1951–1967, San Francisco Museum of Art, 1967.

Lieberman, W. S., and V. Allen, *Tamarind: Homage to Lithography,* Museum of Modern Art, New York, 1969.

Los Angeles Art Community: Group Portrait, University of California, Los Angeles, Oral History Program, 1977, interviews with Edward Biberman, Conrad Buff, Hans Burkhardt, Tony DeLap, Matsumi Kanemitsu, Corita Kent (Sister Mary Corita), Ed Kienholz, Lee Mullican, Millard Sheets, Howard Warshaw, and Emerson Woelffer.

Los Angeles Institute of Contemporary Art Journal, April–May, 1975.

McWilliams, C., *Southern California: An Island on the Land,* Santa Barbara and Salt Lake City, 1973.

Milant, J., and B. Pascal, eds., *Artists/Prints: 1976–1977,* Los Angeles, 1979.

Millier, A., M. Armitage, and H. B. Alexander, *Millard Sheets,* Los Angeles, 1935.

Moran, D., "Helen Lundeberg: The Sixties and Seventies," *Art International,* vol. 33, no. 2, 1979, pp. 35–46.

Morse, P., *Jean Charlot's Prints, A Catalogue Raisonné,* Honolulu, 1976.

Moure, N. D. W., *Dictionary of Art and Artists in Southern California before 1930,* Glendale, California: privately published, 1975.

Plagens, P., *Sunshine Muse,* New York, 1974.

Plous, P., *Richard Diebenkorn: Intaglio Prints 1961–1978,* University of California, Santa Barbara, 1979.

Print Makers Society of California Newsletter, vols. 1–15, 1922–1938.

Prints from Gemini G.E.L., Walker Art Center, Minneapolis, 1974.

Ritchie, W., *Some Books with Illustrations by Paul Landacre,* Los Angeles, 1978.

Sam Francis: The Litho Shop 1970–1979, Brooke Alexander, Inc., New York, 1979.

Sam Francis Monotypes, Los Angeles County Museum of Art, 1980.

Secunda, A., "Tamarind," *Artforum,* vol. 1, no. 3, 1962, pp. 28–31.

Southern California Artists 1890–1940, Laguna Beach Museum of Art, 1979.

Tousley, N., "In Conversation with Kathan Brown," *The Print Collector's Newsletter,* vol. 8, no. 5, 1977, pp. 129–34.

25 Woodcuts by Prescott Chaplin, Los Angeles, 1930.

Wight, F. S., *Lithographs from the Tamarind Workshop,* University of California, Los Angeles, 1962–63.

Ynez Johnston: Graphic Work, 1949–1966, San Francisco Museum of Art, 1967.

Young, J. E., *Three Graphic Artists: Charles White, David Hammons, Timothy Washington,* Los Angeles County Museum of Art, 1971.

Young, J. E., "Lorser Feitelson and Los Angeles Modernism," *Artweek,* Oct. 21, 1972, pp. 9–11.

Young, J. E., *Dimensional Prints,* Los Angeles County Museum of Art, 1973.

Young, J. E., "Contemporary Southern California Printmaking," *Print Review,* vol. 2, 1973, pp. 49–63.

Young, J. E., *Selections from Cirrus Editions Ltd.,* Los Angeles County Museum of Art, 1974–75.

Zigrosser, C., *Between Two Wars: Prints by American Artists 1914–41,* Whitney Museum of American Art, New York, 1942.

Edited by Jeanne D'Andrea,
Alison Hirsch, and Stephen West

Designed in Los Angeles
by Jeffrey Mueller

Text set in Garamond typefaces
by RS Typographics,
Los Angeles

Printed in an edition of 7,000
on Lithofect Suede paper
by Printers, Inc.,
Los Angeles